What's in the word

What's in the Word

Rethinking the Socio-Rhetorical Character
of the New Testament

Ben Witherington III

BAYLOR UNIVERSITY PRESS

Cover Design by Jeremy Reiss, J.Reiss Design

Library of Congress Cataloging-in-Publication Data

Witherington, Ben, 1951-
  What's in the Word : rethinking the socio-rhetorical character of the New Testament / Ben Witherington III.
     p. cm.
  Includes index.
  ISBN 978-1-60258-196-8 (pbk. : alk. paper)
  1. Bible. N.T.--Socio-rhetorical criticism. I. Title.

  BS2380.W58 2009
  225.6--dc22

                                                    2009003944

Printed in the United States of America on acid-free paper with a minimum of 30% pcw recycled content.

To my friends and colleagues at MacQuarie University:
Edwin, Alanna, Chris, Don, Samuel, Stephen, and now Larry.

Thanks to you all for the good stimulus, fellowship,
and scholarship over many years.

Contents

Invitation to the Dance

Paradigms are powerful things. Sometimes they hang on long past their usefulness, like an old sports star who just cannot bear to retire and will not accept that he has passed his prime. And in academic disciplines, it seems that paradigms are especially tenacious and very hard to shift or change. When one talks about a paradigm shift, some scholars react as if one were guilty of sacrilege or heresy. They fear it the way a San Francisco resident fears seismic shifts of tectonic plates. Scholars do not want the ground to move under their feet, especially when they have spent their entire academic careers building tall intellectual skyscrapers on certain assumed unmovable underpinnings or foundations.

One of the things one learns if one stays in the academic arena long enough is that despite a professed commitment to openness and learning new things, many of the guild of biblical scholars do not very often receive the news of a paradigm shift with much, if any, gladness. Indeed, the proposed shift is more likely to be attacked, watered down, contextualized, or trivialized, if it is not simply ignored, following the practice of not-so-benign neglect. All this I know and have experienced as I have continued to write and speak about new, and yet paradoxically old, ways of approaching the study of the New Testament.

This book is about a set of interrelated paradigm shifts in scholarly study of the NT, and its implications. I am talking about examining the NT on the basis of the insights one can learn from studying ancient social history, including the oral nature of ancient cultures, and from studying historical Greco-Roman and Jewish rhetoric. I call this combination *socio-rhetorical criticism*, though I certainly did not coin this phrase, nor do I mean by it what practitioners of the New Rhetoric mean by it. Another way to talk about some of this is to refer to historical rhetorical criticism, as Margaret M. Mitchell does, and to a historical approach to social history, as opposed to applying various modern social scientific and cultural anthropological forms of criticism

I

in the analysis of the NT, as we find in the scholarly circle known as the "Context Group."

In the first place, socio-rhetorical criticism as I am defining it is a historical discipline, not primarily a hermeneutical one. By this I mean that the NT should in the first place be analyzed on the basis of the social and literary realia that actually existed in the first century A.D. and on the basis of the sorts of rhetoric that were actually practiced in the first century A.D.

I do not have a problem with analyzing the NT on the basis of modern sociological ideas, such as group grid analysis or millenarian sect theory, nor do I have a problem with examining the NT by drawing on the "New Rhetoric," following modern theories of language and meaning of various sorts. What I do insist, however, is that if one wants to develop a *historical* understanding of what the "authors" of the NT were doing using the art of persuasion and what *their* social worlds were like, then one must in the first place *avoid anachronism like the plague.*

By this I mean that the proper place to begin when studying NT texts, *in a historical manner,* is to ask a very traditional and historical question: What did this or that author mean to say by writing, or having written, these words? One should begin by respecting the texts as we have them and the historical authors who encoded meaning into these texts in various ways. One should assume that the more one knows about the various ancient contexts, including the social and rhetorical contexts, in which these texts were written, the more one will properly understand them. There can be no talk of the "autonomy of texts" or bandying about of the mythical mantra "all we have is texts" or even of "meaning being largely in the eye of the beholder" if one wants to approach the NT in a truly historical manner.[1]

I am completely in agreement with J. D. G. Dunn when he says in his recent masterwork, *Jesus Remembered*:

> But the "autonomy" of the text is another illusion. For the text will always be read in context, whether the historical context of the text, or of its later editions, or the contemporary context of the reader. The text is not like a free-floating balloon to be pulled to earth every so often, its message read, and then released back again into the atmosphere, as though that were its natural setting. As text it was always earth-bound from the first. The reality is that the less attention given to the text's own context, the more likely the text is to be abused by the hermeneutical process.[2]

Nor am I in any way persuaded by those who want to complain that using the historical method of studying the NT is either unnecessary or a way of protecting oneself from having to engage with the text personally. This is sometimes the complaint of those urging *theologi-*

cal exegesis of the text, as if theology could be neatly separated from dealing with the historical substance of the text. To some advocates of theological exegesis, "going back" implies that the scriptures have to change, whereas theological exegesis is about engaging the text (with all the methodological tools available) with the intent of embodying it. In other words, theological exegesis is seen as the sort that produces contemporary application. Consequently, what historical analysis does is protect the text from us and us from the text. It is perceived to create distance that then has to be bridged by hermeneutical gymnastics.

The assumption is that the traditional historical-critical method along with its paradigm is incapable of producing exegesis that can be embodied by the church. I would stress that there can be no relationship of intimacy with the text or the One who inspired it without first realizing one's distance from the text and its original context. It is simply not true to say that the church today is the same church that it was in the first century, and therefore the continuous ecclesial context allows us to skip the hard work of historical interpretation in order to grasp the meaning of the Bible and apply it today.

Furthermore, I don't understand historical interpretation as "changing" the scriptures. Historical work is reconstructing, as much as possible, the historical context wherein these texts originate. This historical context allows the establishment of meaning that fosters subsequent theological appropriation. This appropriation is aided through the historical-critical methods' capacity to illuminate the development of these texts within the community of God. All things considered, the word *changing* seems to be another example of an easy buzzword created for target practice. I would ask who is being referred to when one states that traditional historical exegesis is incapable of producing theological embodiment.[3] Frankly, there are just too many examples to the contrary to allow such a generalization to stand.

In these respects, it may appear on the surface that we are approaching the NT in a very traditional manner in this book, even being prepared to talk about what certain authors intended when they said this or that. It will appear quite traditional as well when I talk about the historical and social contexts in which these documents were written and that they reflect. But this is only part of the story. The bigger part of the story has to do with some major shifts in thinking about the NT, shifts that need to be embraced and have their implications understood and accepted by more scholars in the twenty-first century.

In this study, I shall talk about how ancient texts are not really texts in the modern sense at all—they are mostly surrogates for oral communication. When we investigate the so-called epistolary literature of the NT, I shall discuss how rhetorical conventions are mainly and dominantly followed and should be more prominently given their due. I am going to suggest as well that when it comes to the issue of pseudepigrapha in the NT, we need to assess accurately whether this was considered an acceptable literary practice in the first century A.D., and whether there was such a thing as a concept of intellectual property in antiquity. Furthermore, I am going to assert that without knowledge of how rhetoric is used in the NT, all sorts of theological, ethical, and practical misinterpretations are possible and have happened, especially when it comes to the so-called epistolary literature in the NT. I am also going to say that some of those "letters" are not letters at all—they are sermons (e.g., if we are talking about 1 John). In addition, I am going to urge that with a clearer understanding of the social and rhetorical world of antiquity, certain key words and phrases that often arise in the discussion of the character of early Christianity and its ethics take on new significance. As it turns out, James was not imposing Jewish food laws on Gentiles, and Paul was not merely suggesting that God is impartial and all are equal in his eyes when he coined Galatians 3:28.

Let me be clear that I am not just arguing for a literary or lexical paradigm shift—I am also urging that several historical ones are necessary as well, once we give the social and rhetorical character of these NT documents their due. For one thing, I shall argue that the persons who wrote these documents represented a socially more elite part of the early Christian movement; indeed, they reflect the fact that the leaders of the movement were not by and large peasants or illiterate persons. On the contrary, Christianity was led from the first by a socially upwardly mobile and, indeed, better-educated group than could be said to characterize the majority of the population of the Roman Empire.[4] I shall argue that one of those better-educated and elite earliest Christians was the Beloved Disciple who stands behind and whose memoirs are enshrined in the powerful rhetoric of the Fourth Gospel.

I shall maintain as well that the rhetoric of Jesus and Paul about marriage and singleness was radical, and perhaps for the first time there was a very positive view held up of being a single person—indeed, it was even seen as a gift or calling from God. This was to change the social landscape regarding which roles were seen as appropriate for women, at least within Christianity, for a good while. I shall argue that one can observe such a changing social landscape even in the way the household codes are modified by Paul and others. I shall also argue that 2 Peter is one of the keys to understanding how the church began to collect and treat its sacred apostolic literature already at the end of the first century A.D.

I shall suggest as well that a proper rhetorical assessment of the meaning of the Apostolic Decree in Acts 15 and 1 Corinthians 8–10 shows that Paul and James did not disagree on what should be expected, ethically, of Gentile converts to Christ. In fact, the degree of theological and ethical diversity among the earliest apostles was not as great as is sometimes thought, and that same *lack* of polarizing diversity is a feature of the NT literature itself. And there will be other surprises along the way.

I shall urge a significant paradigm shift in the ways we view and evaluate the oral tradition behind the Gospels, which should be assessed on the basis of the concept of oral history rather than the older critical theories about oral tradition. I shall devote an entire chapter in this study to interacting with and critiquing Dunn's powerful *Jesus Remembered*, on the basis of recent studies in oral history by S. Byrskog and R. Bauckham.

I shall, in addition, emphasize that there were already the beginnings of a canonizing process for sacred Christian texts (as well as a reasonably fixed understanding of what the limits of the Old Testament were) in the first century A.D. As it turns out, the Muratorian Canon list is a second-century list and provides one of various landmarks and benchmarks along the way toward a recognition that only first-century apostolic and eyewitness resources were fit for inclusion in the NT canon.

What binds all these insights together is the application of a historical socio-rhetorical way of reading NT texts. In short, I urge that socio-rhetorical criticism in a historical mode should become, in this century, one of the dominant paradigms for studying the NT literature. If it does become such, it will change the way we read history and do theology and ethics, and it will even change our preaching as well, shaping all these activities in more biblical and historically informed ways. The thesis of this book is as follows: *Socio-rhetorical criticism, if done rightly, changes various readings and paradigms of NT studies in significant ways, and if we allow these readings to have their due weight, it will change the way we view early Christianity, including the way we view its theology and ethics.*

You have now heard a sound byte of the sort of tune I shall sing and play in this study. Consider this your invitation to dance.

Christmas 2008

I

Oral Examination

How Did "Oral" Texts Function in a Rhetorical Culture?

Christians in the Roman Empire placed a premium on words. Cicero, Quintilian, Fronto, Ausonius—all emphasize the need for the orator to nurture his voice as a musician cares for his instrument; it is his first qualification to be an orator. But in the formulation of Gregory of Nyssa, "the human voice was fashioned for one reason alone—to be the threshold through which the sentiments of the heart, inspired by the Holy Spirit, might be translated clearly into the Word itself."

—Averil Cameron[1]

AN ORAL EXAM

Ours is a text-based culture, a culture of written documents. You need look no further than your computer screen to verify this assertion. An Internet age could exist only with widespread literacy, which in turn leads to widespread production and reading of texts. It is thus difficult for us in a text-based culture to conceive of and understand the character of an oral culture, much less understand how sacred texts function in such an oral culture. Yet however difficult, it is important that we try to understand such a thing, because all the cultures of the Bible were essentially oral cultures, not text-based cultures; their texts were oral texts, which might seem like an oxymoron, but it is not.

The literacy rate in the cultures of the New Testament era seems to have ranged from 10 to 20 percent, depending on the culture and the subgroup within the culture that is being discussed. Not surprisingly then, all ancient peoples, whether literate or not, preferred the living word (i.e., the spoken word). Texts were enormously expensive to produce—papyrus was expensive, ink was expensive, and scribes were ultraexpensive. Being a secretary in Jesus' or Paul's age could be a lucrative job indeed. No wonder Jesus said to his audiences, "let those who

7

have ears, listen." You notice he did not ever say, "let those who have eyes, read." Most eyes could not read in the NT period.

As far as we can tell, no documents in antiquity were intended for "silent" reading, and only a few were intended for private individuals to read. They were always meant to be read out loud, usually to a group of people. For the most part, they were simply necessary surrogates for oral communication. This was particularly true of ancient letters.

Most ancient documents, including letters, were not really texts in the modern sense at all. They were composed with their aural and oral potential in mind, and they were meant to be orally delivered when they arrived at their destinations. For example, when you read the opening verses of Ephesians, loaded as they are with aural devices (assonance, alliteration, rhythm, rhyme, various other rhetorical devices), it becomes perfectly clear that no one was ever meant to hear them in any language but Greek, and, furthermore, no one was ever meant to read them silently. The verses needed to be heard in Greek.

And there was a third reason documents needed to be orally delivered—because of the cost of making documents, a standard letter in Greek would have no separation of words, sentences, paragraphs, or the like; little or no punctuation; and all capital letters. Thus, for example, imagine having to sort out a document that began as follows: PAULAS ERVANTOFCHRISTJESUSCALLEDTOBEANAPOSTLEANDSETAP ARTFORTHEGOSPELOFGOD. The only way to decipher such a collection of letters was to sound them out—out loud! There is of course the famous anecdote about St. Augustine and St. Ambrose: Augustine said that Ambrose was the most remarkable man he had ever met, because he could read without moving his lips or making a sound. Clearly, an oral culture is a different world than a largely literate text-based culture, and texts function differently in such a world. All sorts of texts were simply surrogates for oral speech, and this statement applies to most of the biblical texts themselves.[2]

It is hard for us to wrap our minds around this fact, but texts were scarce in the biblical world and often were treated with great respect. Because literacy was largely a skill only among the educated, and the educated tended to be almost exclusively members of the social elite, texts in such a world served the purposes of the elite—conveying their authority, passing down their judgments, establishing their property claims, indicating their heredity, and the like. But because all ancient people were profoundly religious, the most important documents even among the elite were religious or sacred texts.

What do texts in an oral culture tell us about their authors? It is too seldom taken into account that the twenty-seven books of the NT reflect a remarkable level of literacy and rhetorical skill among the inner circle of leaders of the early Christian movement. Early Christianity was not, by and large, a movement led by illiterate peasants or the socially deprived. The leaders of the movement mostly produced the texts of the movement, and the texts of the NT reflect a considerable knowledge of Greek, rhetoric, and general Greco-Roman culture. This skill and erudition can only seldom be attributed to scribes, except in cases where such scribes as Tertius or Sosthenes (cf. Romans 16 and 1 Corinthians 1) had been converted and donated their skills to the movement. Even then, it appears they were largely just taking dictation from Paul.

The letters we find in the NT are mostly far longer than secular letters of their era. Actually they are *not mainly letters*, although they have epistolary openings and closings sometimes. They are discourses, homilies, and rhetorical speeches of various sorts that the creators could not deliver personally to a particular audience, so instead they sent a surrogate to proclaim them. These documents would not be handed to just anyone. From what we can tell, Paul expected one of his co-workers, such as Timothy, Titus, or Phoebe, to go and orally deliver the contents of the document in a rhetorically effective manner. This would have been almost a necessity because the document would come without division of words or punctuation, so only someone skilled in reading such seamless prose in *scriptum continuum*—indeed, one who *already knew* the contents of the document—could place the emphases in the right places so as to communicate the message effectively.

This brings us to a related crucial matter. Some scholars, on the basis of the occasional reference to "readers" in the NT, have thought that this signaled that Christians were some of the first to be self-consciously trying to produce books or literature meant for reading. For example, sometimes Mark's Gospel has been called the first Christian book, in large part based on the reference in Mark 13:14 where we find the parenthetical remark, "let the reader understand," on the assumption that the "reader" in question is the audience. But let us examine this assumption for a moment. Both in Mark 13:14 and in Revelation 1:3, the operative Greek word is *ho anaginōskōn*, a clear reference to a single and singular reader who, in that latter text, is distinguished from the audience, dubbed the hearers (plural!) of John's rhetoric. As Mark Wilson recently suggested in a public lecture at Ephesus, this surely is likely to mean that the singular reader is a lector of sorts, someone who will be reading John's apocalypse out loud to various hearers.[3]

Sometimes NT scholars have tried to suggest that Christians only used some sort of unique literary genre in telling the gospel story or that their preaching was unlike proclamation on other subjects in the empire. This actually is false. Averil Cameron puts it this way: "A few New Testament critics, taking 'new' in its most literal sense have made extravagant claims: 'a new speech from new depths'; the miraculous unedited newness of the word.' Yet this 'new' Christianity was able to develop a means to ensure its place as a rival to and then inheritor of the old elite culture. . . . Christian discourse too made its way in the wider world less by revolutionary novelty than by the procedure of working through the familiar, by appealing from the known to the unknown."[4] She goes on to add: "Early Christian rhetoric was not always, I shall argue, the specialized discourse its own practitioners often claimed it to be. Consequently, its reception was easier and wider ranging than modern historians allow, and its effects correspondingly more telling. The seemingly alternative rhetorics, the classical or pagan and the Christian were more nearly one than their respective practitioners, interested in scoring off each other, would have us believe."[5]

SACRED RHETORIC

How then did a sacred text function in an oral and rhetorical culture? For one thing, it was believed that words, especially religious words, were not mere ciphers or symbols. They were thought to have power and effect on people if they were properly communicated and pronounced. It was not just the sacred names of God, the so-called *nomina sacra*, that were considered to have inherent power, but sacred words in general. Consider, for example, what Isaiah 55:11 says: "so shall my word be that goes forth out of my mouth: it shall not return to me void, but it shall accomplish that which I please, and it shall prosper in the thing I sent it to do." The Word or words of a living and powerful God were viewed as living and powerful themselves.[6] You can then imagine how a precious and expensive document that contained God's own words would be viewed. It would need to be kept in a sacred place, such as a temple or a synagogue, and only certain persons, with clean hands and pure hearts, would normally be allowed to unroll the sacred scroll and read it, much less interpret it.

From what we can tell, the texts of the NT books were treasured during the first century and were lovingly and carefully copied for centuries thereafter. There is even evidence beginning in the second century of the use of female Christian scribes who had a "fairer" hand to copy and even begin to decorate these sacred texts.[7] But make no mistake— even such texts were seen to serve the largely oral culture. Before the rise of modern education and widespread literacy, it had always been true that "In the beginning was the (spoken) Word."[8] All of this has implications for how we should approach the NT, especially the more ad hoc documents in the Pauline corpus, and the other documents traditionally called letters in the NT, which sometimes are not letters at all. First John is a sermon with neither epistolary opening nor closing. Hebrews is an even longer sermon, with only an epistolary closing, but of course no listener would ever have considered it a letter on first hearing, because there were no signals at the outset of the document to suggest such a thing. And in an oral culture, opening signals are everything if the issue is to identify what sort of discourse or document the audience is listening to. This is why Luke 1:1-4 is so crucial to judging the genre of that Gospel.

Given that the distinction between a speech and an orally performed text was more like a thin veil than a thick wall between literary categories, it will not come as a surprise when I say that oral conventions shape the so-called epistolary literature of the NT more than epistolary conventions do, and with good reason. This is not only because the oral character of the culture was dominant but also more importantly because the Greco-Roman world of the NT period was a rhetorically saturated environment, whereas the influence of literacy and letters was far less widespread so far as we can tell. Thus, we need to understand an important fact: *The rise to prominence of the personal letter used as something of a vehicle for instruction or as a treatise of sorts was a phenomena that only really took root in the Greco-Roman milieu with the letters of Cicero shortly before the NT era.* Contrast this with the long history of the use of rhetoric going back to Aristotle and the use of it in numerous different venues. Rhetoric was a tool useable with the educated and uneducated, with the elite, and also with the ordinary, and most public speakers of any ilk or skill in antiquity knew they had to use the art of persuasion to accomplish their aims. There were not only schools of rhetoric throughout the Mediterranean crescent, but rhetoric itself was part of both elementary, secondary, and tertiary basic education as well. *There were no comparable schools of letter writing* during the NT era as far as we can tell, not least because it was a rather recent art just coming to prominence in the first century A.D. And here we come to a crucial point.

While it can be a helpful exercise to some degree, analyzing the majority of the NT on the basis of epistolary conventions, many of which did not become de rigueur or put into a handbook until *after* NT times, it has no business being the dominant literary paradigm by which we examine the Pauline, Petrine, Johannine, and other discourses in the NT. The dominant paradigm when it came to words and the conveying of ideas, meaning, and persuasion in the NT era was rhetoric, not epistolary conventions.

This is why I will say now that most of the NT owes far more to rhetoric and its very long-standing and widespread conventions than it ever owed to the nascent practice of writing letter essays or letter treatises. Most of the letters of the NT, with the exception of the very shortest ones (2 John, 3 John, and perhaps Philemon), look very little

like the mundane, pragmatic epistolary literature of that era. In terms
of both structure and content, most NT documents look far more like
rhetorical speeches. Some are "words of exhortation," as the author
of Hebrews calls his homily, and some are more rhetorical speeches
suitable for assemblies where discussion would then ensue (e.g., after-
dinner discussions at a symposium), but all are profitably analyzed in
detail by means of rhetorical examination.

RHETORICAL CRITICISM

At this juncture, it would be wise to define more specifically what the
phrase *rhetorical criticism* means in my view and how it applies to the
NT. Rhetorical criticism is by definition the study of rhetoric, whether
ancient or modern; a broad definition of *rhetoric* is the art of persuasion. As applied to the field of NT studies, rhetorical criticism has been
approached in two rather different ways by scholars. The first way,
pioneered and championed by George Kennedy and Hans Dieter Betz
and their students, is more of a historical enterprise, seeking to analyze
the NT documents on the basis of ancient Greco-Roman rhetoric and
asking and answering the question of how the NT authors may or may
not have used this art. Here, we may speak of how the NT authors
adopted and adapted ancient rhetoric for their Christian purposes of
communication.[9]

The second approach, growing out of modern language theory and
modern epistemology when it comes to the issue of texts and meaning,
has been pioneered and championed by Vernon Robbins and his students. Rather than primarily looking for rhetorical structures embed-
ded in the NT texts by NT authors, this approach seeks to apply certain
modern rhetorical categories to the text (e.g., such categories as *inner
texture* or *intra texture*). The terminology, the method, and the theory of meaning of this latter approach has more in common with the
"new" rhetoric of Heinrich Lausberg and others than with the rhetorical guidelines established by Aristotle, Quintilian, Menander, and other
practitioners of ancient rhetoric. In other words, it is more an exercise
in modern hermeneutics than in the analysis of the use of Greco-Roman
rhetoric by the NT authors themselves. The methodological issue here
is whether or not the NT should be only analyzed on the basis of categories the NT authors themselves could have known and used.[10]

In my view, both approaches can yield good insights into the biblical text, but the attempt to fuse the methods of old and new rhetoric
confuses more people than it enlightens. In particular, I would insist
that the primary task is to ask the appropriate historical questions
about the NT text and what its ancient authors had in mind; when that
is the prime mandate, then only analysis on the basis of Greco-Roman

or ancient Jewish rhetoric is appropriate, because ancient authors were completely innocent and ignorant of modern rhetorical theory and epistemology. The remainder of this chapter explains more particularly rhetorical criticism in the Kennedy and Betz vein.

Most NT scholars at this juncture are quite convinced that micro-rhetoric can be found in NT documents, particularly in Paul's letters, but also elsewhere. By *micro-rhetoric*, I mean the use of rhetorical devices *within* the NT documents—for instance, the use of rhetorical questions, dramatic hyperbole, personification, amplification, irony, enthymemes (i.e., incomplete syllogisms), and the like. For example, micro-rhetoric clearly enough shapes: (1) the *chreia* in the Gospels; (2) the speech summaries in Acts; (3) the way portions of a book, such as Revelation, are linked together by catchword and A, B, A structure;[11] and (4) the various enthymemes or incomplete syllogisms we find in the NT (for example, in the Pastoral Epistles).[12] In other words, rhetoric is not just something that illuminates Paul and other portions of the so-called epistolary corpus in the NT. It is a necessary tool for analyzing it all.

More controversial is whether macro-rhetoric is also used in the NT. By *macro-rhetoric*, I mean whether or not the overall structure of some NT documents reflects the use of rhetorical categories and divisions used in ancient speeches. Those divisions are as follows: (1) *exordium*, (2) *narratio*, (3) *propositio*, (4) *probatio*, (5) *refutatio*, and (6) *peroratio*. All six of these normal divisions of an ancient speech could be found in the three different species of ancient rhetoric—forensic, deliberative, and epideictic rhetoric. But these different species of rhetoric served very different functions. *Forensic rhetoric* was the rhetoric of the law court, the rhetoric of attack and defense, and it focused on the past. *Deliberative rhetoric* was the rhetoric of the assembly, the rhetoric of advice and consent, and it focused on changing belief and/or behavior in the future. *Epideictic rhetoric* was the rhetoric of the forum and the funeral, the rhetoric of praise and blame, and it focused on the present. In any given ancient speech, attention was paid as well to the issues of ethos, logos, and pathos—that is, the establishment of rapport with the audience at the outset (in the *exordium*), the use of emotion-charged arguments (logos, in the *probatio* and *refutatio*), and finally the appeal to the deeper emotions (pathos) in the final summation or *peroratio*.

It is fair to say that those NT scholars who have done the detailed rhetorical analysis of all the NT documents have concluded that while micro-rhetoric can be found almost anywhere in the NT, including in genres as varied as the Gospels or Revelation, macro-rhetoric shows up only in the letters, homilies, and speech summaries (in Acts) in the NT. In particular, Paul's letters and the homilies called Hebrews, 1 John, and 1 Peter reflect these larger macrostructures of rhetoric, often in great detail. The macrostructures, however, are used with some flexibility, and they are enfolded within epistolary frameworks in some cases.

Thus, for example, the beginning and end of Paul's letters do almost always reflect epistolary conventions and can certainly be categorized as a form of ancient letters. But these epistolary categories help us very little in analyzing the structure of the material if we are not dealing with the epistolary opening and closing elements (prescript, travel plans, opening or closing greetings). Furthermore, there was no ancient convention to have a "thanksgiving prayer" at the outset of an ancient letter, nor are we helped by lumping the vast majority of a discourse under the heading of "body middle." This tells us nothing about the document, and it is not an ancient epistolary category.

In other words, epistolary conventions and devices help us very little with the bulk of the material in the documents traditionally called NT letters. Here is where rhetoric has proved much more helpful in unlocking the structural and substantive intricacies of the majority of NT documents. Even Paul's letters were not meant to be privately studied. In the first instance, they were surrogates for the speeches Paul would have made had he been present with his audience. As such, they partake of all the ad hoc characteristics of such purpose-driven ancient speeches. They were intended as timely remarks, on target to affect belief and behavior of the various audiences. They were not intended merely as theological or ethical treatises. Rhetorical criticism helps us realize the dynamic and interactive nature of these documents.

A few examples of the usefulness of rhetorical analysis of the NT using the ancient categories of Greco-Roman rhetoric must be offered at this juncture. In the first place, recognizing the rhetorical species of a document will explain much about its content and intent. For example, Ephesians is an epideictic homily written not to a specific situation but to a series of Pauline churches, and it focuses on the rhetoric of praise— in particular, praise of Christ, the church, and the unity between and among them.[13] There is no thesis statement or "proposition" required in epideictic rhetoric, nor are finally honed arguments proving a case necessary. Rather, the audience is intended to be caught up in love, wonder, and praise of someone or some subject. Failure to recognize the rhetorical species of this document, and thus its function and purpose, has led to all sorts of misinterpretations.

Secondly, Romans is a masterpiece of deliberative rhetoric, with its thesis statement plainly laid out at the outset in Romans 1:16-17. This is a discourse about the righteousness of God and the setting right of humankind by grace through faith in Christ, the faithful one. Understanding the rhetorical signals helps with difficult passages, such as Romans 7:7-25, which is a tour de force use of the rhetorical device called *impersonation*, through which Adam and his kin are allowed to speak of their plight in the first person.[14]

In other words, contra Augustine and Luther, these verses are neither Pauline autobiographical remarks nor the plaintive laments of sinful Christians. Furthermore, Paul in Romans is pursuing a delicate rhetorical approach with his largely Gentile audience in Rome, who are not his converts. He uses the technique called *insinuatio*, or indirection. In this approach, one establishes rapport at some length with the audience before dealing with the bone of contention between author and audience—in this case, the Gentile audience's racist views about Jews and even Jewish Christians, which are discussed and rebutted at length in the *refutatio* in Romans 9–11. This same strategy is employed in Galatians, where Paul waits until Galatians 4 to attack the Judaizers head on and demand their expulsion from the churches in Galatia by means of an amazing allegory about Sarah and Hagar.

Finally, in 1 John, which reflects no epistolary features at all and should never have been called a letter, we have a beautiful epideictic homily about love and the character of God and the Christian life, in which virtues are praised and vices are discouraged. Failure to recognize the rhetorical signals in numerous NT documents has led to many false conclusions, especially when it comes to the letters and homilies of the NT. It is safe to say that rhetorical criticism of the NT has established itself as a viable and vital means of analyzing the NT in the last twenty-five years and promises to yield yet more fruit in the years to come. The good news about this approach is that it is not merely modern, it is also ancient, as it was used by many of the great commentators on the Greek NT through the ages, ranging from John Chrysostom to Melanchthon and beyond. It thus has a long and noble pedigree. In my view, it is time for a paradigm shift—the NT documents we have been discussing should *mainly be analyzed by ancient social and rhetorical conventions* and only secondarily by epistolary ones. In this way, we will put the emphasis on the right syllable and analyze the documents as first-century readers or hearers would have primarily evaluated them.

SACRED TEXTS IN A RHETORICAL WORLD

As this chapter draws to a close, I want to return just briefly to the whole issue of the function of sacred texts in an oral and rhetorical culture. I cannot emphasize enough how the living voice was preferred to its literary residue if the speech was taken down or written out beforehand. Rhetoric attended not just to logic and issues of content but to such things as gestures, tone of voice, speed of delivery, and the like, for we are talking about the ancient art of *homiletics*. Function dictated form rather than form following function.

This was all the more the case when it came to the proclamation of a profoundly religious message, especially one based on one or more sacred texts. Sacred texts had an aura, a presence, a palpable character, as the embodiment of the voice of a living God. Ancient peoples would write out their curses on lead foil, roll them up, and place them near or under the altar in a temple, believing that the breath of the deity would animate and act out those words, because the word of a god was a speech-act, an action word that changed things, affected persons, and could serve as either blessing or curse, boon or bane.

In this light, let us study a brief passage of one of Paul's letters, which most scholars think is our very earliest NT document—1 Thessalonians. First Thessalonians 2:13 reads as follows: "And we also thank God continually because when you received the word of God, which you heard from us, you accepted it, not as a human word, but as it actually is, the word of God, which is at work in you who believe."[15]

I will resist the temptation to preach at this juncture, but here is a text that cries out for adequate exposition. First, we note that Paul refers to his own proclamation of the gospel to the Thessalonians as "the word of God"; Paul has no doubt at all that he is speaking God's very word to them, and you will notice he is not likely referring to pre-existing sacred texts from the Old Testament. He is talking about the message conveyed about Jesus. Second, notice that he says that this preaching was by no means only, or even mainly, his own words or the words of human beings or human wisdom. Instead, it was God's living word. Notice, however, that he uses the singular "word." The phrase is "the word of God," on par with previous things that could be called "the word of God" ranging from the utterances of the OT prophets to the sacred texts of the OT themselves. But primacy here is given to the spoken word of God, not to something written—a Good News word of God.

Third, Paul says that this word of God (singular) had lodged in the lives of the Thessalonians, and it was "still at work in you who believe." This word of God had taken up residence in the Thessalonian converts and was doing soul work in and on them. It was a living and active two-edged sword penetrating their very being, just as the author of Hebrews was to suggest in Hebrews 4:12-13, and he also was not talking about a text but an oral proclamation that penetrates the heart.

If we ask whether any of the NT writers believed they were writing sacred, God-breathed texts, it seems to me that the answer must surely be yes. In Paul's case, he believed that he was speaking the very word of God to his converts, not merely his own words or opinions, and furthermore he saw his letters as the surrogates for speeches he would have given in person had he been with his audiences. Letters are just the literary residue of discourses, with epistolary framework added because they must be sent from a distance.

It is no mere rhetoric, full of sound and fury but signifying little, to say that analyzing the NT orally and rhetorically gets us back in touch with the original ethos and character of these oral texts. It remains to be seen whether more students of the NT will heed the call I am making here, change their dominant paradigms, get up from their computers at least for a while, and receive "the living Word of God," about which our earliest NT documents sought to persuade us. In the next chapter, I address a more particular conundrum—namely, if the NT epistolary corpus should not be viewed as texts in the modern sense and in some cases not as letters either, how do socio-rhetorical considerations help us answer whether some of them should be viewed as pseudepigraphical texts, texts with a false attribution of author and audience? Do we have literary fictions in the NT? Inquiring minds want to know.

2

Canonical Pseudepigrapha

Is It an Oxymoron?

We have tried to avoid the pitfalls of "disinterested research" for we have sensed the danger of merely playing in the sandbox of irrelevant scholarship.

— J. M. Robinson and H. Koester[1]

The issue of pseudepigrapha[2] within the canon of Scripture is a critical one from an exegetical, theological, and hermeneutical point of view. Do we really have documents in the New Testament that are falsely attributed to one apostolic figure or another? If we do, what does it say about their authority? Are deception or truth claim issues involved? These issues are too often dodged by NT scholars, or alternately it is assumed that there really is no problem one way or another. Because so many NT "letters" are often assumed to be pseudepigrapha, it is necessary to deal with this issue in some depth. Too seldom is this question posed with a ready grasp of what the actual social and intellectual situation was in the Roman Empire when it came to such issues, and the question is discussed even less often on the basis of what we know about the rhetorical situation during that time period. For example, how did such rhetoricians as Quintilian feel about people stealing their thunder by taking notes at their speeches and then publishing them or proclaiming them under another name? These are some of the questions we must come to grips with in this chapter. Most of all, we must assess whether the rhetorical and historical climate was such that pseudepigrapha would have been seen as an acceptable literary practice without any negative ethical implications.

Often in NT studies over the last hundred years, we have been told that the production of pseudepigrapha was an accepted and time-honored practice without moral issues. But is this another example of scholars ignoring crucial historical and rhetorical evidence to suit their pet theories or perhaps choosing to build intellectual castles in a

19

sandbox that is too small and leads to both erroneous and irrelevant conclusions? These issues are reconsidered in this chapter. The historical evidence must be allowed to carry its proper weight in this matter, and pontifications based on a desired but unproven conclusion need to be held in abeyance.

PRELIMINARY CONSIDERATIONS

A few preliminary remarks are in order. What difference does it make whether some of these documents are pseudepigrapha or not? As it turns out, it makes a great deal of difference in several ways. As David deSilva rightly says, it makes an enormous difference in the way one reconstructs the history of early Christianity and the development of its theological and ethical thinking.

For example, if the so-called Epistles of James and Jude come from the A.D. 40s or 50s and are responding to issues that existed then, including issues rising from the Pauline communities about faith and works, then we have a window into some of the differences in the earliest forms of the Christian faith and in the views of their leading figures. If, on the other hand, these documents are pseudepigrapha from the A.D. 80s or 90s, at least James should be seen as a Jewish Christian document reacting to, rather than being in dialogue with, the Pauline legacy. Again, if the Pastoral Epistles are not by Paul, then we cannot conclude that Paul himself chose to structure his communities as he was about to die, as we see ecclesiology expressed in these letters. These are but two examples, but it should be clear that the authenticity question matters in terms of history, theology, ecclesiology, and ethics, to mention but a few relevant topics.[3]

It is important to argue at the outset that one needs to evaluate the question of pseudepigrapha on a genre-by-genre basis. It is quite clear that pseudepigraphal apocalyptic works existed in early Judaism (e.g., portions of the Enoch corpus) and in early Christianity (the Apocalypse of Peter). Indeed, one could even argue that using a pseudonym was a regular feature of the apocalyptic genre of literature.

One cannot, however, demonstrate that about ancient ad hoc letters. By *ad hoc*, I mean situation-specific letters written to a particular audience. While one could make a case for circular letters of a very general sort accommodating or comporting with the practice of writing pseudepigraphical letters, it is certainly more difficult to make such a case for a particularistic letter.

I have elsewhere given various reasons why I do not think one can make a convincing case for 2 Thessalonians or Ephesians (or Colossians) as pseudepigrapha, although the strongest case has been made for

Ephesians, precisely because it is likely to be a circular document and is more of a homily than a letter.[4] My concern is not to rehearse those arguments here but simply to alert the reader that each document must be examined on a case-by-case basis. We may also want to ask whether it makes a difference if a document is a homily rather than a letter when addressing such questions.

The truth is, the more one studies this issue, the more complex it becomes. For example, we may ask what counts as authorship. Could a document that contained a source document from a famous person (perhaps at the beginning of a composite document) be attributed to that person? The answer to this question is yes. We see this in two very different sorts of documents in the NT. In 2 Peter, we clearly have a composite document that borrows much of Jude but also uses a Petrine source in its first chapter.[5] We also see this phenomenon in the Gospel of Matthew, which uses a special Matthean source that I would argue goes back to the apostle Matthew.[6] The former of these two documents is a composite letter of sorts and falls within the parameters of this study. This reminds us that we must not import into this discussion various modern notions of authorship and intellectual property. The issue must be what the scope or flexibility was when it came to ancient conceptions of authorship and intellectual property. Did ancient notions of intellectual property and plagiarism exist?

Let us consider briefly another possible issue that affects this matter. We know that Paul used secretaries, as Romans 16:22 makes evident, and in addition he tells us at the end of Galatians and 2 Thessalonians that he is taking up the pen, which means he only actually wrote or penned a minority of the words in some of his genuine letters. This raises the pertinent question of whether he might have done something other than just dictate to a secretary. Might he have had them compose a draft to which he would make alterations? Might he have allowed scribes considerable latitude in composing, with plans to revise or correct later? Multiple stages of composition are not all that likely for several reasons: (1) Paul was a man on the move, and he was usually in a hurry; (2) often he had to respond quickly to urgent and emergent circumstances, as demonstrated in various letters of his; (3) paper was expensive, paying a scribe was very expensive, and there are enough infelicities and gaps in the genuine Pauline Letters to suggest these documents were never revised and thus often bear the marks of initial dictation. Incomplete sentences are a dead giveaway.[7]

What is more plausible is that Paul, if he was *in extremis*, might well convey his thoughts orally to a trusted colleague or co-worker who would then write them down and send them off for Paul. This seems to have certainly been within the parameters of ancient views of genuine authorship rather than pseudepigraphy. We do not find this happening in such letters as Philemon or Philippians, in which Paul is still able to dictate letters to those present and send them off while he is under house arrest.

The Pastoral Epistles are perhaps a somewhat different story. One could argue that if Paul were under duress and not far from the time of execution, there would be no leisure time in which he would most likely be able to dictate letters, nor would many people have free access to the man. Perhaps only one trusted friend or colleague who could bring food and convey messages orally (and later write them down) could come to him at a time if he were under close supervision in the Campus Martius, the military camp on the edge of Rome. This *might* be the case with 2 Timothy, and if so, we might well expect the style to be rather different from the earlier Paulines. However, this does not explain why the Pastorals *all* manifest a rather uniform style that in some respects distinguishes them from the earlier Pauline Letters. Furthermore, it does not explain the character of 1 Timothy and Titus at all, both of which were written while Paul was still apparently a free man and not in Rome. We must look elsewhere for an answer to these sorts of questions.

In my judgment, the real dividing line between a genuine letter and a pseudepigraphon is whether the material comes from the mind of a particular person, *not* whether it fully reflects his grammar, syntax, and vocabulary. I would add that a genuine letter not only comes from the mind of the person but is written down by him, or by his request or on his behalf.[8] This seems to have been well within the scope of ancient views of what counted as authorship. We will say more about the Pastorals in this regard shortly.[9]

Epistolary Pseudepigrapha and Intellectual Property in Antiquity — Framing the Discussion

At this juncture, we must consider the issue of epistolary pseudepigrapha in antiquity and the whole question of intellectual property. This must include a discussion of how the early church fathers in the second and third centuries viewed this issue of authorship and intellectual property and the ethics of pseudepigraphy. We may assume that their views would not have differed radically from those of Christians in the first century, although that may be debated. We will tackle these issues together.

First, we may ask, did epistolary pseudepigrapha exist in early Judaism and early Christianity of the first two centuries A.D.? The answer to this question is surely yes. We have such documents as 4 Ezra from the Jewish side and the Epistle to the Laodiceans from the Christian side, although the latter is surely a second-century document created on the basis of the hint that there was such a letter in Colossians 4:16.[10] These examples make clear that such documents existed. Neither of these documents ended up in the Jewish or the later Christian canon, so we may wish to ask why they were excluded or, better said, not considered for inclusion in those canons.[11] In any case, we cannot deny that there were at least a few such documents in play in the NT era or shortly thereafter in the relevant religious communities.

This fact prompts the important question of whether such pseudepigraphical documents raised any ethical questions for early Jews or early Christians, or whether the creation of such documents was simply accepted as part of the literary conventions of the time. We are plagued in part with inconsistent definitions of what might amount to a pseudonymous document within the scholarly community, so answers to the ethical question have often varied.

Richard Bauckham attempts a taxonomy of such documents, dividing them into various categories. He immediately precludes documents that would have been written within the lifetime of an apostolic figure but not by him. He concludes it is very unlikely that any such documents exist in the NT.[12]

Bauckham helps us in various ways to see how difficult it would have been to pull off a pseudonymous letter that was situation specific. For one thing, as he says, not only does the "I" in a pseudonymous letter not refer to the named author, but also the "you" does not likely refer to the named audience, not least because that named audience would likely recognize the document as a forgery! He concludes, "But in no indubitably pseudepigraphical letter known to me are the supposed addressees and the real readers identical."[13] The actual author can only address the actual audience under a literary fiction that involves not only his but also the audience's real identity.

There is then the issue of distance in time and space as well. For a pseudonymous document to work effectively, it needs to be written in the name of a famous-enough person at a great-enough remove from its putative author and audience that its authority and authenticity would be less likely to be challenged. This presents a serious problem for claims about NT letters, all of which, with the possible exception of 2 Peter, were written before the end of the first century A.D., which is to say before the apostolic eyewitnesses or those who had contact with the eyewitnesses had all died out.

For the sake of clarity, by the term *pseudonymous*, I am not referring to anonymous documents, such as Hebrews, nor am I referring to composite documents that at least have some source material by the author whose name is appended to the document. Here, we are helped by the more precise definition offered by I. H. Marshall: "a text is pseudonymous when it is not by the person whose name it bears in the sense that it is written after his death by another person or during his life by another person who was not in some way commissioned to do so."[14]

We may further refine this discussion by pointing out, as David Meade has done, that we should probably distinguish between pseudonyms that are fictitious and those that are borrowed from real human beings.[15] We may also wish to bracket out the use of actual names of ancient or legendary worthies (e.g., Abraham, Isaac), as no one in the first century would be deceived into thinking they were still composing documents during the canonizing era. The issue has to do with the use of real names of contemporary or near-contemporary persons who were known religious authority figures in that era. The motive for pseudonymity would vary from genre to genre; for example, in a pseudonymous apocalypse the attempt is made to pass off history writing as prophecy retrojected into the mouth of an ancient famous religious figure. The issue of prophecy does not necessarily arise in this way with pseudonymous letters.

Another point is in order at this juncture. It could be argued that the canonical documents given the names James and Jude are not pseudonymous, for while they were not written by *the* actual brothers of Jesus, they were rather written by some other unknown early Christian figures who really had such names. This theory is very problematic, precisely because these documents both present themselves as being written by Jesus' actual brothers, and they were certainly viewed in that light in subsequent centuries by Christians. Indeed, they would not likely have been included in the canon had they not been viewed in that way. So, it is doubtful that the issue of these documents and pseudonymity can be resolved with that artful dodge.

There is another consideration from an ancient educational standpoint: the rhetorical exercise called *prosopopoeia*, or impersonation. This exercise was even taken on by school boys, who would try to write a speech as if they were a famous person speaking—Caesar or Alexander, for instance. This rhetorical technique is found in the NT in Romans 7:7-13 when Paul speaks in the first person as Adam, a figure introduced in Romans 5.[16] However, this rhetorical exercise was limited in scope, and to my knowledge it involved only speeches or discourses, not the composition of written documents, particularly letters, using a famous person's name. In addition, in the use of this rhetorical device, there was no attempt to deceive or to use someone else's authority to achieve some nefarious aim. Furthermore, it was always a famous person from the past who was to be impersonated.

Our concern is with documents that could actually be called forgeries because they were created in at least some attempt to deceive some audience, near or far.[17] Deceit is deceit, whether it is for political, financial, personal, or spiritual gain. The issue is whether we have documents in the NT purported to be by one (famous) person but that are really by another who has not been authorized by the famous person to write. It is interesting that it was not until 1792 that an English scholar, E. Evanson, first suggested there might be pseudepigrapha in the NT.[18] Prior to that time, this was not an issue of real debate in the church when it came to canonical books.

NON-DECEPTIVE PSEUDEPIGRAPHA?
VIEWS IN THE EARLY CHURCH

It has often been suggested by scholars in the modern era that while there are definitely pseudepigrapha in the NT, there was no attempt to deceive. It has also sometimes been added by such scholars that the writers were writing in the spirit or as part of the legacy or school of Paul, Peter, or James, or even that they were pneumatic persons who could speak for others or in other's names.

On the surface of things, it is historically plausible that something like the school idea could have happened. We have, for example, the case of Pythagoras. Iamblicus tells us that his disciples wrote in his name, because they attributed to him all that they had learned (*De vita Pythagorica* 158, 198). While it is certainly conceivable this practice could have happened with disciples of Paul, Peter, or James, on closer inspection there is a problem with this sort of reasoning. The disciples of Pythagoras were not writing situation-specific or ad hoc documents to some specific audience using their master's name. They were writing philosophical treatises—a very different matter.

If we consider, for example, 2 Timothy or Titus, these letters contain so many personal details and appear to be addressing a particular historical situation that it is hard to avoid the conclusion that if they are pseudepigraphical, there was an intent to deceive the audience into believing they were written by Paul's own hand, not merely written in the spirit of Paul.[19] We also have no sound historical evidence that Paul, Peter, or James ever had "schools" in the sense that we may talk about Greco-Roman schools where people were trained to speak and write like famous persons. Discipling certainly went on. The sources are quite silent as to whether apostolic co-workers or disciples of apostles were trained to imitate the writings of their apostolic figures.

Furthermore, it is perfectly clear that non-apostles or those who were not even eyewitnesses of much of what they wrote, such as Luke or Mark, felt free to write in their *own* names, and their works were included in the canon under their own names. We also have anonymous NT documents that were deemed to have integrity and authority and were included in the canon (e.g., Hebrews, 2–3 John).[20] In addition, we have composite documents, such as 2 Peter, that do have a link with the reputed author. These things are all demonstrable, and they make it unlikely that there would have been a need for pseudepigraphy in the NT era, *unless* someone really did have the desire to deceive and did not feel he or she had the authority to speak in his or her own voice or anonymously.

There are further problems with the facile reasoning that pseude-pigraphy would not have been a problem in the first-century church. Sometimes this reasoning takes the form that we find in J. D. G. Dunn's work, in which he argues that because pseudepigrapha were not a problem for early non-Christian Jews, they would not have been a problem for early Christian Jews. Dunn of course points to such writings as 1 Enoch, 4 Ezra, and the Letter to Aristeas.[21] The problem with pointing to those examples, as E. E. Ellis has shown, is that the former is an apocalyptic work attributed to an ancient legendary figure, which means it is of a very different ilk than ad hoc letters, and 4 Ezra is likewise a document attributed to an ancient figure. The Letter to Aristeas, while called a letter by Josephus (*Ant.* 12.100), is clearly some kind of treatise, like those produced by the students of Pythagoras, so it does not demonstrate acceptable pseudepigrapha in early Judaism. Furthermore, these documents were not included in the Hebrew canon, which was mostly formed by the end of the first century or early second century A.D.[22]

It is thus hard to see how these examples support the notion that Jews or Jewish Christians would not have had problems with epistolary pseudepigrapha, especially if they claimed to be by a near contemporary or apostolic figure.[23] As Bauckham himself says in evaluating the possibility of such a document as James, Ephesians, or 1 Peter (which are circular documents) being a pseudepigraphon, "the more exegesis tends toward envisaging a specific situation as address in these letters, the less likely pseudepigrapha becomes."[24] We may add also that the closer they were written to the time of their putative author, the less likely the possibility that they could pass as genuine.

It is a helpful point of Bauckham's that only 2 Peter among the NT letters contains indications that it is addressing its immediate *and* a later audience (see 1:12-15, especially the last verse).[25] This suggests it has a broader intended scope than ad hoc letters. In fact, it appears to be the only document that is not really situation specific in the entire NT. It could then be a pseudepigraphon, but only if it does not contain a Petrine source, which it certainly appears to do, just as it contains source material from Jude and elsewhere—but we will say more about this in due course.

It is also not cogent to argue, as Dunn does, that we may distinguish the attitude regarding this sort of matter of Jewish Christians in the first century A.D. from that of Gentile Christians in the second. We have no historical basis for a distinction that suggests pseudepigrapha were acceptable to early Jewish Christians in the first century but not for later Gentile Christians. It is true that there were *additional* reasons to object to pseudepigrapha in the second-century church and later, but that is another matter.

There were clear objections by second- and third-century Christians to such a practice. For example, the Muratorian Canon list, perhaps our earliest canon list (other than that of Marcion),[26] makes note of the Epistle to the Laodiceans and the Epistle to the Alexandrians as being "forged in Paul's name" by Marcion's supporters. Two other classic examples are the supposed correspondence between Jesus and King Abgar or Paul and Seneca.[27] A document named 3 Corinthians was composed by a bishop (!) in the second century, and he said he did it out of admiration for Paul. But when he confessed that he was actually the originator of this document, Tertullian says that he lost his ecclesiastical position (*On Baptism*, 17).

Some of these later documents did take the form of letters, so again we certainly cannot deny there were pseudepigraphical letters in early Christianity. But we also cannot deny that real problems were perceived with such documents. One may also point to Tertullian's judgment in the very same document cited above of the Asiatic presbyter who composed the "Acts of Paul and Thecla." The man was brought to trial and defrocked for the composition of this document, and Tertullian says this is exactly what should have happened with a forger. One could also point to the famous story of Bishop Serapion of Antioch, who around A.D. 200 first approved the reading of the Gospel of Peter in Rhossus in Syria, but when he read the book and realized it was being used to support the docetic heresy, he found some parts of the book to be unorthodox and therefore a forgery (see Eusebius, *Hist. eccl.* 6.12, 3–6).

If we go even further into church history, we can cite the example of Salvian, a priest in Marseilles who was called on the carpet by his bishop for forging a document in the name of Timothy around A.D. 440. Or again, there was Jerome, who actually catalogued types of pseudepigrapha, dividing them into forgeries and falsely attributed works. He listed various criteria for discerning forgeries, including

(1) whether homonyms could be the cause of the false attribution;

(2) whether the book in question was inferior in subject matter or content to other works by the same author;

(3)   when the work was written, in comparison to when the reputed author lived;

(4)   whether statements in the book contradicted or conflicted with the undeniably authentic documents by this person; and

(5)   whether the style of the work was appropriate to its language, author, and time of composition.[28]

A variety of stories like this could be cited from early church history.[29] One then can understand the argument that Dunn has made, which is that these sorts of judgments happened because, by the second century and later, heretics were running around in the church, and there was a heightened concern about what documents were and were not authentic. But I would point out that this concern about forgeries and also about false teaching did not arise for the first time in the second-century church. We already see this concern in 2 Thessalonians 2:2 and elsewhere in the Pauline corpus where Paul takes the trouble to sign his documents to guarantee they are from him (see Gal 6:11; 2 Thess 3:17; and 1 Cor 16:21).

FORGERY AND INTELLECTUAL PROPERTY IN THE GRECO-ROMAN WORLD

Forgery was certainly an issue in the first century A.D., and not just within the confines of the church. In his classic study, B. M. Metzger (followed now by T. Wilder) shows that there was definitely a concept of intellectual property in the ancient Greco-Roman world, and it was seen as a scurrilous practice to put words into someone else's mouth to damage them or even to secure greater credence and authority for one's own ideas (the latter being more to the point for our interests).[30]

First, Metzger is able to show that authors such as Galen had a serious concern about the production of forgeries using his name. For this reason, Galen even wrote a book titled *On His Own Books* to let people know which works were genuine and which were not.[31] In this book, he both listed and described his original works to avoid pseude-pigrapha being pawned off as his own work.[32] Of course, this story also shows that forgeries were not uncommon, but the important point is that Galen objected to such practices and did not see it as a harmless literary convention that everyone accepted. Second, Metzger points out "that persons in antiquity were aware of the concepts of forgery and plagiarism is plain from the existence of a wide range of words used to describe and condemn such practices, e.g., *kibdeleuein, votheuein, paracharattein, plattein, radiourgein.* . . . That scholars in antiquity were able to detect forgeries, using in general the same kinds of tests as are employed by modern critics is also well attested."[33]

Furthermore, some ancient writers used specific literary practices within their documents to protect their intellectual property from being coopted, added to, or subtracted from. Wilder puts it this way: "a writer could protect his work by:

(1) pronouncing a curse in the document to warn others against altering it [see Rev 22:18-19];

(2) binding the authorial attribution with the text by means of a seal or an acrostic;

(3) making known the document's size by citing the exact number of lines/*stichoi* in it [e.g., see the very end of Josephus' *Antiquities*];

(4) informing others of what the work contained in chronological order; or

(5) using trusted friends to circulate his writings before they could be altered or distorted."[34]

All these practices were known and used in the first century A.D., and we find some of them in use in the NT. Another practice used for such authentication was the use of a personal signature, as Paul implemented, which was not a regular practice in ancient letter writing in the Greco-Roman era.

Furthermore, we find evidence that when falsification was discovered, there were moves to correct the problem. The example of Diogenes Laertius may be cited. He tells us (at 7.34) that the librarian of Pergamon, Athenodorus, was caught having falsified some existing Stoic works. Once discovered, the falsified material was eliminated, and the original writings were restored to their original form. Another good example is the lament of Quintilian that only one of his famous rhetorical court speeches was properly published (*Emiseram*). He goes on to complain that though many speeches circulated under his name, they had few words in them that were actually his (*Inst.* 7.2.24).

In his detailed study, W. Speyer[35] points out that there was already in the sixth century B.C. in Greece a concept of intellectual property. For example, Herodotus, the father of Greek historiography, questions whether Homer authored the Cyprian poems (*Hist.* 2.116–17). Aristotle doubted that Orpheus authored the Orphic poems (*De an.* 1.5). Furthermore, there seems to have been a growing awareness and concern about this problem as we progress toward and into the first century A.D. Diogenes Laertius 2.57 speaks of how Xenephon tried to claim the published works of Thucydides were his own, to no avail. We regularly find critical and discerning comments about the issue of authorship by Greco-Roman writers. Cicero comments that he doubts the Sibylline oracles are authentic or inspired (*Diverse* 2.85, 2.110–12). Suetonius, the Roman historian, argues that some works attributed to Horace were likely spurious due to their style (*Lives of Illustrious Men* 2). Suetonius even says that Augustus himself condemned those who wrote under another person's name (*Lives of the Caesars* 2.LV). He adds a story involving the Emperor Claudius about a man found guilty of forgery: He had his hands cut off once he was convicted of the crime (*Lives of the Caesars* V.XV.2). Such examples could be multiplied.[36] These examples are quite enough, however, to make the point.

F. Torm was right when he concluded, "The view that religious circles of Greco-Roman antiquity 'understood pseudonymity as a literary form and straightway recognized its rightness' is a modern invention."[37] It was not seen as an acceptable literary practice but rather as a serious literary problem in the Greco-Roman world, and there could even be criminal repercussions for such acts. Christian reactions to forgery in the second and third centuries as cited above were not atypical of the entire early Christian period. This does not mean that modern conceptions of copyright law applied in antiquity, but a strong case can be made that there was a clear understanding of the matter of intellectual property and the issue of personal integrity when it came to claiming authorship of some document. Plagiarism was recognized as a real problem, not an approved literary device.

AND SO?

Some NT scholars have frankly recognized this problem and have drawn the logical consequence for how one should view such documents as the Pastoral Epistles if they are pseudepigrapha. L. R. Donelson states, "In the interest of deception [the author of the Pastorals] fabricated all the personal notes, all the . . . commonplaces in the letters . . . and any device that . . . might seem necessary to accomplish his deception."[38] This, it seems to me, is the honest and inevitable conclusion once one realizes there was no accepted ancient literary convention that involved epistolary pseudepigrapha if one concludes that the Pastorals, or other NT documents for that matter, are pseudepigrapha.

Ellis goes on to show at length how one has to conclude that if such documents as the Pastorals or 1 and 2 Peter are pseudepigrapha, the authors surely did intend to deceive the audience about this matter, for they excoriate all guile, hypocrisy, and deceit while at the same time practicing it in literary form.[39] Ellis is particularly concerned about apostolic pseudepigrapha (i.e., using the name of Paul, Peter, James, and Jude). He concludes: "The role of the apostle in the earliest church, the evidence for literary fraud in Greco-Roman antiquity, and the New Testament letters themselves combine to show that apostolic pseudepigrapha were a tainted enterprise from the start. At no point in the church's early history could they avoid the odor of forgery. Only when the deception was successful were they accepted for reading in the church, and when they were found out, they were excluded."[40]

One must then ask how in the world this might comport with one further factor. One need also bear in mind that such early Christian writers as Paul believed that both orally and in writing they were speaking the Word of God, a truthful word, not merely the words of human beings. This is already evident in what is generally recognized as Paul's earliest letter. He says, "And we thank God continually because, when you received the Word of God, which you heard from us, you accepted it not as a human word, but as it actually is, the Word of God, which is at work in you who believe" (1 Thess 2:13). The Word of God was spoken and written by such figures as Paul, and this is how they viewed their communications. The documents attest to a concern about truthfulness in all things, especially because the Word of God was being communicated.

Finally, it is worth reiterating why successfully devising a pseudepigraphon would have been especially difficult. C. J. Classen puts his finger on it clearly: "Most poems, works of fiction, novels are written for the world at large for future generations; and this applies to historical accounts as well. Letters, on the other hand, are more immediately relevant, addressed to an individual or a specific group at a specific time in a particular situation, though there are, of course letters composed to be preserved and published and appreciated also later for their literary form or for their content."[41] This remark makes clear how difficult it would be to produce a successful pseudepigraphon—it would likely have to be situation and content specific, but for a situation and with a content that did not actually address the putative audience but rather another later one.

Here are the questions for our study. Do the letters in the NT appear to be situation specific? The answer to this question would seem to be yes, with the exception of 2 Peter. If they are not situation specific, do they show signs of addressing a broader audience over a longer period of time? Again, 2 Peter would seem to be such a document but not these other letters. Do these letters have literary pretensions? We must distinguish here between a facile use of literary and rhetorical devices and literary pretensions. We do find the former in some of our documents, but one would be hard pressed to argue that any of these documents, including 2 Peter, were deliberately written for the purpose of publication or later literary appreciation. We may question whether any of these documents would then have been viewed as valuable or of lasting merit if they are pseudepigrapha.

In light of all these considerations, what must we conclude? At the very least, we must conclude that the older paradigm of F. C. Bauer and others that assumed the general acceptability of epistolary pseude-pigrapha to early Jews and Christians because it was an approved lit-erary genre or literary practice must be rejected. There were various inhibiting factors to such letters being accepted either within or outside of the Jewish and Christian sectors of society. There was indeed a con-cept of intellectual property and also of plagiarism in the Greco-Roman world. Thus, while there may be pseudepigrapha within the NT, the burden of proof must fall squarely on the shoulders of those who claim such a thing.

3

Rethinking and Redescribing Scribal Culture

Our concept of the author as an individual is what underpins our concern with authenticity, originality, and intellectual property. The Ancient Near East had little place for such notions. Authenticity is subordinate to authority and relevant only inasmuch as it underpins textual authority; originality is subordinate to the common stock of cultural forms and values. . . . To us it would seem wrong to credit an editor with the work of an author. The author, in our mind, is the intellectual source of the text, whereas an editor merely polishes; the former is the creative genius, the latter merely the technician. This distinction was obviously less important to the ancients. They did not place the same value on originality. To them, an author does not invent his text but merely arranges it; the content of the text exists first, before being laid down in writing.

—Karel van der Toorn[1]

INSCRIBING A SCRIBAL HERITAGE

New Testament scholars have tried of late to take into account more consciously the role of scribes in the production of letters and other documents in antiquity and thereby to adjust the way we view concepts of authorship as it applies to NT documents.[2]

There are, however, two odd things about this discussion. First, it has failed to take into account adequately the effect of such reflections on the issue of calling one document or another a pseudepigraphon, a matter we discussed in the last chapter; second, the discussion has taken place in a sort of New Testament–era vacuum, without taking into account the long history of scribal work in the ancient Near East and the scribes' role in editing and producing sacred texts.

This chapter attempts to try to remedy that latter deficiency. The way I intend to do this is by having a prolonged dialogue with Karel van der Toorn's landmark new study *Scribal Culture and the Making of the Hebrew Bible*. It must be recognized from the outset that it appears that *all the NT documents were produced by Jews and/or God-fearers, such as Luke*. This being the case, the long history of the role of scribes in Israelite and early Jewish religion is of direct relevance to our discussion of Christian scribes and the NT.

WHEN FEW CAN READ AND WRITE, AND BOOKS ARE NOT BOOKS

Van der Toorn begins his discussion of scribal culture with certain axiomatic statements and assumptions. He stresses the ironic and paradoxical fact that Hebrew religion was birthed in an overwhelmingly oral culture, but the great legacy of that religion was a book—the Hebrew Scriptures. What does it tell us about a religious group that even in an oral culture Jews came to be known as practicing a "religion of the book"?

It is the premise of van der Toorn that scribes manufactured what Christians call the Old Testament, particularly scribes in Jerusalem who were employed by the temple, or perhaps in some case by the rulers who lived there:

> They practiced their craft in a time in which there was neither a trade in books nor a reading public of any substance. Scribes wrote for scribes. . . . The text of the Hebrew Bible was not part of the popular culture. The Bible was born and studied in the scribal workshop of the temple. In its fundamental essence, it was a book of the clergy.[3]

While this thesis certainly can be debated, let us assume for a minute it is true about the OT. This immediately raises the possibility that the NT is something quite different than the OT in this regard. The NT seems on the surface to have been produced by and large by various non-Jerusalem persons who were not themselves scribes. The authors seem on occasion to have used scribes, such as Paul's use of Tertius, but they do not seem to have been scribes themselves, even in their pre-Christian lives. When you have a group of writings produced in a variety of places by a variety of persons, the notion of central control of the sacred text, much less scribal control, would seem to go right out the window. Thus, while it can be argued that the story of the making of the OT portion of the Bible can be said to be the story of the scribes behind the Bible,[4] this thesis seems far less plausible and much less compelling when it comes to the NT. Yet van der Toorn is right to emphasize the fact that prior to the Hellenistic era (i.e., 300 B.C.), there seems to have been no such thing as books as we know them, nor a trade in books, nor a book-buying public: "Insofar as literature reached a larger audience, it was by way of oral performance."[5] This practice, however, of reading out loud or even dramatically performing documents in antiquity was a long-standing one by the time Paul was writing his letters and is of direct relevance in understanding how his letters would have been delivered and dealt with when they reached their destination. Paul wrote as a person seeking to further an evangelistic religion that sought to share the good news with all and sundry. This necessarily meant oral performances of documents written somewhere else when the apostle could not be present to speak to them. In this context, it is worth emphasizing that van der Toorn, were he to stretch his thesis into the NT era, could still assume some continuity with the Ancient Near East (hereafter ANE) world and practices, but clearly the harvest of Hellenism in the Mediterranean world changed a variety of things, one of which was the rise of an actual concern for intellectual property, and the coincident rise of a concern about authorship, as we saw in the last chapter.[6]

Scribes in antiquity were not just secretaries copying documents; they were the scholars of their world. They were usually recruited from the upper echelons of society and, far from just copying and preserving documents, they created and interpreted them as well.[7] They were also the lawyers of their day, which is to say the interpreters and adjudicators of the Law, but they had a variety of other functions as well. This becomes important not only to the study of Jesus' interchange with scribes and Pharisees in various places in Galilee and Judea, but even more tellingly it becomes possibly important when we are told in Acts 4–6 (see esp. Acts 6:7) that various priests and Levites in Jerusalem were converted to the following of Jesus. If this is true, we may assume they brought with them not only their own literacy but probably also their own scribes. This would explain the production of some Christian documents in Jerusalem by James, for instance (see, e.g., Acts 15:23 and perhaps also the letter of James).

Van der Toorn's discussion of books and authors has various revealing points and ramifications for NT studies, so we must walk through this discussion carefully and interact with it. Van der Toorn begins with the assumption that while we do have reference to the "holy books" in such texts as Daniel 9:2 and 1 Maccabees 12:9, both these references are in texts written in the second century B.C. This may be doubted about the former reference. But in general he is right that books as we know them only became a known quantity in the Hellenistic era, an age of increased literacy and the rise of the great libraries in such places as Alexandria and Pergamum, to name but two examples. Thus, when he says there were no books (in the modern sense) in ancient Israel, he is right. There were annals and records kept in royal archives, but public literature really wasn't around in ancient Israel, so far as we can tell.[8] Furthermore, letter writing that involved more than just requests or succinct reports was only becoming a public practice in the first century B.C.

As van der Toorn urges, the conventions in regard to oral performance of anything had a far longer history than the conventions in regard to producing one or another sort of public literature, be it tracts, treatises, letter essays, or other sorts of documents. The conventions of rhetoric long preceded the conventions of letter writing, going back to Aristotle and even earlier. This has considerable ramifications in the way we should understand the documents of the NT.[9] Van der Toorn is right to stress "that the civilizations of the time were at their core oral cultures, literacy being the prerogative of the elite"; furthermore, when one is assessing the social level of a religious group that produces texts, one must take into consideration "the material conditions of writing in antiquity, meaning the writing materials that were used and the labor that was involved in the physical production of texts."[10] Perhaps one of the most important observations van der Toorn makes in his discussion of the rise of book production is that it was in Greece from the classical era onward that one found the highest literacy rates (about 10%), though even there the culture remained through the NT era an oral culture, "rhetoric being the foundation and eloquence the aim of education."[11] The level of literacy is a function of cultural values, social customs, and, perhaps most importantly, access to schooling, though the ability to write a certain script must have also affected the matter as well. For example, some scripts required more technical sorts of tools to produce than others. When one assesses not only the literacy of the earliest Christians but also their abilities with Greek and rhetoric, one quickly realizes these persons had more than a little education and were not from the lower echelons of society.

Van der Toorn argues that in Israel "writing was mostly used to support an oral performance. The native verbs for 'reading' literally mean 'to cry, to speak out loud' (Hebrew קרא . . .). These verbs reflect the way texts were used. Written documents were read aloud, either to an audience or to oneself. Silent reading was highly unusual. Even the student who read in solitude 'muttered' his text (Ps 1.2; compare Acts 8.30). . . . Reading, in other words, was an oral activity."[12] Furthermore, in order for an audience to hear a text properly, this required a specialized messenger, one who already knew the text. Van der Toorn puts it this way: "Even such a mundane form of written communication as the letter usually required the intervention of someone who read its contents to the addressee. A messenger did not deliver the letter like a mailman; he announced its message, and the written letter served as an aide-memoire and means of verification."[13] This practice continued

into NT times, and the implications of this must not be overlooked—
*the audience received the message as an oral performance delivered
according to the conventions of such performances. They did not in the
first instance receive even Paul's letters as "texts."* As van der Toorn
maintains, "oral cultures dictate a particular style in written texts."[14]
In the NT era, the meaning of this was twofold: (1) it meant that there
would almost always be a concern about how the document would
sound, and this in turn meant there would be a concern for the rhetorical dimensions of the text; and (2) because there was much to say, and
book production was expensive, the use of *scriptum continuum* in a
long document especially required a specialized messenger to guide the
audience in understanding what was said and meant. With no division
between words, sentences, or paragraphs, to simply hand a document
to the recipient was to invite at a minimum a period of ponderous puz-
zling over the many letters and lines, and misunderstanding was bound
to follow as well. A division of sentences would be missed. An emphasis
would be misplaced. The ending of one sentence would be mistaken
for the beginning of the next (e.g., in Greek when a sentence ends with
a word that concludes with -ος). Imagine then how much greater was
the need for an interpreter and oral deliverer of the document when
the content was believed to be something the audience crucially needed
to hear, such as a matter of salvation or the prevention of apostasy.
Whether as a script for oral performance or a reminder or aid to the
memory of the messenger or herald, such texts must be seen as "oral"
in character and intent.[15]

It is true that so long as texts or books were rare, the impetus for
literacy would not be very great, but what we notice in the NT era is
that there was more emphasis on the production of texts than ever
before, including the rise of the use of the codex in the first century
A.D., which seems to have become the especial favorite of evangelistic
Christians. This in turn reminds us that there were several reasons for
Christians to become more literate persons, not least being the desire
to help spread their religion. And here is where I point out that it is the
strongly evangelistic nature of early Christianity that makes it stand out
by and large from early Judaism, although there was some proselytizing
in early Judaism as well. What must be remembered is that the early
Christian movement was reaching out to all sorts of persons and to
various ethnic groups, which not only required the production of texts
in Greek, the lingua franca of that world, but also required that those
texts be orally persuasive or winsome, in order to win some. And great
sacrifices would need to be made to produce Christian texts.

In his discussion of the expense of producing ancient documents,
van der Toorn says the following: "The earliest reference to the buying
and selling of Hebrew scrolls are from the Roman period. Price is rarely

mentioned. However one rabbinic tractate from the late Second Temple period states that the price of a Torah [i.e., the Pentateuch scroll] was 100 mineh, which equals 10,000 pieces of silver. Considering the fact that the average laborer earned one piece of silver a day, this price was exorbitant."[16] We may compare the possibly hyperbolic figure in Acts 19:19, which values the magic books of the Ephesians at 50,000 pieces of silver. Nevertheless, one gets the picture. This was a very expensive enterprise. One would reckon that when a codex of the four earliest Gospels was first produced at the beginning of the second century A.D., the cost was quite considerable. We must not make the mistake of thinking there were hundreds of copies of these documents being made in the first or early second centuries A.D, just as we must not make the mistake of thinking the documents would have been treated casually. On the contrary, they would have been preserved and looked after as sacred texts, as is already clear from what 2 Peter 3 says about a collection of Paul's letters.[17]

The cost of even a normal papyrus roll is estimated to have been one to two weeks' wages of an ordinary worker. What ordinary person working to feed his family and survive could afford such a luxury? The answer is, not many. The evidence of the recycling and reusing of papyri and parchment is clear testimony to the expense involved. But the cost of the whole process might have been reduced if a Christian who was a scribe or literate at least would take on the task of copying down a message, thus limiting the cost to the materials involved. Van der Toorn points out a factor that could have aided the proliferation of Christian texts, at least in some contexts: "In Roman times, the price of papyrus fell after the state monopoly on papyrus ended and Palestine was able to control its own papyrus production."[18] But for documents produced nowhere near Egypt, there would still be the need to import and buy the requisite papyri from a dealer. The middle man could not be avoided. If one had to hire a good scribe as well to produce a document in a fair hand, this would add to the cost about two silver denarii a day, as scribes earned twice the normal wage of an average worker. And this leads to a discussion of another factor.

We do not really have any private documents in the NT, with the possible exception of 3 John. Private persons, apart from the very wealthy, could not afford to purchase or own scrolls or books. Even the Torah scroll did not become a private possession of many before the third century A.D., according to Van der Toorn.[19] This being the case, we need to look at all the NT documents, including such a document as Philemon, as public documents that would have been housed in the home of the house church leader and would have been seen as group property. An exception to this would perhaps be the case of

Theophilus, possibly a wealthy patron of Luke's for whom Luke wrote Luke–Acts. We are then not *reading private mail* when we read NT documents. We are reading documents written for groups of Christians for their public edification and instruction.

Van der Toorn goes on to emphasize the difference between a *scroll* and a *codex*. The former was particularly cumbersome if one was looking for some particular passage to copy or cite, which is no doubt one reason that Christians in the late first century quickly gave preference to codexes. Their documents were meant to be used regularly and cited as sacred texts. And as van der Toorn stresses, the scope of a scroll or codex did not necessarily coincide with the scope of a literary work. Because space was at a premium and book production was expensive, a scribe would regularly include more than one document in a scroll or codex, based on the available space, *if there were several documents that the audience might need or want.* The attempt to treat all the NT documents as discrete documents is probably somewhat misguided. For example, there seems clearly to be some kind of literary relationship between Colossians and Ephesians. Could they have circulated together on one scroll—the former for a more specific audience, the latter for a more general one?

The rise to prominence of the already extant Hellenistic schools used to train scribes in how best to use papyrus and scrolls coincides with the rise of the Roman Empire, an enterprise that required many documents and long paper trails. And Jews realized they needed to respond to the propaganda of the Republic and the Empire, especially once they became a conquered and dominated people. So it is of interest for our study that there was a rise of Jewish schools in the Hellenistic and Roman eras. Already around 180 B.C., we hear of the school of Ben Sira (Sir 51:23), and one Talmudic text tells us there were some 480 schools in Jerusalem alone (J. T. Meg. 73b). Doubtless this is an exaggeration even in the post–Second Temple era, but there is no reason to doubt there were many such schools. Van der Toorn emphasizes, "These Jewish schools arose in part in response to the Hellenistic policy of establishing Greek schools in conquered territories. As the tuition fee for the schools was substantial (Sir 51.28) formal education was restricted to the well-to-do. Under the guidance of their teachers, students could familiarize themselves with the classics—Homer in the Greek schools; the Law and the Prophets in Ben Sira's *bet midras* (Sir 39.1-3)." Furthermore, it was possible for a Greek-speaking Jew like Paul to get training in rhetoric in Jerusalem itself. We must not underestimate the extent of Hellenization in the Holy Land and the length of time it had influenced early Judaism before we reach the time of the production of NT documents.[20]

WHEN AUTHORS ARE ANONYMOUS

As van der Toorn stresses, "in the ancient Near East, it was uncommon for an author to sign his or her work. Ben Sira was one of the earliest Jewish authors to put his name to his book (Sir. 50.27). Until the Hellenistic era, anonymity prevailed."[21] It should not be a surprise then that we have various anonymous documents in the NT, such as Hebrews. The Synoptic Gospels and Acts as well are probably formally anonymous, the labels appended to them as superscripts being later additions. The same can be said for 1 John. Letters in the NT era by contrast do indeed mention authors' names and make claims about authorship. It is intriguing that in Israelite history, prophetic scrolls are all attributed to a particular person. Not one is anonymous. This does not help us much with the NT documents, because they are not, with the exception of Revelation, prophetic scrolls (although various non-prophetic books, such as the Gospels, contain prophetic passages), but sure enough, Revelation clearly begins with an attribution of authorship, a normal trait for a Jewish prophetic scroll.[22] However, other forms of apparent authorship existed in antiquity that we might not recognize today as such. Final editorship apparently counted as authorship in some Jewish circles. Consider, for example, the following quote from the Talmud:

> Moses wrote his book, the portion of Balaam, and Job. Joshua wrote his book and [the last] eight verses of the Torah. Samuel wrote his book, and Judges, and Ruth. David wrote the book of the Psalms at the instruction of the Ten Elders, namely Adam, the first human being; Melchizedek; Abraham; Moses; Heman; Yeduthun; Asaph; and the three sons of Korah. Jeremiah wrote his book, the Book of Kings, and Lamentations. Hezekiah and his associates wrote Isaiah, Proverbs, Song of Songs, and Qohelet. The men of the Great Assembly wrote Ezekiel and the Twelve, Daniel, and the Scroll of Esthers. Ezra wrote his book and the genealogies of Chronicles up to his time. . . . Who then finished it? Nehemiah the son of Hachaliah. (B. T. B. Bat. 14b-15a)

This remarkable passage, as Van der Toorn argues, is sometimes referring to authorship in the modern sense, but sometimes it is just referring to who finally wrote down or copied the final form of the text, as in the case with the reference to Hezekiah and the book of Isaiah.[23] All this points to a collectivist rather than individualist view of authorship in antiquity. Traditions and prophecies that began with a prophet would be transcribed by scribes, edited and amplified over the course of time, and put into something like an official form by royal officials for the sake of the use of the rulers. Clearly however, none of the NT documents came out of a royal archive or palace situation, and such practices and concerns did not apply in the case of the NT. The NT is clearly minority literature, which is one of the things that makes it so interesting.

For example, van der Toorn discusses examples where "when a work had been commissioned, the author would ascribe it to the patron. In other instances, an author would pretend to be a famous figure from the past. The former is a case of 'honorary' authorship; the second one of pseudonymity."[24] We do not seem to have examples of either of these sorts of "authorship" in the NT. No documents are ascribed to legendary figures from hoary antiquity, such as the patriarchs or Enoch, and while a patron may be mentioned in Luke–Acts, no documents are ascribed to such persons in the NT. It is possible, however, that the practice of ascribing a document to its most famous contributor does exist in the NT—say, in the case of the Gospel of Matthew, or 2 Peter. Scribes did not tend to take personal credit for a document that they had compiled from various previous authoritative sources. I suggest that Matthew and 2 Peter may reflect such scribal activity, in which case we are not dealing with pseudonymous attribution in either case. The reason for pseudonymity is that in these cultures, antiquity implies authority, as does association with a very ancient worthy figure. But clearly even in OT times, there were serious issues with pseudonymity, as reflected in the Book of Jeremiah. Van der Toorn says the following:

> The controversy provoked by the alleged discovery of Deuteronomy demonstrates that fictive antiquity and pseudonymity *were not simply conventions of the literary genre.* Deuteronomy contains the text of the ancient 'Book of the Torah,' whose discovery served to legitimize a cult reform by King Josiah in 622 (2 Kngs. 22–23). The prophet Jeremiah did not accept the claim of antiquity and denounced the book as a fraud manufactured by 'the deceitful pen of the scribes' (Jer. 8.8-9). He was not the only one to have doubts; shortly after the book had been found, the officials in charge consulted the prophetess Huldah to check whether or not the document was authentic (2 Kngs. 22.11-20). The criticism of Jeremiah and the consultation of Huldah reflect a critical attitude toward the claim of antiquity.[25]

It is not clear to me that Jeremiah is talking about Deuteronomy, but in any case this material shows that there was already an issue with pseudonymity amongst Jews long before the NT era.

Scribes and Their Tasks in the Temple and Elsewhere

One of the major theses of Van der Toorn is that the temple was the center of education in antiquity, rather than the court. He points, for example to the discovery of 1,500 educational exercise tablets in the temple of Nabu in Babylon. Scribal education took place in the temple complex, the library was housed there (and perhaps a further one in the court for the use of royal officials), and sacred texts especially would be kept in the temple precincts. The goal in training a scribe was that he would be able to write clearly, and yet fast enough, to keep up with the speaker, hence the Sumerian proverb, "A scribe whose hand can keep up with the mouth, he indeed is a scribe!"[26] For the scribe the "pedagogy was geared toward the mastery of the technical vocabulary of these various disciplines; the emphasis lay on memorization and scribal skills rather than on the intellectual grasp of the subject matter."[27] What is interesting is that once a scribe acquired these basic compositional skills, he could then go on to become a sage or expert in various disciplines based on the texts he copied. For example, a scribe could continue his study by training to be an astrologer (focusing on star charts and astrological texts), or a diviner, or an exorcist, or a doctor, or a cult singer. There was a textual corpus for each of these trades, and notice that they were all religious in character as well. This leads to the question of whether one reason the scribes and other Jewish authorities objected to Jesus' exorcisms and those of his disciples was because they were stealing their thunder, practicing their trades without training and authorization from above.[28]

There were scribes who simply had skills in copying. We may call them clerks. And some scribes would be hired on private estates by the wealthy to transact business. But there were also public scribes, such as those whom Jesus criticizes for bilking the estates of widows (Luke 20:45-47). Whether they were called scribes or teachers of the law, we are talking about the same persons. It could take up to four years of education to become a scribe, and with that education came the assumption that they were then authorities in their field of expertise, should they have gone beyond the learning of merely how to take dictation rapidly.[29] We begin to see what Peter and John were up against when they sought to teach in the very provenance in which scribes operated, the temple and, more specifically, Solomon's Portico (Acts 4). They were not those who had a scribal education and thus could be called "unlettered" persons (which is not the same as being illiterate). Scribes belonged to the clergy class, and even the priestly class in some cases (e.g., Levites were often scribes),[30] and there is something of the clergy versus laity prejudice reflected in the remarks made in Acts 4:12-15 about Peter and John. Van der Toorn argues that "the 'scribes' of the Gospels are the descendants and successors of the Levites from the days of Ezra, Nehemiah, and Chronicles. One [proof of this thesis] is the association of the scribes with the study and teaching of Torah.

According to the Gospel of Luke, the 'scribes' are coterminous with 'the teachers of the law' (νομοδιδασκολοι, Lk 5.17) or 'lawyers' (νομικοι, Lk 7.30)."[31]

Part of the training of many scribes was also to learn foreign languages and to go abroad to study foreign customs and practices. Sir 39:4 speaks of scribes who do this. Furthermore, there were occasions when scribes had to compose their own texts and "composition being largely an oral art, scribes thus had to acquire rhetorical skills."[32] There were six tasks a scribe might be involved in: (1) transcription of oral lore; this no doubt was what some Christian scribes engaged in to preserve the oral teachings of Jesus and others; (2) invention of a new text; there can be little doubt that someone such as Paul or Apollos had considerable education, including being trained in the skills of composing letters, rhetorical discourses and the like, which he later put to good use in the service of the gospel; (3) compilation of existing lore, either oral or written. Here 2 Peter comes to mind, a document that reflects scribal compilation of material from Peter and from Jude with attribution not to himself but to the most famous contributor; (4) expansion of an inherited text. Here, Matthew's Gospel comes to mind, which takes more than 95 percent of Mark (some 51% verbatim) and then adds other source material. There is another reason to attribute the final form of Matthew to a Christian scribe. Scribes were those who preserved and passed on wisdom literature, such as the book of Job, and both Matthew and John as Gospels are sapiential in character; (5) adaptation of an existing text for a new audience. This in part is what happens to the material in Jude, in the hands of the scribe who composed 2 Peter; and (6) integration of individual documents into a more comprehensive composition.[33] Both the Gospel of John with its epilogue and the book of Revelation with its letters as well as visions may reflect such a compositional approach. In all cases, we must evaluate the NT on the basis of the existing scribal and compositional practices, not our later ones. One thing is clear: "faithful reproduction of the text as received was the scribal norm. The dutiful scribe neither added to nor removed from his text."[34] The warning by John at the end of Revelation 22 is surely a warning to Christian scribes not to go beyond their normal practice in handling his document. We should not expect then for scribes to play a major role in the "creation" of the NT materials and sources, but in its composition as documents we may see their hand in various places and ways. The final question that van der Toorn's study raises is about the role of scribes in the formation of the Hebrew canon, a discussion with some bearing on the formation of the NT canon as well.

SCRIBES AND THE COMPOSITION
OF THE HEBREW CANON

The term *kanon* has as its original sense a table or list, and, in the case of texts, a list of documents or books. Despite protests to the contrary, van der Toorn convincingly argues that the canon of the Hebrew Scriptures was basically closed by the end of the NT era. Pointing not only to Josephus' clear reference to twenty-two books of the Jewish people (*Against Apion* I.38-40), and the reference to twenty-four books both in 2 Esdras 14:44-46 and B. Bat. 14b-15a (the twelve minor prophets are counted as one book, as is Ezra-Nehemiah), van der Toorn adds, "by specifying the number of the books both Josephus and the author of 2 Esdras 14.44-46 implicitly rely on a list. In other words, a limited list of books, or canon." As he goes on to stress, a canon originally is not a volume, but a list.[35] It matters not that the earliest codex of the Hebrew Bible, the Aleppo codex, is from the ninth century A.D. The canon was closed much earlier than that. The point at which the books are put together as a single document is not the point of canonization: "The Hebrew Bible was a list before it was a book. In view of the *numerus fixus* given in several first century C.E. texts, moreover, the list was apparently assumed to be closed."[36] But what role did scribes in Jerusalem play in this process? According to the letter in 2 Maccabees 1:10–2:18, a document that dates to about 60 B.C. if not earlier, there was a temple library in Jerusalem. This telling passage not only mentions Nehemiah as the one who first reestablished a library of sacred books when he returned from exile but also points to Judas Maccabee, who "collected all the books that had been lost on account of the war that had come upon us; they are [now] in our possession. So if you [i.e., the Jews in Alexandria] should lack some of them [in your collection], send people to get them for you" (2 Macc 2:13-15).

Keep in mind that scribes were the maintainers of such libraries and the composers of lists, and it is quite possible that the original Hebrew canon list began as a list of sacred texts held in the Jerusalem temple library. This library would have been accessible only to authorized persons, not to just anyone. We should not draw analogies with modern public libraries; public libraries did not exist before the Hellenistic age and not much after that period, either.

Where would this Jerusalem library have been? Josephus in effect tells us when he says that the priest Hilkiah found the sacred books of Moses as he was bringing out the gold and silver from the temple treasury (*Ant.* 10.57-58). This is exactly what one would expect, because temple treasuries throughout all the ancient world were places where one deposited important documents ranging from wills to astrological charts to accounting ledgers to sacred books. There is no reason to suspect that practices in Jerusalem would have been any different than elsewhere in the ancient world.

If we want to see another example of a Jewish library, we can certainly turn to the sectarians of Qumran and consider their extraordinary collection of texts. Except for the book of Esther, we do not know of a single text dating before 150 B.C. that is not represented in part or whole in their collection. Their library represented a type like that at Alexandra—comprehensive rather than selective. Not only did it include documents with opposing points of view (e.g., the Aramaic Levi document, Jubilees, 1 Enoch on the one hand and Sirach on the other), but it also included its own community documents as well, which we would not expect to find in the library in Jerusalem.[37] The issue then becomes whether the library in Jerusalem was deliberately selective or whether it tried to be more comprehensive like the one at Qumran. The quote cited above about the Jerusalem library suggests that it was a more comprehensive library, because it describes an offer to the Jews in Alexandria of the opportunity to come and make copies and add to their collection, which would be a quite cheeky offer if the Jerusalem library was known to be more selective than the already extant one in Alexandria! The long and short of this discussion is that it suggests that the original Hebrew canon list was not simply a reproduction of the Jerusalem temple library holdings list. Some other social factors must have been in play. While as an alternative theory some have suggested that perhaps the original Hebrew canon list was a list of the curriculum for scribal study, van der Toorn decisively refutes this idea. Scribes in their training were taught to do technical tasks and to copy specialty literature, not epics and long narratives so far as we can tell.[38] Works of literature far outweigh technical studies in the Hebrew canon.

Van der Toorn thus proffers a third thesis—namely, beginning with Ezra a group of scribes provided editions of sacred texts for use in temple, synagogue, and later the home to meet the growing literacy rate and the demands of educated laity and nonscribal teachers alike:

> Between 300 and 200 B.C.E. the scribes of the temple workshop at Jerusalem prepared an edition of the Prophets, the Psalms, the book of Proverbs [the Pentateuch already being extant as a book] to meet the demands of a growing class of literate laymen; their edition was meant to be definitive and to be put at the disposal of the public, to be read in the place of worship, in schools, and by private individuals. At the same time, the temple scholars formulated the doctrine of the closure of the prophetic era. According to the new doctrine, the Spirit of prophecy had departed from Israel after the days of Ezra. Direct revelations were believed not to occur any longer; therefore divine illumination could be obtained only by a study of the Law and the Prophets.[39]

In other words, when the scribes composed the canon of the prophets, they in effect declared the prophetic era closed. Of course various NT figures, including Jesus himself, would dispute or modify such a dictum. Jesus, for instance, would say that John was the last of the line of such prophets, not Malachi, but what is most interesting is that the NT writers operated with a clear sense of a given corpus of the Law and the Prophets that were now being fulfilled in and through Jesus and his movement. What is interesting is that while Jesus and his followers were declaring not only an age of fulfillment of old revelation but also a new age of the Spirit inspiring new prophets and new revelations, other Jewish groups were insisting otherwise. According to Josephus, the time of revelation ended during the reign of Artaxerxes (*Ag. Ap.*, 1.40-41), and the latter Tosephta commentary on the Mishnah tractate Sotah stresses, "When the latter prophets Haggai, Zechariah, and Malachi died, the Holy Spirit departed from Israel" (cf. Y. Sotah 9, 13).[40] By publishing a national library of sorts and helping stock the synagogues with its books, the scribes hastened the process of the closing of the Hebrew canon.

It is important to note the criteria that the scribes used in selecting books for the Hebrew canon—authorship and/or antiquity, the same two criteria that, along with apostolicity, were to be applied in recognizing a NT canon much later. But scribes must be given their due in the formation of the Hebrew canon, perhaps in a way and to a degree that certainly cannot be said about the NT canon. Van der Toorn puts it this way:

> The coming about of the biblical canon is a triumph of scribal culture in the sense that the scribes succeeded in transforming the written traditions of a professional elite into a national library . . . as a result the scribal practices of study, memorization, and interpretation became part of the religious habits of a nation. Scrolls were the symbols of Hebrew scribal culture; as the Bible became the symbol of Jewish religion, Judaism assumed traits of the scribal culture. . . . From its earliest scribblings to the closure of the canon, the Hebrew Bible was the work of Hebrew scribes.[41]

If this hypothesis is anywhere near correct, it helps explains a singular fact about the NT: why, with only one exception, the NT writers never cite any early Jewish literature directly (using, e.g., Scripture citation formula, such as "it is written" or "as God says"), except literature that we now find in the OT! The only exception is from perhaps the earliest, or one of the earliest, of NT documents, Jude, and even there, as we shall see in a later chapter, Jude may not be suggesting that 1 Enoch is a sacred text, only that Enoch was a true prophet.

And So?

While the theory of scribal production of the Hebrew Bible does not explain all our conundrums when it comes to the origins of that book that the earliest Christians used and called the Scriptures, it certainly makes clear that we can indeed talk about a nearly completely closed canon of the OT in the NT times that the NT authors stuck to when they wanted to cite authoritative Scriptures to back up their teachings. This theory also helps us to remember again that the educated were few, and books were produced by even fewer, often mostly by scribes. The issues between Jesus and the scribes were ones not just of moral authority but also of who could correctly interpret the sacred texts. It appears reasonably clear that not only did the earliest Jewish Christians continue to use scribes in the production of their documents, but scribes who had priestly training and heritage, such as Barnabas did, provided some of the elite leadership of the earliest Christian communities. Paul himself seems to have had both a Pharisaic and perhaps also a scribal education, which included an education in rhetoric, while he grew up in Jerusalem. Most importantly, the study of van der Toorn makes it appear incredibly unlikely that we should not see the leadership of early Christianity as part of the early Jewish elite circles—those who not only were literate but were even in some cases learned and scholarly, such as Paul or Apollos. The theories of E. A. Judge about the social level or the leadership of early Christianity find an unexpected ally in the work of van der Toorn. We also gain new appreciation for the sacrifices early Christians made to promulgate their new faith, for considerable sacrifices were required, monetary and otherwise, to produce documents of this quality, length, and abundance. The gospel, if it could not be heard directly from an apostle, needed to be promulgated indirectly through documents delivered orally and in writing by apostolic coworkers. This elevates the importance of the roles a Timothy, a Titus, or a Phoebe played as heralds of the Pauline gospel and harbingers of the apostle's arrival to further the discourse.

In the context of a culture where various religious authorities said that the Scriptures and the prophetic era were closed and done, Christianity saw a need to say "not so fast" and then go on to produce its own collection of sacred texts, all the while knowing that if antiquity, authorship, and apostolicity were to be the criteria by which to decide which documents passed muster as Scripture, then the NT Scripture was effectively closed once the apostolic and eyewitness age ceased to exist. But we shall say much more about this in a later chapter. Here, it must suffice to say that van der Toorn has placed the discussion of these matters on fresh and more solid scribal ground and has reminded us that all these biblical texts arose in an oral culture and are oral texts, and for that we should be thankful.

4

The Question of Sermons and Homilies in the New Testament

Jesus did not say, "let those with two good eyes, read." He said, "let those with two good ears hear." One of the implications of taking seriously the dominantly oral and rhetorical character of first-century culture is that some New Testament documents, upon reexamination, turn out to be not letters at all but rather sermons, samples of early Christian preaching.

Two chapters ago, we discovered that the modern penchant for categorizing all sorts of NT documents as letters had led to the conclusion that we have falsely attributed letters or pseudepigrapha in the NT. We saw good reason to doubt that conclusion. But there is a long precedent for misidentifying some early Christian documents as letters. Two good examples of this phenomenon will have to suffice. First, there is the document known as 2 Clement, which although called a letter by Eusebius (*Hist. eccl.* 3.38) clearly gives evidence of being a sermon read aloud to a congregation (15.2; 17.3; 19.1). Second, there is the book of Hebrews, which P46, one of our earliest witnesses, positions between Romans and 1 Corinthians. In the uncials (A, B, C, H, I, K, L, P), it is placed after 2 Thessalonians but before the Pastorals. In both instances, the placement of the document shows that it is viewed by the composers of the manuscript as a letter, indeed as some sort of Pauline letter.

It is important as well to recognize that one could argue that rhetorical discourses, such as Paul's letters, which were orally delivered in worship services as part of those services, also served as sermons of a sort even though they had epistolary openings and closings. It is interesting that almost the entire discussion of homilies in the *Anchor Bible Dictionary* is taken up with the issue of the use of rhetoric in shaping early Christian proclamation.[1] But what do we really know about ancient Jewish and Christian sermonizing? Apart from what we find in the NT, there is sadly very little we know about early Jewish sermonizing. But perhaps we are not looking in the right places or in the right ways. Perhaps we have been looking in the wrong social context, using the wrong literary models to analyze such documents, all the while ignoring the dominant rhetorical character of all oral proclamations and speeches in antiquity. What can we really say about early Jewish sermons when examined from these angles?

ON JEWISH SERMONS

We need to understand from the outset that ancient sermons may have looked quite different from modern ones. For example, ancient sermons were not necessarily expositions of a particular, or even two or three, biblical texts. Of course, there was no NT when the NT writers were living, and thus for them the Old Testament was the sacred Scripture (see 2 Tim 3:16).

But even so, early Christian sermons were based on a variety of resources. There were sermons based on OT texts, but there were also sermons based on early Christian tradition, including the Jesus tradition, and sermons based on general biblical themes. Also, there were rhetorical discourses using all kinds of resources, to mention just several possibilities. Expository preaching of the Bible was not the only thing happening in the first-century world of Jewish or Christian preaching. Where then should we begin to explore this matter?

Part of our problem in talking about this matter is that there is considerable debate about the existence of synagogues in the first century A.D., by which is meant purpose-built Jewish religious buildings. This clouds the issue of what could have been going on in such places.[2] Most scholars have concluded there were synagogues in the first century A.D., not merely because they are mentioned in the book of Acts, but because Josephus also mentions them (*Wars* 2.285-91—a *sunagoge* adjoining another plot of land in Caesarea Maritima; cf. *Wars* 7.43-44 about one in Antioch), and because of the inscriptional evidence (SEG 17, no. 16) from Berenice in Northern Africa, dated to A.D. 56, which speaks of the repair of a *sunagoge*, clearly not a reference to people! We may also point to the purpose-built structures at Masada, the Herodium, and at Gamala. We now have also the careful argument of R. Riesner that there is evidence in Jerusalem itself of the existence of synagogues in the NT era. We may also point in particular to the Theodotus inscription.[3] It may be concluded, then, that there were such synagogue buildings. But what went on in them?

It seems clear that the synagogue was not yet the very formal institution it was to become after A.D. 70. The very fact that Paul, as an unknown visiting speaker, could be repeatedly invited to speak in such places all over the eastern Empire should tell us that early synagogues, at least in the Diaspora, did not exactly have a fixed rotation of proclaimers.

The earliest clues we have on the matter of synagogue worship come from Alexandria and Philo (*Leg.* 3.162-68 and *Mut.* 253-63), and what he tells us indeed suggests a less formal institution that met sometimes in homes and sometimes in purpose-built buildings for prayer and what we might call Bible and religious study—an early version of Hebrew school, and some form of worship on Shabbat (Friday evening). Later Talmudic evidence about a lectionary cycle of readings, sometimes anachronistically projected back into the first century, probably is not that relevant. But what we can say is that there is clear evidence of the reading of the Torah in the worship service and its exposition in some form.[4]

We may think of the brief synopsis offered by Luke in Luke 4:16-27, which may provide us with some clues. There we have reading of Scripture, exposition of a sort, and an exhortation responding to the response of the audience. There clearly seems to have been an interactive dimension to this experience. Questions could be put to the speaker and he would answer, perhaps after the initial exposition. We know that there were early rules of exegesis laid down by Hillel in the first century (the so-called seven rules). One would comment on a particular text and then relate it to other texts, sometimes in a sort of chain reference or catena-like citation (cf. Philo, *Spec.* 2.15 no. 62; *Prob.* 12 no. 81-82).[5]

On the Rhetoric of Jewish Christian Sermons

What comports with this picture is what we find recorded in Luke's synopses of synagogue sermons offered by early Christians such as Paul. We may compare, for example, Acts 13:15-41. Notice in the first verse that there is an invitation to offer "a word of exhortation" (*logos parakleseos*), the very same phrase used to describe the highly Jewish and textually oriented discourse we call Hebrews (Heb 13:22). This suggests that at least one form of synagogue homily involved paraenesis based on Scripture exposition. In other words, it had an ethical and practical aim, it was not just an expounding of interesting ideas. This is hardly surprising because early Judaism was more focused on orthopraxy than orthodoxy.[6]

L. Wills, in an important essay, has argued that this "word of exhortation" form of homily had three parts: (1) the *exempla*, which was a reasoned exposition of the main thesis, usually with illustrations from one or more scriptural texts. This exempla laid out the facts, sometimes in narrative form, and illustrated them. This was followed by (2) the *conclusions*, which were based on those facts laid out in the first part of the homily. This section was introduced by such words as *dio* (therefore), *dia touto* (through or because of this), or some other Greek particle or conjunction. This conclusion was then followed by (3) an *exhortation*, usually with imperatives.[7]

It is argued that this three-part form can be seen in the following Jewish and Christian texts: Wis 13–15; *T. Reub.* 5.1-5; *T. Levi* 2.6–3.8; *T. Benj.* 2.5, 3.1, 6.6, 7.1, 8.1; Acts 2:14-40, 3:12-26, 13:14-41, 20:17-35; 1 Corinthians 10:1-14; Heb 1:1-2:1; 1 Pet 1:3-11; 1 Clem 6:1-7:2, 42:1-44:6; Ign. *Eph.*; and the Epistle of Barnabas. Building on the work of Wills, and to some extent critiquing and refining it, C. C. Black notes that this threefold pattern is an ancient rhetorical one, such that the first part of the homily corresponds with the rhetorical *narratio*, the second major part corresponds with the proposition and the arguments based on the narration (*probatio*), and the final exhortation corresponds with the peroration. This form reflects a primitive sort of deliberative rhetoric by which one is trying to modify the audience's belief or behavior in some way in the near future.[8]

This following of a rhetorical format in early Jewish and Christian preaching should in no way surprise us. It was part of the harvest of Hellenism even in Israel. The rhetorical handbooks or guidebooks to persuasive speaking in Greek had been in circulation from the fourth century B.C., and there can be no doubt that this heavily influenced even early Judaism. One may see the Qumran community as a reaction to the over-Hellenization of early Judaism in Jerusalem. But their protest did not stem the tide of Hellenization. The building program of Herod the Great was intent on turning Jerusalem into a cosmopolitan city influenced by Greek culture, as the building of the theater and the hippodrome right in the shadow of the temple made evident. There was a school of rhetoric in Jerusalem during Paul's day, and we need not doubt it affected the preaching of those who spoke in synagogues where Greek was spoken, including in Jerusalem.[9]

We must also reckon with the influence of Jewish schooling in a more general sense. Speaking of students at a Sabbath school in Alexandria, Philo tells us that what was taught to these students included the following: "they were trained in piety, holiness, justice, domestic and civic conduct, knowledge of what is truly good or evil, or indifferent, and how to choose what they should do and avoid the opposite, taking for their defining standards these three—love of God, love of virtue, love of people" (*Every Good Man Is Free* 83). This almost reads like a summary of many of the major topics discussed in these early Christian letters and homilies (see, e.g., 1 John), and we may be reasonably sure that these same sorts of topics of orthopraxy were regularly preached in the synagogues as well as in early Christian house churches.

It is then not sufficient to note that Luke presents his early Christian sermon summaries in rhetorical format in the book of Acts, as if this were something Luke imposed on sermons that had no such format. It is more likely that his work reflects the earlier patterns that he had seen and heard in synagogues and elsewhere.[10] For example, the rhetorical form of Hebrews is now well established, although there is debate about the particulars. This is a profoundly Jewish Christian sermon in rhetorical format. As such, it fleshes out for us what such sermons could have looked like in the synagogue and in the church, and this one was intended for Jewish Christians, so it gives us an even clearer picture of what sort of discourse was thought to be viable by and for Jews, including Jewish Christians.

It becomes clear, as we shall see, that story telling and drawing lessons from biblical, early Christian, and even personal stories were often the basis of such preaching. The narration of salvation history, Christ's story or personal history, or some combination of these was the platform from which conclusions were drawn and exhortations made. As L. Hurtado has recently rightly emphasized, it was the experience of God in the risen Christ in crisis events, in worship, in fellowship that led to the expressions of faith and sermonizing that we find in the NT. The experiences led to the profound searching and researching of the Scriptures, now read through Christocentric glasses, and what resulted were remarkable Christian prayers, hymns, sermons, and a host of other things.[11] These documents are part of the literary residue of such remarkable Christian experiences and reflections.

It is the case that not all early Christian sermons followed a rhetorical pattern. One would be hard pressed to find such a pattern in some NT material. What we can say at this juncture is that 1 John, James, Hebrews, and probably Jude should all be seen as homilies of one sort or another, with Hebrews most closely following rhetorical conventions. These documents either have no or very minimal epistolary elements, and they should never have been analyzed primarily as letters in the first place. On the other hand, we have the Pastoral Epistles (perhaps excepting 1 Timothy, which is more of an exhortation), 2 and 3 John, and 1 Peter that definitely can and probably should be analyzed primarily as letters. This is the sort of genre division of material that will guide our study.

What is important to recognize about all these documents is that they are intended to be pastoral in character and are not theological or ethical treatises in any case. Their uses of Scriptures and other resources are primarily homiletical rather than exegetical in character by and large, and what we actually find in these documents is not theology and ethics but theologizing and ethicizing into specific situations, hopefully in a persuasive manner. These documents are, mainly, words of exhortation, with ethics and practical matters to the fore, although theology is also not neglected.

If we ask what the real importance is of these documents tucked away toward the back of the NT canon, we can answer that they are very important. They give us a window on early Christian life between the middle of the first century and the early second century A.D. Indeed, they are some of the very few resources that directly deal with this largely hidden period of time. Acts, as we are well aware, stops its narrative in about A.D. 60–62 with Paul in Rome, and it is the only historical monograph we have from and about the first-century church. The Gospels, while written later, do not provide direct evidence, only indirect evidence, of what Christian communities were like in the last third of the century. In this regard, they are unlike these sermons and letters that do provide a more direct window into this important period as the apostles were dying and the torch of Christian faith was being passed to another generation. While the book of Revelation, especially chapters 1–2, does give us a glimpse of church life in the 90s in Asia, it is only a glimpse in passing, for John's focus is primarily on the future. There is much to be gained from close analysis of this material if we are to understand the end of the apostolic era and how the transition was made to a time when there would no longer be apostles. But there is another reason why this literature is crucial.

THE RHETORIC OF CHRISTIAN PREACHING

In her detailed and brilliant lectures, A. Cameron has shown that Christian discourse going all the way back to the first century A.D. and forward into the Middle Ages was a discourse that was shaped by and sought to shape society. It was not shaped merely by and for its own conventicles and churches. Christianity was profoundly an evangelistic enterprise, so it is not a surprise that it would adopt and adapt the familiar and popular forms of speaking and writing of the day and use them to its own ends to convict, convince, and convert many for Christ. Cameron aptly says:

> Christianity was not just ritual. It placed an extraordinary premium on verbal formulation; speech constituted one of its basic metaphors, and it framed itself around written texts. Quite soon this very emphasis on the verbal formulation of the faith led to a self-imposed restriction—an attempt, eventually on the whole successful, to impose an authority of discourse. And eventually—though only after much struggle and with many variations—this approved discourse came to be the dominant one in the state. The story of the development of Christian discourse constitutes

part of the political history. . . . Early Christian rhetoric was not always
. . . the specialized discourse its own practitioners often claimed it to be.
Consequently its reception was easier and wider ranging than modern historians allow, and its effect correspondingly more telling. The seemingly
alternative rhetorics, the classical or the pagan and the Christian, were
more nearly one than their respective practitioners, interested in scoring
off of each other, would have us believe.[12]

If we wish to understand early Christian preaching, then at least a
good measure of our attention must be focused on various of these NT
documents. Likewise, if we wish to understand pastoral advice and
exhortation in an age in which apostolic influence is waning or even,
in the case of 2 Peter, is perhaps over, we will do well to look closely
at these documents. Furthermore, if we want to understand why it is
that later great church fathers, like Clement of Alexandria, Tertullian,
Chrysostom, Melito of Sardis, Gregory of Naziansus, Augustine, and
many others, used rhetorical forms in their preaching and teaching,
we shall want to look closely at these documents, for it was both the
wider culture and the original Christian source documents that drew
on rhetorical forms and practices, which led to that sort of rhetorical
sermonizing after the apostolic age. We even have such a figure as
Lactanius (A.D. 250–300), who taught rhetoric prior to his conversion, continued to use it afterward, and gained fame as the "Christian
Cicero." In other words, I am arguing that there is some real continuity between the way the early church sermonized and advised in
the first century and the way the church continued to sermonize and
advise using rhetoric in various ways.

Of course, there were some, such as Tertullian or Jerome, once
heresy began to arise in a persistent way, who raised questions about
the use of rhetoric in early Christian discourse and acts of persuasion.
Tertullian famously asked, "What has Athens to do with Jerusalem?
What concord is there between the Academy and the Church?" (*Praescr.*
7). Jerome asked, "What has Horace to do with the Psalms, Virgil with
the Gospels, or Cicero with the Apostles?" (*Epist.* 22.29). Perhaps they
were both feeling something of a guilty conscience, because they had
both used rhetoric in the service of the faith in the past!

The point I wish to make, however, is that this tension is not really
much in evidence in the first-century documents. While A. Overman is
right in saying that "as early Christian preaching was more and more
influenced by classical rhetoric and its techniques and conventions,
certain Church Fathers began to feel a tension between rhetoric and
Christian preaching,"[13] this tension is not really evident in the earliest
period. Paul and the author of Hebrews especially were happy to use
rhetoric as a means of shaping proclamation and acts of persuasion.

In short, we should not think that it was the adaptation of Christianity to Greek philosophy and rhetoric in the second and following centuries that entirely accounts for what we find in prominent later proclaimers and pastors, such as Chrysostom and Augustine. The church began to go down this path already in the first century, especially in the person of Paul, and this means there is a formal continuity of sorts between the earliest proclamation and the developing discourse of early Christianity. Recognizing this factor can help us better understand the development of early Christianity in the post-apostolic period.

But there are also some important social corollaries to what I am saying. Christian literature was far from simple or ordinary. For example, Christian letters were often far longer, more complex, and more intellectually challenging than common letters of the era. This means in turn that at least the writing leadership of the early Christian movement was not merely literate but in some cases rather well educated, especially in such areas as rhetoric, which was a part of Greco-Roman education in its early levels.

The Christian movement was led by some who, at least educationally, were among the elite of society, for only 10 percent of the general populace was literate to this degree or in this way. While this Christian elite may have been small in number, they were huge in influence in their own day and later, for it is their documents that have been preserved in the canon of the NT. And if one reads Paul's letters and Acts closely, one can see a regular pattern of some of the elite being converted and then offering their homes and resources to provide a venue for Christianity to exist in a particular locale. This seems to have continued to be the case in the second-century church and beyond.

The social and discursive situation had already been set in motion in the first century A.D., especially by the apostle to the Gentiles and his co-workers, for the future of the church was to largely be with Gentiles. And if we look for one reason why Christian proclaimers had so much success, it was in part because, as Cameron says, "certain elements in the body of discourse loosely called Christian in the first two centuries were in fact extremely well suited to the cultural conditions of the early Empire."[14] I and many others have been pointing out how Paul, for example, takes up the rhetoric of the Imperial Cult and simply transfers it and applies it to Jesus, but this is only one example of a sophisticated rhetorical move meant to persuade a largely Gentile audience about Jesus.[15] There were many such sophisticated intellectual and rhetorical moves used by early Christians to persuade a diverse Greco-Roman world, which had in common Greek language, Greek culture, and Greek rhetoric.

Christianity did not strive to be a reclusive cult—it wished to convert as much of the populace as possible. In that process, it offered discourse that both insiders and outsiders could understand. Indeed, discourse was offered that those who used to be outsiders but were now insiders could grasp, appreciate, and embrace. What is perhaps surprising to us is that rhetoric even affected and structured what has been sometimes seen as the most Jewish of the documents in the last third of the NT—Hebrews. We must look at it a little more closely as a sample of early Christian preaching.

THE HOMILY TO THE HEBREWS

One of the most controverted issues when it comes to Hebrews is why this document is anonymous. Is it because the author is neither an eyewitness nor an apostle? This hardly seems likely to be the cause because we have other documents in the NT attributed to non-eyewitnesses and non-apostles, such as Luke's two volumes or the Revelation of the seer John of Patmos. Is it because the author is a woman? This is perhaps possible, but elsewhere women who played important ministry roles are named in Christian circles without any reservation. It is possible that the author was so well known to the audience that there was no need for a specific identification. I would suggest, however, that while that may be true, there is another primary reason for the anonymity of this document.

This document, like 1 John, is a homily;[16] D. J. Harrington has called it "arguably the greatest Christian sermon ever written down."[17] It does not partake of the qualities of a letter except at the very end of the document (Heb 13:22-25), and these epistolary features are added because this sermon had to be sent to the audience rather than delivered orally to them by the author. In fact, H. Thyen, after studying all the evidence for early Jewish homilies, has argued that Hebrews is the only completely preserved Jewish homily of the period, but this statement overlooks 1 John and James as well.[18]

Sermon manuscripts, ancient or modern, do not conform to the characteristics of the beginning of a letter, with addressor or addressee expected at the outset. Other rhetorical forms of speaking also do not conform to this pattern, and make no mistake—this document involves rhetoric of considerable skill. It is then, to use an oxymoron, an oral document and a particular type of oral document—a homily in the form of a "word of exhortation," as Hebrews 13:22 puts it. It is not an accident that this is the very same phrase used to characterize Paul's sermon in Acts 13:15. Hebrews is not a haphazard discourse but a piece of polished rhetoric that has been variously categorized as either epideictic, deliberative, or some combination of the two (see below). Here the point that needs to be made is that the document's authority rests in its contents, not in its author's claims to apostolic authority. To judge from the end of Hebrews 13, it is assumed, but not argued, that this author has some authority over this audience, who knows very well who he is and who can anticipate a visit from him and Timothy before long. The oral and homiletical character of the document cannot be stressed enough. Here is how T. Long, a professor of homiletics, puts it:

> Hebrews, like all good sermons, is a dialogical event in a monological format. The Preacher does not hurl information and arguments at the readers as if they were targets. Rather, Hebrews is written to create a conversation, to evoke participation, to prod the faithful memories of the readers. Beginning with the first sentence, "us" and "we" language abounds. Also, the Preacher employs rhetorical questions to awaken the voice of the listener (see 1.5 and 1.14 for example); raps on the pulpit a bit when the going gets sluggish (5.11); occasionally restates the main point to insure that even the inattentive and drowsy are on board (see 8.1); doesn't bother to "footnote" the sources the hearers already know quite well (see the familiar preacher's phrase in 2.6: "Someone has said somewhere . . ."); and keeps making explicit verbal contact with the listeners (see 3.12 and 6.9, for example) to remind them that they are not only supposed to be listening to this sermon, they are also, by their active hearing, to be a part of creating it. As soon as we experience the rise and fall of the opening words of Hebrews, the reader becomes aware that they are not simply watching a roller coaster hurtle along the rhetorical tracks; they are in the lead car. In Hebrews, the gospel is not merely an idea submitted for intellectual consideration; it is a life-embracing demand that summons to action.[19]

The other formally anonymous document of relevance to this discussion of Hebrews that is also likely addressed to Jewish Christians is 1 John. A few words here about it will not go amiss. It is a homily or some form of oral proclamation now written down, as even its opening paragraph makes apparent. Yet it has such differences from the character of Hebrews, and unlike the ending of Hebrews, it has no epistolary elements at all. Why is this? I would suggest that 1 John, while it has a christological proem much as we find in Hebrews 1:1-4, thereafter does not toggle between more expository and more exhortatory sections of discourse but rather spends nearly the entire discourse on ethical exhortation in a Jewish sapiential manner (and so in this regard is much like James).

Philo, speaking of students at a Sabbath school in Alexandria, informs us that what was taught these students was the following: "they were trained in piety, holiness, justice, domestic and civic conduct, knowledge of what is truly good or evil, or indifferent, and how to choose what they should and avoid the opposite, taking for their defining standards these three—love of God, love of virtue, love of people" (*Every Good Man Is Free* 83).

What is striking to me about this brief summary is how well it comports with the character and content of 1 John, which is all about distinguishing good and evil and about love of God and each other, with the additional important element of Christology. The ethical or paraenetic aim of most early Jewish preaching, such that it could be characterized as a "word of exhortation," should be emphasized, as should the influence of rhetoric on early Jewish preaching in the first century A.D., particularly outside the Holy Land. The christological or doctrinal sort of beginning to 1 John and the continuing reminders about the correct christological beliefs should not fool us into thinking that 1 John is primarily or in essence a theological tract. The theology is introduced to undergird and guide the ethical response being prompted and urged in this discourse. The focus is actually more on behavior than belief, though the latter is fundamental as well.

In addition to these basic observations (we are dealing with a rhetorically adept exhortation, like other early Jewish homilies) we must further stress the important observation that this homily is profoundly sapiential in character. It is a form of wisdom utterance not unlike some of the exhortations we find in Proverbs or Ben Sira, with our author assuming the same sort of pedagogical posture that we find the sage doing in Proverbs 1–7, where he speaks as a father to his spiritual children.

As in this earlier Wisdom literature, we shall find a great deal of repetition and amplification on basic themes, with much wordplay and rhetorical finesse as the author makes his discourse both memorable and memorizable through the interlocking and intertwined use of polar opposite key terms and phrases, such as light and darkness, sin and cleansing/sanctification, and love and hate.

An aspect of this discourse is rather like a musical round, with the author offering us permutations and combinations of certain basic themes in order to reinforce the audience's understanding and to ensure the desired response. We might compare the similar sort of effect in Ecclesiastes. Finally, we must add that the Christology that is manifested in this discourse is also a form of Wisdom Christology in which Wisdom has come in person—in this case, in the flesh as Jesus to instruct and save his people—and the echoes of what is said about Wisdom coming and attempting to rescue God's people in Wisdom literature ranging from Proverbs to Wisdom of Solomon to Ben Sira needs to be kept in mind.[20]

In this chapter we have briefly examined what we can know about early Christian homilies or sermons, noting their indebtedness to both rhetorical forms and conventions on the one hand, and to Jewish ser-monizing styles and practices on the other. The sermons we have in the NT, such as 1 John or Hebrews or even James, reflect this harmonic convergence of Greco-Roman and Jewish influences and as such should be seen as "oral documents" surrogates for live proclamation. In our next chapter we will discover that even in the NT documents which more obviously reflect some epistolary conventions and which we freely call letters, the dominant conventions shaping such 'letters' were in fact oral and rhetorical.

5

Romans 7:7-25

Retelling Adam's Tale

There is no more controverted text in all of ancient literature, and no more commented on text, than Romans 7. This is the stuff of which whole theologies, not to mention dissertations and scholarly careers, are made. One trait that has characterized the discussion of this text in the twentieth and into the twenty-first centuries is that until recently scholars have almost universally failed to apply the insights of Greco-Roman rhetoric to the analysis of this text. This is unfortunate, because it provides several keys to unlocking the mysteries within.

Romans 7 demonstrates not only Paul's considerable skill with rhetoric but also his penchant for using even its most complex devices and techniques. This text proves beyond a reasonable doubt that Paul did not use rhetoric in some purely superficial or sparing way (e.g., using rhetorical questions).[1] To the contrary, the very warp and woof of his argument here reflects and requires an understanding of sophisticated rhetorical techniques to make sense of the content of this passage and the way it attempts to persuade the Roman audience. It will repay our close attention at this juncture.

WHEN "IMPERSONATION" GETS PERSONAL

"Impersonation," or *prosopopoia*, is a rhetorical technique that falls under the heading of figures of speech and is often used to illustrate or to make vivid a piece of deliberative rhetoric (*Inst.* 3.8.49; cf. Theon, *Progymnasmata* 8). This rhetorical technique involves the assumption of a role, and sometimes the role would be marked off from its surrounding discourse by a change in tone, inflection, accent, or form of delivery, or by an introductory formula signaling a change in voice. Sometimes the speech would simply be inserted "without mentioning the speaker at all" (9.2.37).[2] Unfortunately for us, we did not get to hear Paul's discourse delivered in its original oral setting, as was Paul's intent. It is not surprising then that many have not picked up the signals, having only Paul's words left to us, that impersonation is happening in Romans 7:7-13 and also in 7:14-25.[3]

Quintilian says impersonation "is sometimes introduced even with controversial themes, which are drawn from history and involve the appearance of definite historical characters as pleaders" (*Inst*. 3.8.52). In this case, Adam is the historical figure being impersonated in Romans 7:7-13, and the theme is most certainly controversial and drawn from history. Indeed, Paul has introduced this theme already in Romans 5:12-21, and one must bear in mind that this discourse would have been heard seriatim, which means the audience would have heard about Adam only a few minutes before hearing the material in Romans 7.

The most important requirement for a speech in character in the form of impersonation is that the speech be fitting, suiting the situation and character of the one speaking: "For a speech that is out of keeping with the man who delivers it is just as faulty as a speech which fails to suit the subject to which it should conform" (*Inst*. 3.8.51). The ability to pull off a convincing impersonation is considered by Quintilian to reflect the highest skill in rhetoric, for it is often the most difficult thing to do (3.8.49). That Paul attempts it tells us something about Paul as a rhetorician. This rhetorical technique also involves *personification*, sometimes of abstract qualities (such as fame or virtue, or in Paul's case sin or grace; 9.2.36). Quintilian also informs us that impersonation may take the form of a dialogue or speech, but it can also take the form of a first-person narrative (9.2.37).

Of course, since the important work of W. G. Kümmel on Romans 7, it has become a commonplace, perhaps even a majority, opinion in some New Testament circles that the "I" of Romans 7 is not autobiographical.[4] This, however, still does not tell us what sort of literary or rhetorical use of "I" we *do* find in Romans 7. As S. Stowers points out, it is also no new opinion that what is happening in Romans 7 is the rhetorical technique known as impersonation.[5] In fact, this is how some of the earliest Greek commentators on Romans, such as Origen, interpreted this portion of the letter, and later commentators, such as Jerome and Rufinus, took note of this approach by Origen.[6] Didymus of Alexandria and Nilus of Ancyra also saw Paul using the form of speech in character, or impersonation, here.[7] The point to be noted is that we are talking about church fathers who not only knew Greek well but also understood the use of rhetoric and believed Paul is certainly availing himself of rhetorical devices here.[8] Even more importantly, there is J. Chrysostom (*Homily 13 on Romans*), who was very much in touch with the rhetorical nature and the theological substance of Paul's letters. He also does not think that Romans 7 is about Christians, much less about Paul himself as a Christian. He interprets it as talking about: (1) those who lived before the Law, and (2) those who lived outside the Law or lived under it. In other words, it is about Gentiles and Jews outside of Christ.

But I want to argue that because the vast majority of Paul's audience is Gentile, and one of his rhetorical aims is to effect some reconciliation between Jewish and Gentile Christians in Rome,[9] it would be singularly inept for Paul here to retell the story of Israel in a negative way and then turn around in Romans 9–11 and try to get Gentiles to appreciate their Jewish heritage in Christ and to be understanding of Jews and their fellow Jewish Christians. Instead, Paul tells a more universal tale here of the progenitor of all humankind, followed by the story of all those "in Adam," not focusing specifically on those "in Israel" who are within the Adamic category.[10] Even in Romans 7:14-25, Paul can be seen to be mainly echoing his discussion in Romans 2:15 of Gentiles who had the "Law" within and struggled over its demands.[11] Because of the enormous debate about this text, it is important to rehearse a bit of the history of interpretation here, as it bears on the study of Romans in general and also particularly Romans 7. It will be seen that much of the discussion of Romans 7 after Augustine not only is indebted to Augustine but was misled by Augustine.

FATHER KNOWS BEST?
ROMANS 7 INTERPRETATION AS FOOTNOTES TO AUGUSTINE

If the measure of the importance of a text is who it has impacted in a major way, then in many regards Romans is, perhaps after one or the other of the Gospels, the most important NT book. From Augustine to Aquinas to Erasmus to Melanchthon to Luther to Calvin to Wesley and, in the modern era, to K. Barth, R. Bultmann, and many others, the influence has been decisive. But what must be kept squarely in view is that the nature of the impact is in part determined by the way in which and the tradition from which each of these persons has read the text, and this is especially the case with Romans.[12]

There is a direct line of influence from Augustine to these other interpreters, who all are in his debt. But it needs to be borne in mind that there were interpreters of Romans, and especially of Romans 7, prior to Augustine, and many of them, including luminaries among the Greek Fathers, such as Origen and Chrysostom in the East and Pelagius and Ambrosiaster in the West, did not take Augustine's line of approach to Romans, and in particular to Romans 7.

It is my view that to a real degree Augustine skewed the interpretation of this crucial Pauline text, and we are still dealing with the theological fallout these many years later. P. Melanchthon wryly complains,

"This part of the Pauline epistle must be pondered in a particularly careful manner, because the ancients also sweated greatly in explaining these things, and few of them treated them skillfully and correctly."[13] The problem is Melanchthon thought that Augustine had it right, and the great majority of the Fathers were wrong!

The need to use Romans to dispute the Marcionites and the Gnostics preoccupied the patristic interpreters of Romans before Augustine, and as T. J. Deidun says, there were emphases on very un-Augustinian themes, such as the created goodness of human flesh and at least some human desire, the integrity of human nature (Chrysostom), free will (Pelagius), and the harmony of gospel and Law (several of the Fathers). In Pelagius' view, sin comes from humans' free imitation of Adam and can be overcome by imitating Christ. He also suggests that justification, at least final justification, is through determined moral action. Augustine was to counter Pelagius by insisting on the necessity of grace for justification (see his *On the Spirit and the Letter*, A.D. 412).

Deidun aptly summarizes the key points of Augustine's mature interpretation of Romans, and we will turn to this in a moment, but we need to bear in mind that Augustine's interpretation immediately had enormous weight in the West and was to be, in effect, canonized for the Roman Catholic tradition at the Council of Carthage in A.D. 418 and of Orange in A.D. 529. It was to be canonized, so to speak, for the Protestant line of interpretation by Luther and Calvin. It must be urged that Augustine's interpretation of Romans, and especially Romans 7, seems to be in various regards an overreaction to Pelagius.[14]

Consider now Deidun's summary of Augustine's main points on Romans:

> (1) The "works of the Law" which Paul says can never justify, mean moral actions in general without the grace of Christ, not Jewish practices as Pelagius and others maintained. (2) The "righteousness of God" . . . is not an attribute of God but the gift he confers in making people righteous; (3) Romans 5:12 now became the key text for Augustine's doctrine of original sin: all individuals (infants included) were co-involved in Adam's sin. As is well known, Augustine's exegesis of this verse largely depended on the Latin translation *in quo* ("in whom") of the Greek εφ ὁ ("in that," because) and on the omission in his manuscripts of the second mention of "death," with the result that "sin" became the subject of "spread": sin spread to all (by "generation," not by "imitation").[15] (4) Romans 7:14-25, which before the controversy Augustine had understood to be referring to humanity without Christ, he now applied to the Christian to deprive Pelagius of the opportunity of applying the positive elements in the passage (esp. verse 22) to unredeemed humanity. To do this, Augustine was obliged to water down Paul's negative statements:

the apostle is describing not the bondage of sin but the bother of concupiscence; and he laments not that he cannot do good (*facere*) but that
he cannot do it perfectly (*perficere*). (5) During this period Augustine
came to express more boldly his teaching on predestination. It does not
depend on God's advance knowledge of people's merit as Pelagius and
others maintained in their interpretation of Romans 9:10ff. nor even on
his advance knowledge of "the merit of faith," as Augustine himself had
supposed in 394 in his remarks on the same passage: "it depends rather
on God's 'most hidden judgment' whereby he graciously chooses whom
he will deliver from the mass of fallen humanity. Everything is pure gift
(1 Corinthians 4:7)."[16]

All these points of Augustine's are today under dispute among interpreters of Romans, and some points are clearly wrong, such as the conclusions based on the Latin text of Romans 5:12. For our purposes, it
is interesting to note that Augustine, having changed his mind about
Romans 7:14-25 in overreacting to Pelagius, must water down the stress
on the bondage of the will expressed in this text in order to apply it to
Christians. Luther takes a harder and more consistent line, even though
in the end he refers the text to the wrong subject—namely, everyone
including Christians. It is also noteworthy that Pelagius does not dispute God's destining of persons, only that God does it on the basis of
his foreknowledge of the response of believers. It is also important that
Augustine talks about God's gift of making people righteous. The later
forensic emphasis comes as a result of the translation work of Erasmus.

It is interesting that the discussion of merit that Pelagius introduced
into the conversation about Romans resurfaces in the medieval exegetes
after Augustine. Paul's doctrine of "justification" is filtered through
Aristotelean thinking, so that grace becomes a *donum super additum*,
something added on top of God's gift of human faculties (see Aquinas):
"Divine *charis* became 'infused grace.'"[17] The nominalist school of
William of Occam focused on merit, even in a Pelagian way, and it was
to this repristinization of Pelagius' case that Luther, an Augustinian
monk much like his founder, was to react in his various lectures and
then in his commentary on Romans. But it was not just Pelagius he was
reacting to. In due course, Luther came to see self-righteousness as the
most fundamental of human sins (not concupiscence), and his polemics
are directed against both Judaism and Catholicism, which he sees as
religions that embody this besetting sin, as well as being preoccupied
with "merit." Luther thinks that Romans 7:14-25 is about that sin of
self-righteousness.

Deidun notes, rightly, that Luther's exploration of what Augustine
says about the righteousness of God led him to criticize Augustine for
not clearly explaining the imputation of righteousness. But, as Deidun

says, Augustine's "understanding of justification is thoroughly incompatible with the notion of imputation."[18] Luther gets this idea from Erasmus, but he is not afraid to critique Erasmus at other points. For instance, drawing on his own understanding of Romans 7:14-25 as validating the notion of the Christian as being *simul justus et peccator*, Luther argues against Erasmus and other humanists in regard to human freedom of the will. It is also noteworthy that Luther's influential two-kingdom theory (spiritual and temporal) is derived from his exegesis of Romans 13. Christians are subject to earthly powers out of respect and love, but in the spiritual sphere they are only subject to God, not to human authorities, such as the pope. Calvin was to follow Luther's line on justification and predestination, except that he at least more explicitly highlights the notion of double predestination, based on a certain reading of Romans 8:29 (cf. the 1539 edition of Calvin's *Institutes*).

The English Reformation or revival of the eighteenth century did not produce any great commentaries on Romans, not by Wesley, Coke, or Fletcher, nor later in the Wesleyan tradition by Clarke, Watson (though he offers much exposition on Romans in his *Institutes*, a rebuttal to Calvin), or Asbury. This helps explain why the Protestant tradition of interpretation of the nineteenth and twentieth centuries continued to be dominated by Lutheran or Calvinist interpreters, including Bultmann, Barth, Kasemann, Cranfield, and others of note. Even the foremost Methodist NT scholar of the last half of the twentieth century, C. K. Barrett, in his Romans commentaries (both editions) reflects primarily the influence of the Reformed tradition of interpretation, including an acknowledged indebtedness to Barth (and Bultmann).

Winds of change, however, have blown through NT studies since the late 1970s, and the changed views of early Judaism and, as a result of Paul and the Law, a reassessment of the social setting of Romans and its rhetorical character have led to various fresh lines of interpretation that seem to be better grounded in the historical setting and matrix of Paul rather than in the longer history of Protestant interpretation of Romans. It needs to be said that especially since Vatican II, there have also been notable contributions to the discussion of Romans by a series of Catholic scholars, such as Cerfaux, Lyonnet, Kuss, Fitzmyer, and Byrne. It is interesting, however, that these expositors, especially Fitzmyer, seem more indebted to Augustine and Luther than to the scholastic and medieval Catholic traditions. Another way to measure the importance of a document is by whether it has continued to exercise the best minds in the field with fresh attempts to understand it. This Romans continues to do, for it is not only an enduring classic and the most commented on work in human history, it is also a constant challenge to rethink the Christian faith.

ADAM'S PLIGHT REEXAMINED

But who is the "I" who is speaking in Romans 7:7-25? In my view, the "I" is Adam in verses 7-13 and all those who are currently "in Adam" in verses 14-25.[19] Adam, it will be remembered, is the last historical figure Paul introduced into his discourse at Romans 5:12, and we have contended that the story of Adam undergirds a good deal of the discussion from Romans 5:12 through Romans 7.[20] More will be said on this below, but suffice it to say here that the old traditional interpretations that Paul was describing his own pre-Christian experience, or alternately the experience of Christians in this text, fail to grasp the rhetorical finesse and character of this material and must be deemed very unlikely not only for that reason but for others we will discuss in due course.[21]

I have commented on this text to some degree elsewhere,[22] but here it is important to give full attention to the narrative. Three things are crucial if one is to understand this text. First, Paul believes that Moses wrote the Pentateuch, including Genesis. Second, the "law" in Moses' books includes more than the Law given to Moses and with the Mosaic covenant; it would include the first commandment given to Adam and Eve.[23] Third, it appears that Paul saw the "original sin" of coveting the fruit of the prohibited tree as a form of violation of the tenth commandment (cf. *Apoc. Mos.* 19.3).

I would suggest an expansive rendering of verses 8-11 that takes into account the Adamic story, which is being retold here as follows:

> But the serpent [Sin], seizing an opportunity in the commandment, produced in me all sorts of covetousness. . . . But I [Adam] was once alive apart from the Law, but when the commandment came, Sin sprang to life and I died, and the very commandment that promised life, proved deadly to me. For Sin [the serpent] seizing an opportunity through the commandment, deceived me and through it killed me.

Here we have the familiar primeval tale of human life that began before the existence of the Law and apart from sin, but then the commandment entered, followed by deception, disobedience, and eventually death. We must consider the particulars of the text at this juncture.

First, those who claim that there is no signal in the text that we are going into impersonation at verse 7 are simply wrong.[24] As Stowers points out,

> The section begins in verse 7 with an abrupt change in voice following a rhetorical question, that serves as a transition from Paul's authorial voice, which has previously addressed the readers explicitly . . . in 6.1-7.6. This constitutes what the grammarians and rhetoricians described as change of

voice (εναλλαγη or μεταβολη). These ancient readers would next look for
διαφονια, a difference in characterization from the authorial voice. The
speaker in 7.7-25 speaks with great personal pathos of coming under the
Law at some point, learning about desire and sin, and being unable to do
what he wants to do because of enslavement to sin or flesh.[25]

It is indeed crucial to see what we have here as not only a continu-
ation of Paul's discussion of the Law, but a vivid retelling of the fall
in such a manner that he shows that there was a problem with commandments and the Law from the very beginning of the human story.
Paul has transitioned from talking in 7:5-6 about what Christians once
were before they came to Christ[26] to talking about why they were that
way and why the Law had that effect on them before they became
Christians—namely, because of the sin of Adam. This is the outworking
of and building upon what Paul says when he compares and contrasts
the story of Adam and Christ in Romans 5:12-21.

Furthermore, there is a good reason not to simply lump verses 7-13
together with verses 14-25, as some commentators still do. In verses
7-13, we have only past tenses of the verbs, while in verses 14-25, we
have present tenses. Either Paul is somewhat changing the subject in
verses 14-25 from that of verses 7-13, or he is changing the time frame
in which he is viewing the one subject. Here, it will be worthwhile to
consider the issue of the "I" as it has been viewed by various commentators who do not really take into account Paul's use of rhetoric
and rhetorical devices, nor note the Adamic narrative subtext to Paul's
discourse here (see "The Pauline 'I' Chart" on p. 69).

There is no consensus of opinion whatsoever among scholars who
do not take into account the rhetorical signals in the text and do not
recognize the echoes and allusions to the story of Adam in verses 7-13.
Sometimes too, as in the case of E. Kasemann, we have combinations
of some of these views. Kasemann argues that 7:14-20 reflects the pious
Jew, while 7:21-25 reflects all fallen humanity.[27] The very fact that
there are so many varied conjectures about these texts counts against
any of them being very likely.

The fact that many commentators through the years have thought
Paul was describing Christian experience, including his own, we owe
in large measure to the enormous influence of Augustine, including
his influence especially on Luther and on those who have followed in
Luther's exegetical footsteps. P. Gorday says, "This entire section of
Romans 7.14-25 is absolutely omnipresent in Augustine's work, and is
linked with every other passage in the epistle where the concern is to
reinforce the complex interplay of grace and law that Augustine saw in
Romans."[28] Furthering the impact of this view is that Augustine shared
his opinions on this text in his most influential work, his *Confessions*,

THE PAULINE "I" CHART

Verses 7-13	Verses 14-25
(1) The "I" is strictly autobiographical.	(1) The "I" is autobiographical, referring to Paul's current Christian experience.
(2) The "I" reflects Paul's view of a typical Jewish individual.	(2) The "I" is autobiographical, referring to Paul's pre-Christian experience as he viewed it then.
(3) The "I" reflects the experience of Jews as a whole.	(3) The "I" is autobiographical, referring to Paul's pre-Christian experience as he views it now.
(4) The "I" reflects humanity as a whole.	(4) The "I" represents the experience of the non-Christian Jew as seen by himself.
(5) The "I" is a way of speaking in general, without having a particular group of persons in mind.	(5) The "I" represents how Christians view Jews.
	(6) The "I" refers to the "carnal" Christian.
	(7) The "I" reflects the experience of Christians in general.
	(8) The "I" reflects a person under conviction of sin and at the point of conversion (thus 7:14–8:1 provide a sort of narrative of a conversion).

as well as in later works, relating the text to his own experience.[29] Various important later expositors, such as Luther, resonated with this approach. This fact, however, does not constitute any sort of proof that this was what Paul had in mind when he wrote Romans 7. It probably says more about Augustine and Luther than it does about a rhetorically adept first-century Jewish Christian such as Paul, who, as K.

Stendahl was later to aptly say, does not seem to reflect the introspective consciousness of the West.[30] Paul hardly ever talks about his own personal guilt feelings or repentance, and when he does so, it is a discussion of his pre-Christian period when he persecuted Christians, not about any internal moral conflict he struggled with as a Christian.[31]

DETAILING ADAM'S SIN

What are the markers or indicators in the text of Romans 7:7-13 that the most probable way to read this text, the way Paul desired for it to be heard, is in the light of the story of Adam, with Adam speaking of his own experience?[32] First, from the beginning of the passage in verse 7, there is reference to one specific commandment: "thou shalt not covet/desire." This is the tenth commandment in an abbreviated form (cf. Exod 20:17; Deut 5:21). Some early Jewish exegesis of Genesis 3 suggested that the sin committed by Adam and Eve was a violation of the tenth commandment.[33] They coveted the fruit of the tree of the knowledge of good and evil.

Second, one must ask who in biblical history was only under one commandment, which was one about coveting? The answer is Adam.[34] Verse 8 refers to a commandment (singular). This can hardly be a reference to the Mosaic law in general, which Paul regularly speaks of as a collective entity. Third, verse 9 says, "I was living once without/apart from the Law." The only person said in the Bible to be living before or without any law was Adam. The attempt to refer this to a person's life before the time of his bar mitzvah, when he takes the yoke of the Law upon himself at twelve to thirteen years of age, while not impossible, seems unlikely. Even a Jewish child who had not yet personally embraced the call to be a "son of the commandments" was still expected to obey the Mosaic law, including honoring parents and God (cf. Luke 2:41-52).[35]

Fourth, as numerous commentators have regularly noticed, sin is personified in this text, especially in verse 11, as if it were like the snake in the garden. Paul says, "Sin took opportunity through the commandment to deceive me." This matches up well with the story about the snake using the commandment to deceive Eve and Adam in the garden. Notice, too, how the very same verb is used to speak of this deception in 2 Corinthians 11:3 and also 1 Timothy 2:14. We know that physical death was said to be part of the punishment for this sin, but there was also the matter of spiritual death, due to alienation from God, and it is perhaps the latter that Paul has in view in this text.

Fifth, notice how in verse 7 Paul says, "I did not know sin except through the commandment." This condition would only properly be the case with Adam, especially if "know" in this text means having personal experience of sin (cf. v. 5).[36] As we know from various earlier texts in Romans, Paul believes that all after Adam have sinned and fallen short of God's glory. The discussion in Romans 5:12-21 seems to be presupposed here. It is, however, possible to take *egnon* to mean "recognize"—I did not recognize sin for what it was except through the existence of the commandment. If this is the point, then it comports with what Paul has already said about the Law's turning sin into trespass and sin's being revealed as a violation of God's will for humankind. But on the whole, it seems more likely that Paul is describing Adam's awakening consciousness of the possibility of sin when the first commandment was given. All in all, the most satisfactory explanation of these verses is if we see Paul the Christian rereading the story of Adam here, in the light of his Christian views about law and the Law.[37]

Certainly one of the functions of this subsection of Romans is to be something of an *apologia* for the Law. Paul asks whether the Law is something evil because it not only reveals sin but has the unintended effect of suggesting sins to commit to a human being. Is the Law's association with sin and death then a sign that the Law itself is a sinful or wicked thing? Paul's response is, of course, "absolutely not"! Verse 7 suggests a parallel between *egnon* and "know, desire," which suggests Paul has in view the experience of sin by this knower. Verse 8 says sin takes the Law as the starting point or opportunity to produce in the knower all sorts of evil desires.[38]

Stowers reads this part of the discussion in light of Greco-Roman discussions about desire and the mastery of desire, which may have been one of the things this discourse prompted in the largely Gentile audience.[39] But the story of Adam seems to be at the fore here. The basic argument here is how sin used a good thing, the Law, to create evil desires in Adam. It is important to recognize that in Romans 5–6, Paul has already established that all humans are "in Adam," and all have sinned like him. Furthermore, Paul has spoken of the desires that plagued his largely Gentile audience prior to their conversions. The discussion here then just further links even the Gentile portion of the audience to Adam and his experience. They are to recognize themselves in this story as the children of Adam who also have had desires, have sinned, and have died. The way Paul illuminates the parallels will be seen in Romans 7:14-25, which I take to be a description of all those in Adam and outside Christ.[40]

Paul then is providing a narrative in Romans 7:7-25 of the story of Adam from the past in verses 7-13 and the story of all those in Adam in the present in verses 14-25. In a sense, what is happening here is an expansion on what Paul has already argued in Romans 5:12-21. There is a continuity in the "I" in Romans 7 by virtue of the close link between Adam and all those in Adam. The story of Adam is also the prototype of the story of Christ, and it is only when the person is delivered from the body of death, only when a person transfers from the story of Adam into the story of Christ, that one can leave Adam and his story behind, no longer being in bondage to sin and being empowered to resist temptation and walk in the newness of life, as is described in Romans 8. Christ starts the race of humanity over again, setting it right and in a new direction, delivering it from the bondage of sin, death, and the Law. It is not a surprise that Christ only enters the picture at the very end of the argument in Romans 7, in preparation for Romans 8, using the rhetorical technique of overlapping the end of one argument with the beginning of another.[41]

Some have seen verse 9b as a problem for the Adam view of verses 7-13, because the verb must be translated as "renewed" or "live anew." But notice the contrast between "I was living" in verse 9a with "but sin coming to life" in verse 9b. C. E. B. Cranfield then is right to urge that the meaning of the verb in question in verse 9b must be "sprang to life."[42] The snake/sin was lifeless until it had an opportunity to victimize some innocent prey and had the means, namely the commandment, to do so. Sin deceived and spiritually killed the founder of the human race. This is nearly a quotation from Genesis 3:13. One of the important corollaries of recognizing that Romans 7:7-13 is about Adam (and 7:14-25 is about those in Adam and outside Christ) is that it becomes clear that Paul is not specifically critiquing Judaism or Jews here any more than he is in Romans 7:14-25.[43]

Verse 12 begins with *hoste*, which should be translated as "so then," introducing Paul's conclusion about the Law that Paul has been driving toward. The commandment and, for that matter, the whole Law is holy, just, and good. It did not in itself produce sin or death in the founder of the human race. Rather, sin/the serpent/Satan used the commandment to that end. Good things, things from God, can be used for evil purposes by those with evil intent. The exceeding sinfulness of sin is revealed in that it will even use a good thing to produce an evil end—death.[44] This was not the intended end or purpose of the Law. The death of Adam was not a matter of his being killed with kindness or by something good. Verse 13 is emphatic: "The Law, a good thing, did not kill Adam. But sin was indeed revealed to be sin by the Law, and it produced death." This argument prepares the way for the discussion of the legacy of Adam for those who are outside Christ. The present tense verbs reflect the ongoing legacy for those who are still in Adam and not in Christ. Romans 7:14-25 should not be seen as a further argument but as the last stage of a four-part argument that began in Romans 6, being grounded in Romans 5:12-21, and will climax with Paul's discussion about sin, death, the Law, and their various effects on humankind.

SEEING EYE TO "I" IN ROMANS 7:14-25

It will not be necessary for us to go into as much depth with Romans 7:14-25 as we have with the tale of Adam in 7:7-13. Rather, we will focus on the points of rhetorical significance that should have guided the interpretation of this text all along. First, once it is realized that a fictive "I" is being used in 7:7-13 to create a speech in character, then it requires a change of rhetorical signals at 7:14 or thereafter if that were to cease to be the case in 7:14-25. We have no such compelling evidence that Paul is now using "I" in a nonfictive way in these verses now under scrutiny. There is, it is true, a change in the tenses of the main verbs; here, we have present tenses, signaling that Paul is talking about something that is now true of someone or some group of persons, but it must be some group that has an integral connection with the "I" of 7:7-13. Fortunately, Paul has already set up such a link in Romans 5:12-21, in particular at the outset of that *synkrisis*, or rhetorical comparison— one man sinned, and death came to all people, not just because he sinned, but because they all sinned. The link has been forged, and we see here how it plays out as Adam's tale in 7:7-13 leads directly to the tale of all those who are in Adam in 7:14-25. Kasemann puts the matter aptly: "Εγω [here] means [hu]mankind under the shadow of Adam: hence it does not embrace Christian existence in its ongoing temptation. . . . What is being said here is already over for the Christian according to chapter 6 and chapter 8. The apostle is not even describing the content of his own experience of conversion."[45] It is telling that most of the church fathers thought as well that Paul was adopting and adapting the persona of an unregenerate person, not describing his own struggles as a Christian. Most of them believed that conversion would deliver a person from the dilemma described here, deliver him or her from the bondage to sin or the law of sin and death, as Romans 8:1-2 puts it.[46] But what about the reference to the struggle with the "law of the mind" here? Does that not suggest a person, perhaps a Jew, under the yoke of the Mosaic law? While not an impossible interpretation of the struggle described here, there is a better and more likely view if we are attentive to the rhetorical signals of the whole document. In Romans 2:15, Paul is quite explicit that Gentiles not beholden to the Mosaic covenant or its law nonetheless have the generic law of God written on their very hearts, and therefore they do from time to time do what God requires of them.

Notice that the struggle described in Romans 7:14-25 is between a law residing in one's mind and a quite different ruling principle residing in one's "flesh" or sinful inclinations. Nothing is said here about rebellion against a known external law code, nor is the book of the Law or Moses mentioned here. Remember, too, that it was said that even

Adam himself had a singular commandment of God to deal with, well before Moses, such that when Adam violated that one commandment, sin and death reigned from Adam to Moses, even prior to the existence of the Mosaic code (Rom 5:14). Notice the difference between Romans 7:14-25 and debates in Romans 2–3 with the Jewish teacher over the meaning of the external law code. It is thus most likely that we have here a more generic description of the condition of those who are in Adam and are fighting but losing the battle with sin in their lives. The only way out of their dilemma is deliverance. Paul is speaking as broadly as he can in this passage, addressing the human plight outside Christ in general, and is not singling out Jews for special attention here. That would have been rhetorically inept in any case, because the great majority of his audience is likely Gentiles (see Rom 11:13). We must bear in mind as well that we are dealing with a Christian interpretation of a pre-Christian condition. Paul does not assume that this is how either Gentiles or Jews themselves would view the matter if they were not also Christians. But clearly Gentiles could relate to this discussion. For example, Ovid, in his famous work *Metamorphoses*, speaks in very similar terms of the struggle with sin: "Desire persuades me one way, reason another. I see the better and approve it, but I follow the worse" (7.19-20). Even closer is the words of Epictetus: "What I wish, I do not do, and what I do not wish, I do" (2.26.4). Paul has not traipsed into *terra incognita* for his largely Gentile audience; rather he is standing on familiar ground. The effect of law, law of any sort, on a fallen human being, whether the law of the heart or the law in a code, is predictably the same, in Paul's view.

In the earlier parts of Romans, and especially in Romans 2–3, Paul resorts to the rhetorical device of the diatribe: a rhetorical debate with an imaginary interlocutor. Romans 7:7-25 has just a taste of that at Romans 7:25a, where Paul himself, in his own and most pastoral voice, responds to the heart cry of the lost person—"Who will deliver me from this body of death?" His answer is swift and powerful: "Thanks be to God—through Jesus Christ our Lord!" What was lost on Luther is that the voice in verse 25a is not the same voice as the one that precedes it, or that follows it in verse 25b.

Paul is following a well-known rhetorical technique called *chain-link*, or interlocking construction, which has now been described in detail with full illustration of its use in the NT by B. Longenecker.[47] The basic way this technique works is that one briefly introduces the theme of the next argument or part of one's rhetorical argument just before one concludes the argument one is presently laying out. Thus in this case, Romans 7:25a is the introduction to Romans 8:1 and follows where Paul will once more speak in his own voice in the first person. Quintilian is quite specific about the need to use such a technique in a complex argument of many parts. He says that this sort of ABAB structure is effective when one must speak with pathos, force, energy, and pugnacity (*Inst.* 9.4.129-30). He adds, "We may compare its motion to that of men, who link hands to steady their steps, and lend each other their mutual support" (9.4.129). Failure to recognize this rhetorical device by which one introduces the next argument before concluding the previous one has led to all sorts of misreadings of Romans 7:14-25.[48]

As Longenecker emphasizes, this reading of Romans 7:25a comports completely with the thrust of what has come immediately before Romans 7:7-25 and what comes immediately thereafter. He puts it this way:

> Paul has taken great care to signal the transition from Romans 7 to Romans 8: first by contrasting the 'fleshly then' and the "spiritual now" in 7.5-6, two verses which provide the structural foundation for the movement from 7.7ff. and 8.1ff., and second, by introducing the "spiritual now" in 8.1 with the emphatic "therefore now" (αρα ουν). Such structural indicators are strengthened further by the intentional inclusion of a thematic overlap in 7.25. . . . Since in Paul's day chain-link construction was not an uncommon transitional device in assisting an audience . . . the placement of 7.25 within its surrounding context would not have been unusual or confusing. It would not have been seen as a structural anomaly requiring either textual reconstruction . . . or psychological explanation. Instead it would have been seen as a transition marker used for the benefit of Paul's audience.[49]

And So?

It is the mark of any good and correct interpretation of a complex and controverted passage that it explains not only the passage in question, but it clears up other conundrums as well. One such conundrum for Augustine, Luther, and others who have seen Romans 7:7-25 not in the light of rhetoric but as some sort of agonized transcript of Paul's own experience is that there is a flat contradiction to such a reading of this passage when one examines Philippians 3:4-6. Here again we have a *synkrisis*, only here Paul is indeed contrasting his own past with his present condition and frame of mind. The key to understanding the passage is that on the one hand Paul says he has much to brag about "in the flesh," but on the other hand he says that however good those things were, he now counts them as refuse or dung because of the exceedingly great joy and glory of knowing Christ.

We need not make the mistake of assuming that this colorful rhetorical language leads us to the wrong conclusion about Philippians

3:4-6. Paul was an outstanding and exceptionally pious Jew. On his own admission in Galatians 1:14, he was advancing in Judaism well beyond many Jews of his own age, and he was exceedingly zealous for and about his faith. Paul was no slacker.

Thus, it will come as no surprise that Paul gets to the point of describing his rich Jewish heritage and is even able to say that when he was a Pharisaic Jew, when it came to the matter of keeping the Mosaic law, he was faultless! His exact words are, "as for righteousness of the Law—faultless" (Phil 3:6). I submit that the person who says this as a Christian looking back on his Jewish past cannot also be describing his own personal experience in Romans 7:7-25, or else Paul is capable of flatly contradicting himself, even when he is talking about something he knows more intimately than any other human being—his own spiritual pilgrimage. The only thing about Paul's past that he does indeed agonize over is his persecution, perhaps even to the death, of some Christians when he was a zealous Pharisee. This, as Galatians 1, 1 Corinthians 15, and the later text 1 Timothy 1:13-15 show, he did indeed regret, repent of, and have considerable remorse and anguish about. That, however, is very different from the described state in Romans 7:14-25 where the person knows better but is quite unable to do better and cries out for deliverance in his bondage.

Paul, as Stendahl rightly stresses, should not be overpsychologized, and we should not read back into his story the more tormented one of Augustine or Luther. He did not reflect the "introspective consciousness of the West," as Stendahl correctly urges.[50] I was fortunate enough to take Romans with Stendahl in the late 1970s and hear his exposition of these crucial matters first hand. Needless to say, he convinced me. What is remarkable, however, is that he was able to come to this conclusion without fully recognizing the rhetorical character of the material and its signals. But when one reads Paul with rhetorical spectacles, Stendahl's conclusion moves from being plausible to being by far the clearest and most convincing reading of this material in its original social and rhetorical contexts. Paul, as it turns out, was not a Lutheran before his time, nor even an Augustinian. Paul was a master rhetorician, and he fully believed that when Christ has set people free, they are free indeed from the bondage to sin, no longer entangled by the ruling principle of sin and death, for they have the Spirit of life within them, and they need not, indeed they must no longer, dwell in the past: "If anyone is in Christ, behold a whole new creation, *the old has already passed away*." Thanks be to God in Jesus Christ.

6

What's in a Name?

Rethinking the Historical Figure of the Beloved Disciple in the Fourth Gospel

O, be some other name! What's in a name? That which we call a rose by any other name would smell as sweet.

—William Shakespeare, *Romeo and Juliet*, Act II, Scene 2

Earlier in this study, we pointed out at some length that the environment in which the New Testament was written was both oral and rhetorical in character.[1] We stressed the fact that texts, especially religious texts, functioned differently in a culture that was 90 percent illiterate and in which even the texts that exist are oral texts, meant to be read aloud. These important insights, when coupled with the realization that orally delivered and rhetorically adept discourse and storytelling was at the heart of first-century culture, should have long ago led us to a new way of reading the Gospels themselves.

The telling of the story of Jesus was from the beginning crucial for the new Christian movement, and surely it was important well before the whole story was written down in any one fashion. M. Mitchell in a seminal essay has shown that in various places in the Pauline corpus, "Paul grounds his arguments solidly upon an underlying gospel narrative, which he accesses through various forms of rhetorical shorthand—brevity of speech, synecdoche, and metaphor. Though Paul is thoroughly consistent in his frame of reference—the gospel narrative—his references to it are fluid and flexible."[2] A good example of this sort of short rhetorical citing of the gospel can be found in 1 Corinthians 15:3-8, in which Paul mentions the climax of the gospel narrative, the death, burial, and resurrection of Jesus, and its immediate sequels, the appearances of Jesus. The gospel apparently first appeared in any written form in these summaries in Paul's highly rhetorical discourses, framed as letters.

What this means is that there was permission to tell the story in rhetorically effective and persuasive ways, even when, and perhaps especially when, the story involved the memoirs of someone who actually heard Jesus in person—an eye- and earwitness of some part of Jesus' life and teachings. I submit that there is no more rhetorically effective (and affective) telling of the gospel story in long form, but nonetheless edited down on the basis of rhetorical and other considerations (cf. John 20:30 and 21:25) than the Gospel of John. What we have in this Gospel is not the boiling up of a story on the basis of shards of information, but rather the boiling down of copious notes, memoranda, and eyewitness accounts from the Beloved Disciple and their organization into a rhetorically effective order and shape by some final editor (on which more is said at the end of this chapter). I also submit that when one looks at the Gospel of John as an oral document that was meant to be heard rather than read privately or individually, and heard in the order in which it is now presented, certain things come to light, including fresh insights into the identity of the Beloved Disciple.[3]

THE PROBLEM WITH THE TRADITIONAL ASCRIPTION
TO JOHN ZEBEDEE

M. Hengel and G. Stanton, among other scholars, have reminded us in recent discussions of the Fourth Gospel that the superscripts to all four of the canonical Gospels were in all likelihood added after the fact to the documents; indeed, they may originally have been added as document tags to the papyrus rolls. Even more tellingly, they were likely added only after there were several familiar gospels, for the phrase "according to" is used to distinguish this particular Gospel from other well-known ones.[4]

This means that all four Gospels are formally anonymous, and the question then becomes, how much weight one should place on internal evidence of authorship (the so-called inscribed author) and how much on external evidence? In my view, the internal evidence should certainly take precedence in the case of the Gospel of John, not least because the external evidence is hardly unequivocal. This does not alleviate the necessity of explaining how the Gospel came to be ascribed to someone named John, but we will leave that question to the end of our discussion.

As far as the external evidence goes, it is true enough that various church fathers in the second century thought John, son of Zebedee, was the author. There was an increasing urgency about this conclusion for the mainstream church after the middle of the second century, because the Fourth Gospel seems to have been a favorite among the Gnostics, and, therefore, apostolic authorship was deemed important if this Gospel was to be rescued from the heterodox. The tendency to associate authenticity and accuracy with apostolicity and eyewitness testimony is evident throughout this church crisis, but the emphasis on eyewitness testimony is already in evidence in Luke 1:1-4 and in various places in the Pauline corpus. It was not an urgency first forced on the church by the Gnostic crisis.

Irenaeus, the great heresiarch, around A.D. 180 urged that the Fourth Gospel was written in Ephesus by one of the Twelve—John. It is therefore telling that this seems not to have been the conclusion of perhaps our very earliest witness, Papias of Hierapolis, who was surely in a location and in a position to know something about Christianity in the provenance of Asia at the beginning of the second century A.D. Papias ascribes this Gospel to one elder John, whom he distinguishes presumably from another John, and it is only the former that he claims to have had personal contact with. Eusebius, in referring to the preface to Papias' five-volume work, stresses that Papias only had contact with an elder John and one Aristion, not with John of Zebedee (*Hist. eccl.* 3.39.3-7), who is distinguished by Eusebius himself from the John in question. It is notable as well that Eusebius reminds us that Papias reflects the same chiliastic eschatology as is found in the book of Revelation, something at which Eusebius looks askance. Eusebius is clear that Papias only knew the "elders" who had had contact with the "holy apostles," not the holy apostles themselves. Papias had heard *personally* what Aristion and the elder John said, but he had only heard *about* what the earlier apostles had said.[5]

As most scholars have now concluded, Papias was an adult during the reign of Trajan and perhaps also Hadrian, and his work that Eusebius cites should probably be dated to about A.D. 100,[6] which is only shortly after the Fourth Gospel is traditionally dated. This is interesting in several respects. First, Papias does not attempt to claim too much, even though he has great interest in what all the apostles and the Twelve have said. His claim is a limited one of having heard those who had been in contact with such eyewitnesses. In the second place, he is writing at a time and in a place where he ought to have known who it was that was responsible for putting together the Fourth Gospel, and equally clearly he reflects the influence of the millennial theology we find only distinctly in the book of Revelation in the NT and not, for example, in the Fourth Gospel. This suggests that the John he knew and had talked with was John of Patmos, and this was the same John who had something to do with the production of the Fourth Gospel. It is significant that Hengel, after a detailed discussion, concludes that this Gospel must be associated with the elder John, who was not the same as John, son of Zebedee,[7] but more on this in due course. As I have suggested, while Papias' testimony is significant and early, we must also give due weight to the internal evidence in the Fourth

Gospel itself, to which we will turn shortly. One more thing: Papias' Fragment 10.17 has now been subjected to detailed analysis by M. Oberweis, and Oberweis, rightly in my judgment, draws the conclusion that Papias claimed that John, son of Zebedee, died early as a martyr like his brother (Acts 12:2).[8] This counts against both the theory that John of Patmos was John of Zebedee and the theory that the latter wrote the Fourth Gospel.

THE GROWING RECOGNITION OF THE JUDEAN PROVENANCE OF THE FOURTH GOSPEL

A. Lincoln, in his new commentary on the Gospel of John, has concluded that the Beloved Disciple was a real person and "a minor follower of Jesus during his Jerusalem ministry."[9] While Lincoln sees the Beloved Disciple traditions as small snippets of historical tradition added to a larger core of the gospel that did not come from this person, he draws this conclusion about the Beloved Disciple's provenance for a very good reason—he does not show up at all in this Gospel in the telling of the Galilean ministry stories, but he seems to be involved with and know personally Jesus' ministry in and around Jerusalem.

One of the things that is probably fatal to the theory that John, son of Zebedee, is the Beloved Disciple and also the author of this entire document is that none, and I do mean *none*, of the special Zebedee stories are included in the Fourth Gospel (e.g., the calling of the Zebedees by Jesus, their presence with Jesus in the house where Jesus raised Jairus' daughter, the story of the transfiguration, the request for special seats in Jesus' kingdom when it comes, and so forth). In view of the fact that this Gospel places some stress on the role of eyewitness testimony (see especially John 19–21), it is strange that these stories would be omitted if this Gospel were by John of Zebedee, or even if he were its primary source. It is equally strange that the Zebedees are so briefly mentioned in this Gospel as such (see John 21:2), and John is never equated with the Beloved Disciple, even in the appendix in John 21 (cf. verse 2 and verse 7—the Beloved Disciple could certainly be one of the two unnamed disciples mentioned in verse 2).

Also telling is the fact that this Gospel includes none or almost none of the special Galilean miracle stories found in the Synoptics, with the exception of the feeding of the five thousand and walking on water tandem. The author of this document rather includes such stories as the meeting with Nicodemus, the encounter with the Samaritan woman, the healing of the blind man, the healing of the cripple by the pool, and the raising of Lazarus; what all these events have in common is that *none of them transpired in Galilee.*

When we couple these revelations with the fact that our author seems to have some detailed knowledge about the topography in and around Jerusalem and the historical particulars about the last week or so of Jesus' life (e.g., compare the story of the anointing of Jesus by Mary of Bethany in John to the more generic Markan account), it is not a surprise that Lincoln and others reflect a growing trend by recognizing the Judean provenance of this Gospel. Recognition of this provenance clears up various difficulties, not the least of which is the lack of Galilean stories in general in this Gospel and more particularly the lack of exorcism tales, none of which, according to the Synoptics, are said to have occurred in Jerusalem or Judea. Furthermore, there is absolutely no emphasis or real interest in this Gospel in the Twelve as Twelve or as Galileans. If the author is a Judean follower of Jesus, is not one of the Twelve, and in turn is sticking to the things he knows personally or has heard directly from eyewitnesses, this is understandable. This brings us to the question of who this Beloved Disciple might have been.

THE ONE WHOM JESUS LOVED—FIRST MENTIONED IN JOHN 13?

It has been common in Johannine commentaries to suggest that the Beloved Disciple as a figure in the narrative does not show up under that title before John 13. While this case has been argued thoroughly, it overlooks something very important. This Gospel was written in an oral culture for use with non-Christians as a sort of teaching tool to lead them to faith. It was not intended to be handed out as a tract to the nonbeliever to be read, but nevertheless its stories were meant to be used orally for evangelism.

In an oral and rhetorically careful document of this sort, the ordering of things is especially important.[10] Once introduced into the narrative by name and title or name and identifying phrase, figures may thereafter be only identified by one or the other, because economy of words is at a premium when one is writing a document of this size on a piece of papyrus (John 20:30-31). This brings us to John 11:3 and the phrase *hon phileis*. It is perfectly clear from a comparison of 11:1 and 11:3 that the sick person in question who is first called Lazarus of Bethany and then is called "the one whom you love" is the same person. Ths is made certain in the context by the mention of sickness in each verse. This is the first time in this entire Gospel that any particular person is said to have been loved by Jesus. Indeed, one could argue that this is the only named person in the whole Gospel about whom this is specifically said directly. I would argue that in a rhetorically saturated environment, the audience would be well aware and attuned to the fact that first mention of crucial ideas, persons, and events was critical to the understanding of what was being suggested and how it was meant to persuade the audience. This brings us to John 13:23.

At John 13:23, we have the by-now-very-familiar reference to a disciple whom Jesus loved (*hon agapa* this time) as reclining on the bosom of Jesus, by which is meant he is reclining on the same couch as Jesus. The disciple is not named here, and notice that nowhere in John 13 is it said that this meal transpired in Jerusalem. It could just as well have transpired in the nearby town of Bethany, and this need not even be an account of the Passover meal. John 13:1 in fact says it was a meal that transpired *before* the Passover meal. This brings us to a crucial juncture in this discussion. In John 11, there is a reference to a beloved disciple named Lazarus. In John 12, there is a mention of a meal at the house of Lazarus. If someone was hearing these tales in this order without access to the Synoptic Gospels, it would be natural to conclude that the person reclining with Jesus in John 13 was Lazarus. There is another good reason to do so as well. It was the custom in this sort of dining that the host would recline with or next to the chief guest. The story as it is told in John 13 implies, then, that the Beloved Disciple is the host. But this in turn means he must have a house in the vicinity of Jerusalem. This in turn probably eliminates *all* the Galilean disciples.

This identification of the Beloved Disciple as Lazarus not only clears up some conundrums about this story, it also neatly clears up a series of other conundrums in the Johannine Passion narrative as well. For example, it was always problematic that the Beloved Disciple had ready access to the high priest's house. Who could he have been to have such access? Surely he was not a Galilean fisherman. John 11:36-47 suggests that some of the Jewish officials who reported to the high priest had known Lazarus and had attended his mourning period in Bethany. This in turn means that Lazarus likely had some relationship with them. He could have had access to Caiphas' house, being a high-status person known to Caiphas' entourage.[11] If Lazarus of Bethany is the Beloved Disciple, this, too, explains the omission of the Garden of Gethsemane prayer story in this Gospel. Peter, James, and John were present on that occasion, but the Beloved Disciple was not. It also explains John 19:27. If the Beloved Disciple took Jesus' mother "unto his own" home (it is implied), this surely suggests some locale much nearer than Galilee, for the Beloved Disciple will show up in Jerusalem in John 20 immediately thereafter, and Mary is still there, according to Acts 1:14, well after the crucifixion and resurrection of her son. How is it that the Beloved Disciple gets to the tomb of Jesus in John 20 before Peter? Perhaps because he knows the locale and knows Joseph of Arimathea and Nicodemus, being one who lived near and spent much time in Jerusalem and with various of the elders in Jerusalem. One more thing about John 20:2, which T. Thatcher kindly reminded me of: here, the designation of our man is a double one—he is called both "the other disciple" and also the one "whom Jesus loved," only this time the verb is *phileō*. Why has our author varied the title at this juncture, if in fact it was a preexisting title for someone outside the narrative? We would have expected it to be in a fixed form if this were some kind of preexisting title. Notice now the chain of things: Lazarus is identified in John 11 as the one whom Jesus loves, and here "the other disciple" (see John 20:1-2) is identified as the one whom Jesus loves, which then allows him to be called "the other disciple" in the rest of this segment of the story, but at 21:2 we return once more to his main designation—the one whom Jesus loved is Lazarus. This makes good sense if John 11–21 is read or heard in the sequence we now find it. Of course, the old problem of the fact that the Synoptics say all the Twelve deserted Jesus once he was taken away for execution, even Peter, and record only women being at the cross is not contradicted by the account in John 19 if the Beloved Disciple, while clearly enough from John 19:26 a man (called Mary's "son," and so not Mary Magdalene!), is Lazarus rather than one of the Twelve. There is the further point that if indeed the Beloved Disciple took Mary into his own home, then we know where the Beloved Disciple got the story of the wedding feast at Cana—he got it from Mary herself. I could continue mounting up small particulars of the text that are best explained by the theory of Lazarus being the Beloved Disciple, but this must suffice. I want to deal with some larger issues in regard to this Gospel that are explained by this theory, in particular its appendix in John 21. But one more conjecture is in order here.

Scholars have often noted how the account of the anointing of Jesus in Bethany as recorded in Mark 14:3-11 differs from the account in John 12:1-11 while still likely being the same story or tradition. Perhaps the most salient difference is that Mark tells us that the event happens in the home of Simon the Leper in Bethany, while John 12 indicates it happens in the house of Mary, Martha, and Lazarus in Bethany. Suppose for a moment, however, that Simon the Leper was in fact the father of these three siblings. Suppose that Lazarus himself, like his father, had also contracted the dread disease and succumbed to it (and we now know for sure that the deadly form of Hansen's disease did exist in the first century A.D. from recent archaeological and medical work on ancient corpses from the region). This might well explain why it is that none of these three siblings seems to be married. Few have remarked about the oddness of this trio of adults not having families of their own but rather still living together, but it is not at all odd if the family was plagued by a dread disease that made them unclean on an ongoing basis. It also explains why these folks never travel with Jesus' other disciples and they never get near this family until that fateful day recorded in John 11 when Jesus raised and healed Lazarus. Jesus, of course, was not put off by the disease and so had visited the home previously alone (Luke 10:38-42). But other early Jews would certainly not have engaged in betrothal contracts with this family if it was known to be a carrier of leprosy.

How Seeing Lazarus as the Beloved Disciple Explains a Host of Conundrums

Most scholars are in agreement that John 21 makes clear that while the Beloved Disciple is said to have written down some gospel traditions, he is no longer alive when at least the end of this chapter was written. The "we know his testimony is true" is a dead giveaway that someone or someones other than the Beloved Disciple put this Gospel into its final form and added this appendix or, at a minimum, the story about the demise of the Beloved Disciple and the conclusion of the appendix. This line of reasoning I find compelling. And it also explains something else. We may envision that whoever put the memoirs of the Beloved Disciple together is probably the one who insisted on calling him that.

In other words, the Beloved Disciple is called such by his community perhaps, and by his final editor certainly, and this is not a self-designation; indeed, it was unlikely to be a self-designation in a religious subculture where humility and following the self-sacrificial, self-effacing example of Jesus was being inculcated. This then explains one of the salient differences between 2–3 John and the Gospel of John. The author of those little letters calls himself either the "elder" or "the old man," depending on how you want to render *presbyteros*. He nowhere calls himself the Beloved Disciple, not even in the sermon we call 1 John, in which he claims to have personally seen and touched the Word of life, which in my view means he saw and touched Jesus. We must conjure then with at least two persons responsible for the final form of the Fourth Gospel, while only one is necessary to explain the epiphenomena of the Johannine Epistles. This brings us to the story itself in John 21:20-24.

Why is the final editor of this material in such angst about denying that Jesus predicted that the Beloved Disciple would live until Jesus returned? Is it because there had been a tradition in the Beloved Disciple's church that he would live until then? If so, what generated such a tradition? Not, apparently, the Beloved Disciple himself. But now he has passed away, and this has caused anxiety among the faithful about what the case was with the Beloved Disciple and what Jesus had actually said about his future in A.D. 30. I suggest that no solution

better explains all the interesting factors in play here than the suggestion that the Beloved Disciple was someone that Jesus had raised from
the dead, and so quite naturally there arose a belief that surely he would
not die again before Jesus returned. Such a line of thought makes perfectly good sense if the Beloved Disciple had already died once and the
second coming was still something eagerly anticipated when he died.
Thus I submit that the theory that Lazarus was the Beloved Disciple
and the author of most of the traditions in this Gospel is a theory that
best clears up the conundrum of the end of the appendix written after
his death.

Finally, there is one more thing to say. It is true that the Fourth
Gospel takes its own approach to presenting Jesus and the gospel tradition. I am still unconvinced by the attempts of Lincoln and others to
suggest that the author drew on earlier gospels, particularly Mark. I
think he may well have known of such gospels and may even have read
Mark, but he is certainly not dependent on the Synoptic material for
his own Gospel. Rather, he takes his own line of approach and has an
abundance of information that he is unable to use in his Gospel, including much non-Synoptic material (see John 20:30 and 21:25) because
of the constraints of writing all this down on one papyrus. He did not
need to boil up his Gospel based on fragments and snippets from the
Synoptics. On the contrary, he had to be constantly condensing his
material, as is so often the case with an eyewitness account that is rich
in detail and substance. But it is not enough to say that the author was
an eyewitness to explain the Gospel's independence and differences
from the earlier Synoptic Gospels. There are other factors as well.

As I pointed out more than a decade ago, this Gospel is written
in a way that reflects an attempt to present the Jesus tradition in the
light of the Jewish sapiential material.[12] Jesus is presented as God's
Wisdom come in the flesh in this Gospel, serving up discourses like
those of Wisdom in earlier Jewish Wisdom literature rather than offering aphorisms and parables as in the Synoptics. I have suggested that
this reflected Jesus' in-house modus operandi for his private teaching
with his own inner circle of disciples. We need not choose between the
public form of Wisdom discourse found in the Synoptics (i.e., parables
and aphorisms) and the private form of Wisdom discourse (see, e.g.,
John 14–17) in John when trying to decide which went back to the
historical Jesus—both did, but they had different *Sitz im Leben* and
different functions. But I have concluded even this line of thinking is
insufficient to explain the differences from the Synoptics we find in the
Fourth Gospel. There is yet one more factor in play.

Our author, the Beloved Disciple, had been raised not merely from
death's door but from being well and truly dead—by Jesus! This was
bound to change his worldview, and so it did. It became quite impossible

for our author to draw up a veiled messiah portrait of Jesus such as the one we find in Mark. No, our author wanted and needed to shout from the mountaintops that Jesus was the resurrection—not merely that he *performed* resurrections, but that he was what E. Kasemann once said about the presentation of Jesus in the Fourth Gospel, that he was a God bestriding the stage of history. Just so, and our author pulls no punches in making that clear in various ways in this Gospel, especially by demonstrating that everything previously said to come only from God, or the mind and plan of God known as God's Wisdom, is now said of and said to come from Jesus. He is the incarnation of the great I Am.

The Beloved Disciple would not have been best pleased with modern minimalist portraits of the historical Jesus. He had had a personal and profound encounter of the first order with both the historical Jesus and the risen Jesus and knew that they were one and the same. This was bound to change his worldview. It is no accident that the book of Signs in the Fourth Gospel climaxes in John 11 with the story of Lazarus' own transformation, just as the book of Glory climaxes in John 20 with the transformation of Jesus himself. Lazarus had become what he admired—he had been made, to a lesser degree, like Jesus. And he would not mince words about his risen savior and Lord. Rather, he would walk through the door of bold proclamation, even to the point perhaps of adding the logos hymn at the beginning of this Gospel. This was the Jesus he had known and touched and supped with before and after Easter, and he could proclaim no lesser Jesus.

This then leads us to the last bit of the puzzle that can now be solved. How did this Gospel come to be named according to John? My answer is a simple one—it is because John of Patmos was the final editor of this Gospel after the death of Lazarus. Once Domitian died, John left Patmos, returned to Ephesus, and lived out his days. One of the things he did was edit and promulgate the Fourth Gospel on behalf of the Beloved Disciple. Somewhere very near the end of John's own life, Papias had contact with this elderly John. It is not surprising, because this contact seems to be brief, that Papias learned correctly that this John was not the Zebedee John and that this elderly John had something to do with the production of the Fourth Gospel. This I think neatly explains the various factors involved in our conundrum. It may even have been Papias who was responsible for the wider circulation of this Gospel with the tag "according to John." It is not surprising that Irenaeus, swatting buzzing Gnostics like flies, would later conclude that the Fourth Gospel must be by an apostle or one of the Twelve.

If I am right about all this, it means that the historical figure of Lazarus is more important than we have previously imagined, due to his role in founding churches in and around Ephesus and his role in the life of Jesus and Jesus' mother. Jesus must have trusted him implicitly to hand over his mother to him when he died. Lazarus was far more than one more recipient of a miraculous healing by Jesus. He was "the one whom Jesus loved," as the very first reference to him in John 11 says. We have yet to take the measure of the man. Hopefully now, we can begin to do so.

7

What's in a Word?

Part One—*Eidolothuton*

"In the beginning was the Word"—but some students of the Bible seem to think when it comes to the study of New Testament words that "in the beginning was the dictionary." Words, however, even NT words, only have meanings in contexts. Dictionaries do not define words, they record their meanings. Lexicons are just the result of careful study of the semantic range of words in various contexts.

The social history of language is an interesting subject, especially when one is talking about a biblical language that was seen as a vehicle for the communication of revelations from God. Such history becomes all the more crucial because the NT was written in the context of an oral and rhetorical culture that believed that sacred words had special resonance and power, and this of course included polemical language, including pejorative terms and even curse formulae. The study of invective and its rhetorical uses has not made much progress for the very good reason that traditionally the invective found in the NT has simply been evaluated in light of earlier Jewish literature and without an understanding of the various functions of invective in a Greco-Roman rhetorical setting.

One of the things one learns immediately from a close reading of experts in rhetoric ranging from Aristotle to Menander to Quintilian is that not only did these rhetoricians believe in the power of words, including pejorative terms, but they also believed that one of the most effective ways to stigmatize something or someone and warn an audience off from that thing or person was to coin new words.

Such a word is *eidolothuton*, the origins of which have been assumed to be general Jewish polemics against idolatry. However, on closer inspection, that is probably not the case. As we shall see, *eidolothuton* seems to have been a term coined by Paul, James, or perhaps another Greek-speaking early Jewish Christian in response to the increasing numbers of Gentiles who were becoming followers of Jesus.

Such an innovation of a new word as a leading polemical term that could encapsulate what was wrong with going to pagan temples could be a rhetorically effective tool in the struggle for identity formation in early Christianity. And clearly enough, if one takes the homily titled James as a sample of the rhetorical skill of James himself, including his skills at polemics, then he was quite capable of coming up with a *juste mot*, a memorable term or phrase that would imbed itself in the memories of his audiences.[1] The study of the origins, meaning, and rhetorical use of this key term then will repay major dividends if we seek to understand the socio-rhetorical climate and strategies of the earliest Christians.[2]

THE SEMANTIC ORIGINS AND RANGE OF *EIDOLOTHUTON*

It has long been a commonplace of NT scholarship that the term *eidolothuton*, most often translated as "idol meat," is a Jewish term coined to have a polemical counterpart to the Greek term *hierothuton*, which simply means "stuff," or in this case "meat" that comes from or is found in a temple. The latter term does not have the polemical edge of the former, for pagans would not call their gods idols. It is surprising how often NT scholars have been content to simply pass along the view, without close examination of the evidence, that *eidolothuton* is a term that comes out of Hellenistic Jewish polemics.[3] Surprisingly, before I took the time in the early 1990s to do a complete Ibycus and Thesaurus Lingua Graecae (TLG) search of all the occurrences of this term, it does not appear that anyone had bothered to check all the data. In fact, when one looks at all the relevant evidence from the period, in the Greek sources that antedate Paul's letter that we call 1 Corinthians, *there are no examples whatsoever of the use of* eidolothuton *unless 4 Macc 5:2 or Sibylline Oracles 2.96 count! Furthermore, these same two examples are the only ones that come from possibly non-Christian sources.* In regard to the reference in the *Sibylline Oracles*, it is found in only one manuscript, which the experts tell us is dependent on Ps-Phocylides *Sententiae* 31, which in turn is dependent on Acts 15:29.[4] In other words, this text provides no evidence for its non-Christian use. As is widely recognized by scholars, there were numerous Christian interpolations into the *Sibylline Oracles*, and this is one of them. What about the reference in 4 Maccabees?

Traditionally, 4 Maccabees was thought to have been produced by Josephus. However, as most recent treatments of this document show, this is unlikely because its rhetorical style differs from Josephus' and it includes views that Josephus would not entirely embrace. What is far more clear and certain is that 4 Maccabees is likely dependent on 2 Maccabees, which in turn means that there is a slight chance it might be from as early as 63 B.C. or so, but most scholars today believe it was not written prior to A.D. 63–70, and some would date it as late as the Hadrian persecutions of the second century.[5] There is in addition the further problem that it possibly endured some Christian interpolations as well, but probably not.[6] We may date the document to sometime in the A.D. 60s or later, which certainly places it too late to have been the origins of the usage of the term *eidolothuton* by Paul, and by James, if Acts 15 and 21 reflects James' actual decree to Gentiles, which I have argued elsewhere it certainly does.[7]

In addition to this, there are no examples anywhere of the use of this term in the papyri, in any inscriptions, or in any Coptic sources whatsoever. This means that this term was used exclusively in Christian circles with one possible exception, and that exception cannot be said to be the origin of the usage in Paul, nor is it likely the source of the usage in Acts or elsewhere in Christian literature. In sum then, of the 112 references to *eidolothuton* generated by the TLG, all but one seem clearly enough to come from Christian sources, and that one materialized too late to explain the origins of this term. We must conclude that there is probably no basis at all for the suggestion that this term comes to Christianity from Hellenistic Judaism. On the contrary, it is far more likely to be a term coined as part of the rhetoric of early Christianity in dealing with paganism. In particular, it is part of the Jewish Christian polemic against paganism, which is very prevalent in the NT in various forms and in numerous sources as varied as Paul's Letters, 1 Peter, Jude, and Revelation.

In regard to the specific meaning of *eidolothuton*, most scholars are right to draw a parallel with the common term *hierothuton* ("offered in the temple") or *theothuton* ("offered to a god"), and thus they have concluded it means "offered to an idol," denoting something sacrificed to an idol or idols. The absence of the former term and the frequent presence of the latter two terms in inscriptional evidence and literary texts are eloquent testimony that pagans would not have coined or ever used such a term. It is outsider language and is deliberately polemical in character. But where did it actually come from?

One suggestion I would make is that it is possible that we should see it as the negative counterpart to the Jewish term *Corban* (see Mark 7:11), which means something dedicated to the true God, a subject about which Jesus commented (negatively), and James could well have known of these traditions of Jesus' teaching on the subject. Note that *Corban* does not just refer to dedicating something to God; it refers in addition to placing that resource in the temple itself.[8]

Here is where I say that in regard to the pagan parallel terms, the literal meaning says it all—whether offered to a god or offered in a temple, the social setting is implied in the very term itself. Sacrifices took place in temples. There is good reason to think that under any normal circumstances the term *eidolothuton* would have been heard to refer to something that goes on in a temple, not merely to "idol meat" in general, wherever it might have been consumed. In what follows, I argue that in its NT occurrences the term *eidolothuton* does not merely connote something—namely, an offering to an idol—it also denotes or at least implies the venue in which such things transpired—the precincts of a pagan temple. *It then does not refer to a sacrifice taken from the temple and eaten elsewhere for the very good reason that the statue of the gods to whom the offering was made and who were believed to participate in the temple feasts were found in the temples themselves.* The term *hierothuton* could, by contrast, occasionally refer to something offered in the temple but eaten elsewhere, such as in a private home, where the god was not thought to dwell and where a statue of that specific god was unlikely to be found, and thus the god was not thought to participate in a feast in that home. I shall discuss this topic in more detail shortly. In summary, in all the first century A.D. references to *eidolothuton*, including all the Christian ones, the association of this term specifically with what was happening at one particular social venue, namely a pagan temple, is likely and is made absolutely clear by the larger context in which this new rhetorical term was used.

USE OF THE TERM *EIDOLOTHUTON* OUTSIDE THE NEW TESTAMENT

The reference to *eidolothuton* in 4 Maccabees 5:2 describes the misdeeds of the tyrant Antiochus. We are told that he ordered his troops to "drag every single one of the Hebrews to a certain high place" where he was seated with his counselors and courtiers, and they were to compel the Hebrews to eat pork and *eidolothuton*. What is most crucial about this story is its locale—"a certain high place," which means a place where sacrifices were offered to a god. It is clear enough that the Jewish person who wrote 4 Maccabees was deeply influenced by the Hebrew Scriptures and the social and religious connotations of the phrase "a high place" (*bamah* in Hebrew). This word had a very clear association with pagan worship in Jewish literature, especially in the polemics of later prophets, such as Ezekiel (cf., e.g., Ezek 6:3, 16:24-39; Hos 10:8; Amos 7:9; but also Num 33:52; 1 Kgs 12:28-33 (calf worship); 2 Kgs 17:7-29; 2 Chr 21:11, 31:1; Isa 15:21, 16:12; Jer 48:35). Antiochus was not merely trying to force the Hebrews to eat non-kosher food. He was trying to do it in a setting where it would obviously carry the connotations of participating in an act of pagan worship. Social venue as well as menu is the issue here.

Turning to the reference in *Sibylline Oracles* 2.96, we find the reference in one of many passages in that document excoriating idolatry. The specific prohibition there of "eating blood" coupled with the term *eidolothuton* makes it likely indeed that the author has in mind eating in a temple where the blood might be poured out and consumed or at least would still be sufficiently in the meat that it would be consumed with the idol offering. Meat sacrificed in the temple, drained, and later taken to the *macellum,* or meat market, would not likely have so close an association of consuming blood and consuming meat. If we connect this teaching with 2.95, where there is a warning against drinking in excess, something that certainly happened in pagan dinner feasts in temples, we may then have a further hint that the author is thinking about what went on in pagan temples.[9]

It needs to be said that while drinking blood was not part of the traditional Greek ritual of dining, and Greeks saw it as the practice of barbarians and marginalized groups,[10] the Romans did not follow all the restrictions of Greek dining, and Greeks were known to say that Romans dined like barbarians. Paul in 1 Corinthians, and probably James in Acts, is dealing with a social world in which there was a Roman overlay on Greek culture and many Greek cities had been reconstituted as Roman colonies, bringing their own practices into the cultus in those places, especially in the Imperial Cult temples.

There is one further reference to *eidolothuton* from outside the NT that could come from the first century, and it is found in the early Christian document called the *Didache*. The passage (Didache 6.3) deserves to be quoted in full: "And concerning food tolerate what you are able but keep well away from *eidolothuton*; for it is the worship of dead gods." Here is a clear contrast between eating whatever one is able and what one finds in the meat market, when it is simply a matter of food, but abstaining from *eidolothuton* because *it is the worship of dead gods.* The issue then is certainly not merely food, but more specifically food eaten in a context where it entails and is an expression of idolatry (i.e., in a pagan temple). There is nothing at all in any of these three texts to cause one to dispute the thesis that *eidolothuton* means meat consumed in the presence of a god in a temple, where the god's power and presence were thought to reside. In Roman religion, while the statue of a god was not seen as the god itself, it was seen as the vehicle through which one had contact with the god, such that to eat in the presence of the god's image was to eat in the presence of the god. Thus for an early Jew, such as Paul or James, this was clearly enough an act of idolatry. Paul in fact says in 1 Corinthians 10 that demons are present when one dines in a pagan temple. The gods, as it turned out, were not viewed as phantasms of the human imagination. Rather, they were viewed by early Jewish Christians as dangerous spiritual beings—

evil spirits. But this brings us to the point of asking what did go on in temples, especially when it came to sacrifices. Why all the polemics against what went on there?

SACRIFICES — GRECO-ROMAN STYLE

While there were some variations from one Greco-Roman temple to another and from the worship of one god to another, there is enough known about ancient sacrifices that we can talk about a general pattern or the common features involved in Roman worship.[11]

Ancient temples were in most respects different from modern churches or synagogues in that the "business" of religion took place outside the building proper. Inside a pagan temple, there was a central walled room (the *cella*) in which stood the usually quite large statue of the deity (a good example would be the Parthenon with its huge statue of Athena). The god's statue would often be adorned with flowers or jewels and other gifts from devotees. Usually there was nothing else at all in that room except perhaps an incense altar. There were no seats and no altars.

When a Roman wished to secure the good will of a god, he or she would usually make a vow, most often written on a wax or lead tablet, and would go to the temple to arrange a time with the custodian when he or she could come and have a sacrifice offered on his or her behalf. There were professional officials who actually cut the animals' throats and usually a flute player as well. There were both set fees and a list of approved animals that this god would accept as a sacrifice (*CIL* 6.820). The one consistent rule was that male gods required male animals and female gods required female ones as sacrifices.

When the day came for the sacrifice, the devotee would enter the *cella*, attach the tablet to the statue of the god, and pray facing the statue with hands uplifted and head covered. While there were a rare few sacrifices actually offered in the temple (see Festus 356L), the vast majority were offered outside, usually in front of the temple, so that strangers walking by, even Jews or Christians, could see what was happening if they cared to do so. The sacrifice would take place on a stone altar if a blood sacrifice was involved. The sacrificial animal would be led to the altar, where a fire would often already be kindled. Care was taken to make sure no strangers were close enough to pollute or disturb the proceedings (cf. Plutarch, *Quaes. Rom.* 10, on the exclusion of dogs and women from the sacrifice to Hercules or Mars—i.e., male deities; cf. Servius, *On the Aeneid* 8.172).

It is thus possible that Paul at least, though perhaps not James, would have seen a pagan sacrifice, but from afar. Certainly neither of them was able to see what happened after the sacrifice was made and the participants retreated into the temple or an indoor dining area adjacent thereto. The devotee would normally invite family and friends to the meal, not least because there was normally a great deal of meat to eat, and it needed to be done quickly in a world without real refrigeration. Furthermore, because it was normally only the rich who had meat to eat, except at festivals, for only they could afford it as a regular part of their diets (Tacitus, *Ann.* 14.24), eating in the temple was seen as a special occasion for most and was eagerly attended.

In terms of preparation for the sacrifice, both the devotee and the priest had to come with clean hands and clean clothes. A great deal of stress was placed on cleanliness, being next to godliness, as we might say. Livy (45.5.4) puts it this way: "Every sacrifice is introduced by the statement that those with unclean hands should depart." At the moment of the sacrifice itself the command would be given for absolute silence (*favete linguis*, or "check your tongues" in Latin). There was no speaking at that juncture, but a flute player would play to drown out background noise. The priest would then cover his head with the top folds of his toga (see 1 Corinthians 11) and sprinkle flour between the horns of the animal and on the sacrificial knife. Sometimes this was followed by pouring wine over the animal's head, and the animal was stripped of any ribbons or garlands that had been put on it. A carefully written and rehearsed prayer was then said, followed by a sharp blow with a hammer to the animal's head to stun him. This was done by the *popa*, or priest's assistant, and then the *cultrarius*, or knife man, would slit the animal's throat. There are occasional references in the literature to the priest then tasting the animal's blood—again, which could be seen by onlookers because this transpired outside the temple.[12]

If all went well up to this point, the animal was dismembered and disemboweled, and the entrails were very carefully inspected. Any blemish or fault found would invalidate the whole proceeding, and one would need to start over again. The internal organs would be cut up thereafter, and this is what would be placed on the altar for the god to consume, with the flames actually doing the work. It was rare indeed for the whole carcass of the animal to be burned. Normally, most of the meat would be quickly cooked in the temple kitchen, with the priests and staff getting a portion along with the family and friends of the one making the offering. This food would be eaten in the adjacent *cenaculum*, or temple dining room, with the guests reclining on couches.

Needless to say, a person who went through this whole procedure was consuming meat in a very different setting, a setting with a very different religious ethos and social impact, than someone who simply bought meat in the market and ate it at home. Eating in the temple was the successful climax of an act of worship, not merely just another meal. Temple dining rooms were the restaurants of antiquity for big celebrations, not to be confused with the *taberna* where one might go for drinks or a snack. In the case of the wealthy, eating in temples may well have been a regular, even a weekly, occasion. I must emphasize that even if this were the case, such a person invited to a meal in the temple complex would never have viewed it as merely a mundane meal or secular venture. There is even clear historical evidence of a small statue of the god being brought out to recline on couch with the diners, and we have inscriptional evidence that it was the god who sent out the RSVP cards to the prospective diners—"the god calls you to a banquet being held in the Thoreion from the ninth hour" (P. Koln 57). Furthermore, we even have evidence from Alexandria in Egypt of coins being minted that showed Serapis reclining on a couch with the diners.[13] Even when a trade guild or *collegium* met for a meal in the temple precincts, this would have been preceded by an act of worship as described above, so it is clear that these banquets had a necessary religious dimension and function.[14] While the temple staff might well turn meat over to the meat market vendors if some was left over and make a little money off the deal, there is no evidence that temples simply kept quantities of meat on hand for such meals. Such meals were always connected with a religious sacrifice. An act of worship would have concluded with a dinner, or, put the other way around, the dinner would have been preceded by the main portion of an act of worship as a necessary prerequisite. Bearing these things in mind, we can now turn to the NT evidence.

THE NEW TESTAMENT AND *EIDOLOTHUTON*

We shall treat the NT evidence in chronological order, and thus we begin with 1 Corinthians 8–10, turn to Acts 15 and 21 thereafter, and finally look at Revelation 2. First Corinthians 8–10 looks at an issue brought up in the Corinthians' letter to Paul, as the quotation from that letter in 1 Corinthians 8:1 makes quite apparent.[15] The nub of the argument comes at 1 Corinthians 8:10, where Paul states, "But if others see you, who possess knowledge *eating in the temple of an idol* might they not, since their understanding is weak, be encouraged to the point of eating *eidolothuton*?"

The scenario involves higher status Gentile Christians who continue to attend such feasts tempting Jewish Christians who have scruples about going to such meals. The strong apparently thought they were demonstrating their strength and knowledge that there is but one God by attending such meals while saying that idols are nothing. In their view, if one was a monotheist, one could simply see the meal as just another meal. It is interesting that in classical Greek literature, the term *eidolon* originally had the sense of a phantom or a ghost (see Homer

Il. 5.451 and *Od.* 4.794; Herodotus 5.92). It is thus possible that Paul, knowing this, coined this term to indicate that sacrifices made to pagan gods were being made to some sort of real or spiritual entity, though not to gods. That is, the term *eidolothuton* might have conjured up the idea of sacrifices offered to spirits or demons in a temple setting but then eaten in the temple dining room. Notice the reference to the "table of demons" in 1 Corinthians 10:20-21, which is clearly not a reference to the sacrifice altar.

The explanation suggested above makes very good sense of the typology Paul undertakes in 1 Corinthians 10. There, Paul cites Exodus 32:6 (see 1 Cor 10:7) as providing a prototype of the sort of behavior currently going on in Corinth, which involved participation in pagan worship, eating meat in a pagan temple dining complex, and engaging in sexual play, presumably after inebriation set in. The Exodus citation is clearly complaining about full-fledged idolatry and immorality. First Corinthians 10:14 is also explicit, for it does not merely say do not dine in areas adjacent to a pagan temple, but rather it says to flee the worship of idols (*eidololatria*), and thereafter Paul speaks of the act of pagan sacrifice (v. 20), followed by the reference to partaking of the cup and table of demons (v. 21).[16]

What then should we make of the reference to *hierothuton* in 1 Corinthians 10:28? Notice that here Paul is discussing a very different social setting indeed—a meal in a home. The discussion has been prefaced by a reference to the buying of meat in the meat market and taking it home. Here Paul gives advice about what one should do if invited to a dinner party in a home. But what if there is an awkward moment when someone (the host?) says, "this is *hierothuton*"? Paul's response is that the person in question should not eat the meat, for "their sake." Notice he does not say "abstain for your *own* sake" but for "*their* sake." This is the same Paul who has said they could eat this meat without raising issues of conscience. There are two possibilities. One is that "their" refers to the host and his or her family, who have provided a pagan religious interpretation of the meat by calling it "temple offerings." The Christian then abstains because he does not want to be seen as endorsing pagan religion. The other possibility is that at this dinner are both strong and weak Christians, those with too many scruples about such meat and those with few or none. Paul then would be asking the strong to abstain lest they cause the weak Christian to stumble by eating "temple offerings." I cannot stress enough that meat was a luxury item that for the poor or nonelite person would almost always have religious associations because it came from the temple, and this would be doubly so for a Jew or a Jewish Christian.[17] I would suggest in addition that the reason we have here the term *hierothuton* rather than *eidolothuton* is because the former connotes merely meat that has come from a pagan temple sacrifice and is now being consumed elsewhere, rather than in the presence of a god.

This leads us to the much controverted material in Acts 15 and 21. Here I shall simply assume with most scholars that the correct or original text form of the decree is (1) *eidolothuton*, (2) blood, (3) things strangled, and (4) *porneia*.[18] What is often overlooked in the discussion of the decree is what is said in Acts 15:20, where we have the first reference to James' ruling—namely, that Gentiles must abstain from "the pollutions of idols" as well as sexual immorality, things strangled, and blood. This first phrase, *ton alisgematon ton eidolon*, is odd if the issue is simply avoiding meat that has been sacrificed in a pagan temple but is eaten elsewhere. Surely the most natural way to interpret this key phrase that precedes and helps exegete the meaning of the decree is that James is referring to what happens when one is in the presence of idols—namely, one gets spiritually polluted. It is idols and their worship that are the pollutants here, affecting the meat, as verse 29 makes evident, and so affecting those who consume the meat offered to a pagan god. Gregory of Nyssa had no doubts as to what Acts 15:20 has in view—the pollution around the idols, the disgusting smell and smoke of the sacrifices, the defiling gore around the altars, the taint of blood from the offerings (*Vita Thaumaturg* PG 46.944).

It becomes clear, the more one delves into the origins and use of the term *eidolothuton* in early Christianity, that it is the wrong question altogether to ask where one might find a ruling in the Old Testament about this or that item in the decree. The term *eidolothuton* does not occur at all in the LXX at Genesis 9:4 (don't eat flesh with blood in it) or Leviticus 3:17 (don't eat fat or blood; cf. Lev 17:10-14). These texts are absolutely not about the specific issue of food partaken within an act of idolatry; while we are at it, they make no mention of things strangled or *porneia*. The regulations to be followed by Noah are not identical in content or intent with the Apostolic Decree. I would urge that the proper thing to ask about the decree is where one would find all four of these items together. The answer is in an act of pagan worship in a pagan temple complex. While sexual immorality may well not have occurred on an everyday basis in a pagan temple dinner party, the point is that early Jewish Christians believed it happened with enough regularity in those venues to warn against it. We should have all along been paying more attention to Acts 15:20 before we interpreted the decree itself. James is inveighing, in a polemical way, about the pollutions of idols, and hence idol worship and its various related activities. In regard to the prohibition of "things strangled," this is a reference to the strangling of birds so as to squeeze the lifeblood out of them and into a statue, hence further animating the god.[19] This was not a Jewish practice at all, but it was a pagan one, and it provides a further clue that

James is not imposing kosher or Noahic food restrictions on Gentiles. There is no reference to such a Jewish practice in the OT.

I would also submit that this interpretation make perfect sense of Acts 15:21, where James reminds his audience that Moses is taught in the synagogues throughout the empire. If we ask what was the very heart of Mosaic law, it was the Ten Commandments, and if we summarize the heart of that central portion, it would be "avoid idolatry and immorality," which is precisely what the decree is exercised about. James does not want the Diaspora synagogues to be able to complain about Gentile Christian behavior; henceforth, the Gentiles must stay away from the activities going on in pagan temples—namely, idolatry and immorality. Acts 21:25 in no way conflicts with this conclusion. There again, stereotypical Gentile behavior, not Jewish food laws, is the issue. In other words, *there is no hint in the decree that the major issue is table fellowship between Jews and Gentiles.* Rather it is a matter of specifically Gentile behavior. Notice that Acts 15:29 says that these Gentiles are turning to God, indicating what they are turning *to*, while the decree indicates what they are turning *from*. James is urging, as does Paul in 1 Corinthians 8–10, a clean break with pagan worship and dining in temples. Paul puts it succinctly in 1 Thessalonians 1:9—"you turned to God from idols, to serve a living and true God." In other words, Paul does not differ from James about the Apostolic Decree and its application. Indeed, we see him implementing it especially in 1 Corinthians 8–10.

We must now turn briefly to Revelation 2:14 and 20. Here the seer warns against the teachings of Balaam and the prophetess Jezebel. The latter is associated with "the deep things of Satan." Two things are being warned against—*eidolothuton* and *porneia*. Notice as well that John associates these things with the teachings of Balaam and so with stumbling or apostasy (v. 14), the very same thing Paul associates them with in his typology in 1 Corinthians 10. Again, the issue is not where one might find these things separately but where one might find them together. Revelation 2:13, which speaks of Satan's throne, is normally and rightly seen as a reference to a pagan temple, presumably the one built to Augustus in Pergamum in 29 B.C. For John, an emperor who expected worship was indeed "the Great Satan."[20] In other words, the emperor worship that went on in imperial cult temples was the worst form of idolatry. Thus Revelation 2:14-15 should be interpreted in the very same way that the other references in the NT to *eidolothuton* should be interpreted—as a warning against participating in pagan worship, which involved idolatry and immorality with the sacrifice and its conclusion in a sacral meal, which was all part of worship.

Is there any evidence that the church fathers understood these texts in this fashion? We have already cited Gregory of Nyssa and his understanding of Acts 15, but to this we could add Clement of Rome (7.8.1-2), who says that *eidolothuton* means partaking of the table of idols. Even more clear is John Chrysostom (*Hom.* 20 on 1 Corinthians), who distinguishes between meat eaten in a non-idolatrous context and meat eaten as a part of a sacrifice to an idol, which in his view constituted idolatry (see also his comments on 1 Cor 8:4-8, 10:10; and Acts 15). More could be cited along these lines, but this must suffice. It is time to sum up the remarkable implications this has for NT studies, especially when it comes to assessing the relationship of James and Paul and their teachings directed to Gentiles.

A RIPOSTE ABOUT A REPAST

Acts 15:21 provides us with a summary of the minimal requirements imposed on Gentiles who wanted to be Christians. The concern in Acts 15 is not, or at least not mainly, about fellowship meals between Jews and Gentiles in Christ but rather about the deleterious effect on witnessing to Jews in the Diaspora if Gentile Christians continue to go to pagan temples and partake in idol feasts. The church needed to make clear it in no way sanctioned idolatry or immorality as it continued its witness to Jews as well as to Gentiles. This was an issue close to the heart of James.[21] Refuting the charge that worshiping Jesus was idolatry was hard enough without adding the need to explain why some Christians were still going to pagan temples and yet claimed to worship only the biblical God. James then was not, as he has often been portrayed in NT studies, a conservative hardline Judaizer at odds with Paul at many turns. Rather his own views were much closer to Paul's than those of the Judaizer, and Paul on his part made every effort to implement James' decree with his largely Gentile Christian audience. Notice as well that John seems to have implemented the decree as well in his churches in Asia Minor, as is revealed in Revelation 2. The council then, spoken of in Acts 15, is not about imposing food laws on Gentiles from the OT, not even a modicum of them. This in turn makes it likely that things were in gestation when Paul wrote Galatians, which in turn means he must have written it before the council of Acts 15.[22]

We began this chapter by asking, what's in a word? The answer is much in many ways if the word in question is a loaded term, such as *eidolothuton*. Whole theories about early Christianity and its unity or diversity have hung on certain interpretations of that word. *Eidolothuton* is not a Hellenistic Jewish term but rather one that seems to have been coined in early Christianity by Paul, James, or another Jewish Christian, providing a term of rhetorical power to warn Gentile converts against committing idolatry and immorality in the context of pagan worship and dining.

While Paul, James, and John agreed that pagan gods were not gods, they did not agree with the notion that pagan idolatry or pagan idol feasts were spiritually harmless. On the contrary, they believed they were places of spiritual pollution, as if one sat down to dine with devils without being able to enjoying the devil's food cake, especially if one was a Jewish Christian with strong scruples about food. It may be no accident that in the very next chapter, 1 Corinthians 11, after the long harangue about food offered to idols, Paul then turns around and warns that if one partakes of the Lord's Supper in an unworthy manner, one could get sick and even die. Social missteps had spiritual consequences, whether at a pagan act of worship or a Christian one—all the more reason for the riposte about the repast, and all the more reason for the strong battle cry: Flee idolatry and immorality. As it turns out, the leading lights of Pauline, Johannine, and Jamesian Christianity all agreed on this matter. And the agreement was neither superficial nor merely rhetorical.

8

What's in a Word?

Part Two—*Porneia*

In Matthew 5, *porneia* and *moicheia* stand side by side and are clearly distinguished. The latter is the common term for adultery, or marital unfaithfulness. What then could *porneia* mean when used by Jesus or Paul?

In our last chapter, we discussed the terms *eidolothuton* and *porneia*, though clearly the focus was on the former word.[1] Here, we shall concentrate on the latter term, with regard to its use in an early Jewish Christian source—namely, the Gospel of Matthew. If we doubted that social location and social situation affects what certain words mean in both their connotations and denotations, the study of the loaded term *porneia* can quickly disabuse us of such a view. In this case, we are interested in what Matthew 5:32 and 19:9 mean, particularly the exception clauses.

It is true that some interpreters of the exception clauses think they know exactly what the exception refers to (no divorce except on grounds of marital unfaithfulness or adultery), but there are numerous problems with such facile reasoning. For one thing, neither Mark nor Paul think that Jesus allowed any exceptions to his prohibition of divorce. If one takes even a cursory look at Mark 10:9-12 or 1 Corinthians 7:10-11, this becomes rather apparent. Where then do the exception clauses fit into this picture, if at all? Or has the First Evangelist simply modified the strict teaching of Jesus in a more lenient direction? That is certainly possible, but one should not leap to that conclusion, because Matthew takes over about 95 percent of Mark's material and follows Mark quite closely at most points. Furthermore, *porneia* is not the term used elsewhere in Matthew 5 for adultery or marital unfaithfulness—that would be *moixeia* (see Matt 5:27-28). Is there something in the origins of this term, or in the social situation of Jesus (or the First Evangelist), that might help us make sense of this material?

PRELIMINARY CONSIDERATIONS

The root meaning of the term *porneia* is "sex with a prostitute." Indeed, *pornē* is the basic term in Greek for a prostitute, and it is of course also the origin of the English word *pornography*. Could Jesus or the First Evangelist have been critiquing prostitution? This is certainly not impossible, but what makes this an interesting discussion is that Jesus seems to be rather forgiving toward women who are involved in this trade. Besides the famous pericope about the "woman caught in adultery" in John 7:53–8:11, there is in addition the story of Jesus' forgiveness of the anonymous sinner woman in Luke 7:36-50 who seems to have been a prostitute, not to mention the story of the Samaritan woman in John 4. In other words, there are multiple traditions from various sources that Jesus did not take a hard line against a woman who had committed adultery or even prostitution. Would then he have allowed Jewish men to divorce their wives for prostitution? It is at least a question worth asking. But let us take another angle on this problem and reflect for a bit on the social situation in Galilee under the reign of Herod Antipas.

One recent interpretation of what was going on in Galilee during Jesus' day when it came to the issue of marriage and divorce has been offered by D. Instone-Brewer. He argues on the basis of Matthew 19:3 that Jesus was opposed to the then-popular practice of "any cause" divorce. He contends that there were Hillelite rabbis who interpreted the crucial material in Deuteronomy 24:1 to indicate that a man could divorce a woman for "a cause," which meant basically on almost any grounds. The Shammaite Jewish teachers, by contrast, understood *erwat dabar* to mean "adultery," or marital unfaithfulness.[2] Although Instone-Brewer has certainly done his homework on this difficult subject, I have to say that I find his discussion unconvincing for several reasons.

First, our earliest evidence about Jesus' view of divorce comes from Paul and, in the case of the Gospels, from Mark, not Matthew. Both Mark and Paul are clear that Jesus said "no divorce" for those God has joined together.[3] Second, while Instone-Brewer has suggested that the reaction of the male disciples to Jesus' view ("if that is the way it is between a man and woman, it is better not to marry") is caused by the rejection of an "any cause" view of when divorce was permitted, which he seems to think was the most prevalent view and form of divorce at the time in early Judaism, I find this most unlikely from a historical point of view. Even the Pharisees were divided in their views on this subject, and Hillel's view was the most lenient one. What we know about the varieties of forms of early Judaism, including Qumran, does not encourage us to think that the most liberal view of divorce in early Judaism was the most prevalent one. Third, if Jesus had simply agreed with the more restrictive Shammaite view, which is what Instone-Brewer suggests, it is very difficult to explain the disciples' enormous reaction to what Jesus said, as if they were hearing a view that was much more restrictive than anything they had heard before. Surely they had heard of "no divorce except on grounds of adultery." There is the further problem as well that in Matthew 5 the word for adultery is not *porneia* but rather *moixeia*, so it makes no sense that *porneia* would be used in the exceptive clause to refer specifically to adultery. Clearly a solution to this conundrum needs to be sought from some other quarter and by means of some other lexical and socio-historical explanation.

The Galilean Setting of Matthew's Gospel

I have argued at length elsewhere that the Gospel of Matthew likely has a Galilean provenance, though Antioch is not impossible. The reason not to favor the Antioch hypothesis is that there is clear evidence in both Galatians and Acts that there was a mixed community of Jewish and Gentile Christians there and that they were having table fellowship with each other until certain Judaizers showed up and objected. Indeed, that community had so many Gentile Christians in it that they were noticeable to outsiders and could be called *christianoi*. The ethos of Matthew's Gospel certainly does not suggest that we are dealing with an audience that is largely Gentile. On the contrary, this is the Gospel that is most exercised about in-house Jewish debates and issues. As my friend A. J. Levine has put it, Matthew "can seem so redolent with such 'Jewish' concerns that one wonders if the five thousand were fed with pickled herring and a nice piece of challah."[4] Galilee is surely a more likely location for having a Christian audience that resonates with the content of this Gospel and must deal on a daily basis with their non-Christian Jewish counterparts who are the dominant religious presence there. In Antioch, a city of some two hundred fifty thousand in the first century, a small Jewish Christian group could easily get lost and certainly would not have seen the synagogue as the dominant religious presence in their city. We have to ask as well what sort of audience would be most receptive to a portrait of Jesus, who is specifically said to be sent only to the lost sheep of Israel. My suggestion would be Jewish Christians in Galilee, who had no significant number of Gentile converts in their midst. It can be said that the archaeological evidence suggests that there was no significant Gentile presence in Galilee during Jesus' era.[5] This audience would especially be likely to remember and to relate to the period when Herod Antipas ruled Capernaum and the other cities and villages of southern Galilee.[6]

Social context becomes especially crucial when we are dealing with a *crux interpretum*, such as the exception clauses in Matthew 5 and

19. And the first question that should be asked is whether there were marital situations, perhaps famous or infamous ones, from the period of Jesus' adult life in Galilee that might have prompted him to comment on what exceptions there might be to a prohibition of divorce. First, two facts should be mentioned: (1) John the Baptist was jailed and then beheaded for criticizing the marriage of Herod Antipas to his brother's wife (see Josephus *Ant.* 18.136, 18.240); and (2) John was apparently Jesus' relative (see Luke 1–2). Furthermore, when he spoke of Herod, Jesus had nothing good to say about him, calling him "that fox" (Luke 13:31-33). Could Jesus have also criticized the "immoral" marriage of Herod and Herodias? Could that be what the exception clauses are about?[7] We must pursue this line of inquiry.

INCEST AND *PORNEIA*

Words only have meanings in certain contexts. They do not have meanings in isolation from contexts, and in this case the historical and social context matters a great deal. The first question to be asked is whether there is New Testament evidence that the word *porneia* can refer to incest in certain contexts. The answer to this question is yes—1 Corinthians 5:1 would seem to be a clear example of such a usage of the term. A good example from early Jewish literature from slightly before the relevant period is Tobit 8.7. In addition, J. Fitzmyer has presented first century A.D. evidence from Qumran that favors the view that *porneia* in Matthew 5:32 and 19:9 refers quite specifically to a *zenut* marriage, a marriage that was null and void from the outset and therefore not a legitimate or moral marriage.[8] It is especially significant that the technical term that seems to have been used for incestuous marriage, marriage within prohibited degrees of relatedness, *'erwa*, was also a term that could be used for fornication as well. *'Erwa*, it will be remembered, is the term we find in Deuteronomy 24:1, which is the basis for the Mosaic permission of divorce. I shall discuss more on this point in a moment.

A. Mahoney, in my judgment, has correctly assessed the social context of the discussion about divorce between Pharisees and Jesus. They are most certainly trying to catch Jesus in his words. Mahoney puts it this way:

> Their insidious question was probably directed toward the then-current and divisive cause célèbre in this matter, the *affaire* Antipas-Herodias. In the crowd, there could have been disciples of John the Baptist, the victim of the hate of Herodias; Herodians, supporters of Herod Antipas; devout Jews angered by the flagrant violation of the law; and, especially if the

question was posed in Perea, Nabateans, the daughter of whose King Aretas had been repudiated in favor of Herodias.[9]

Whether Mahoney is right about the Perean context, the rest of what he says is not affected by that conjecture and is right on target. We can hardly imagine what a scandal was caused in Galilee by that particular marriage. Pious Jews would have been upset for a long time about that flagrant violation of the Law by the ruler of a land belonging to Jews and overwhelmingly populated by Jews.

In regard to what the Law says about incestuous marriages, one need look no further than Leviticus 18:6-16, which lays out the degrees of kinship within which sexual union and marriage was prohibited. This was indeed a matter much discussed in early Judaism, including when the discussion was about the Genesis story about the first "marriage" between Adam and Eve. Thus, for instance, R. Akiba offered the following exegesis: "'Therefore a man shall leave his father and mother' refers to the fact that one must not marry his father's sister or wife, or his mother and her sister." He adds, "And he shall cleave to his wife" prohibits pederasty (B. T. San. 58a). The point of mentioning this discussion is of course that Jesus quotes this very same text when he discusses marriage and divorce in Matthew 19. Thus, both the choice of text to discuss marriage and divorce and the social context with John's recent death favor the suggestion that the exception clauses are dealing with an incestuous situation. But there is more.

The Pharisees, when they came to Jesus, themselves refer to Deuteronomy 24:1, which has the famous *erwat dabar* clause. They apparently want to hear Jesus' interpretation of this controverted phrase, which can be variously interpreted and translated. For example, it could be translated as "a thing of nakedness," or it could be translated as "some unseemly thing" (notice how in Deuteronomy 23:11, it refers to uncovered excrement), but we have already noticed how *'erwa* at Qumran was used to refer to *zenut* marriages—inappropriate marriages that were null and void *ab initio*, which included incestuous marriages. Notice that in the LXX, the key Hebrew phrase in Deuteronomy 24:1 is translated as *aschēmon pragma*, "a shameful thing."

I submit then that we have all the necessary historical, social, and linguistic ingredients here for Jesus, or at least Matthew writing in Galilee, to have commented on the incestuous marriage of Herod and Herodias. Even if we see the exception clauses as added by the Evangelist himself, the outcome is still basically the same. What Jesus told his disciples was no divorce, except in the case of so-called marriages that were not proper marriages to begin with—incestuous relationships such as that between the ruler and his brother's wife being especially flagrant illustrations of what was meant.

The exception clause in 19:9 was prepared for by Jesus' use of a Genesis text that the Pharisees may well have seen as referring to incest. Jesus uses the Genesis text in a different manner to refer to proper marriage and God's creation order intent long before Moses permitted divorce, but then he (or the Evangelist) adds the exception clause to make clear that an incestuous relationship was not a marriage in God's eyes and that if God had joined people together, no one should put them asunder.

This solution to the old conundrum of the meaning of the exception clauses has numerous advantages:

(1) it fits a specific historical situation during the time of the ministry of Jesus in Galilee;

(2) it draws on known early Jewish interpretations of the key text Jesus cites from Genesis but also the meaning of key terms, such as 'erwa, which were being used to refer to illegitimate marriages and incest at Qumran;

(3) it allows the exception clauses in Matthew 5 and 19 to be true exceptions; Jesus does not think that incestuous marriages are joined together by God, so they should end;

(4) it draws on a known specific meaning of porneia that is found at least once elsewhere in the NT as well as in other early Jewish literature;

(5) it allows the distinction between moixeia, which certainly does mean adultery in Matthew 5:27-28, and porneia to stand rather than suggesting that Matthew has confused or fused the two terms;

(6) it comports with the expected contrast between Jesus' teaching on divorce and some other teaching—namely, the permissive teaching of Moses—and most adequately explains the reason why the disciples went ballistic when they heard how strict a view Jesus was taking on divorce;

(7) furthermore, Jesus' appeal to the original creation order design set over against the Mosaic teaching ("but from the beginning it was not so") is best explained by there being a real contrast between the permission of Moses and the teaching of Jesus;

(8) marriages that violate God's laws by their very character are not true marriages, because in Jesus' view, God has not joined these people together; and

(9) 1 Corinthians 7:10-11 presupposes a teaching by Jesus that amounted to a "no divorce" view for those whom God had joined together.

The same applies to the teaching found in Mark 10. In other words, whether we predicate the exception clauses of Jesus or of the Evangelist, in either case Matthew's Gospel does not permit what Mark's forbids. There is no contradiction here between the two accounts, nor for that matter is there a contradiction with the Pauline teaching.

Finally, one more thing should be said. It is always wise to ask how the earliest interpreters of the Gospel of Matthew viewed these exception clauses. In a careful survey of what the church fathers said about Matthew 5 and 19, J. P. Arendzen almost a century ago made very clear that despite the fact that Matthew's Gospel was the most popular, most copied, and most widely used Gospel in the second and subsequent centuries, *there is no evidence at all before Nicea (A.D. 325) that any interpreter understood the exceptive clauses to refer to the authorizing of the breaking of a legitimate and ethical marriage between a man and woman that God had brought together.*[10] This fact must be given its due weight. What it surely strongly suggests is that these exception clauses were not seen to be about true exceptions by those for whom the Greek language was their own language and who were more likely to understand the nuances of Matthew's grammar and syntax and word use than we are. The close reading of such texts in light of their possible social and linguistic context not only illuminates the discussion of controverted issues, such as marriage and divorce, but it helps us to see Jesus as a person who did indeed address controversial issues of his day and context, just as John the Baptist had done before him.

PAUL ON *PORNEIA* AND *MOICHEIA*

Heading the vice list found in Galatians 5:19-21, which is contrasted with the fruit of the Spirit, is the term *porneia*. Most scholars see the usage here as general in character, covering a multitude of sins, and they translate the term as "sexual immorality" and see the two terms that immediately follow it as general in character as well—sexual impurity and indecency.[11] There is little doubt that the term *porneia* can be used in this broad way. Ephesians 5:3 has a similar cluster of terms, and again *porneia* is listed first, followed by reference to "all sexual impurity." Once again, the use seems to be more generic in character, an umbrella term for all sorts of sexual sin. Of a very similar sort is Colossians 3:5, which again begins with *porneia* followed by reference to unclean passions and evil desires. Second Corinthians 12:21 has the same sort of cluster of terms referring to sexual impurity and *porneia* and shameful acts. In 1 Thessalonians 4:3, we have a straightforward contrast between *sanctification*, which is said to be God's will for our bodies, and *porneia*, which is said to be just the opposite of sanctification and therefore must be abstained from. Once again, the sense seems to be that Paul is using the word as a catchall for all sorts of sexual sin. In 1 Corinthians 7:2, Paul contrasts being married and having one's own wife with avoiding *porneia*. Here, the term could actually be translated as "fornication," although it is possible that the larger semantic field is in view and so it is translated as "sexual immorality." We may compare this to 1 Corinthians 6:13-18, where we have two references to *porneia*. The larger context, especially 1 Corinthians 8–10, suggests that Paul is already discussing here what, in his view, goes on in a pagan temple (note the reference to "meat"—in this case, idol meat). The reference to sex with a *pornē* in 1 Corinthians 6:15 strongly points to the conclusion that here the term must refer to having sex with a prostitute, in this case a temple prostitute. In 1 Corinthians 5:1, however, we see a reasonably clear case where the term *porneia* has the connotation of incest, a meaning we have already suggested for Matthew 5 and 19.

For our purposes, the most important of all the Pauline verses is 1 Corinthians 6:9, where Paul provides us with a list of those who will be excluded from God's eschatological kingdom if they persist in their pattern of sinful behavior. Paul says, "do not be deceived, neither *pornoi*, nor idol worshipers, nor *moichoi*, nor the *malakoi*, nor a male who copulates with a male will inherit God's kingdom." Here finally we find at least cognate terms of *porneia* and *moicheia* in the same context, but notice that here as well the terms are distinguished, and interestingly they are separated by the term *idol worshipers*. In view of the discussion that follows, not only about proper marriage in 1 Corinthians 7 but about improper behavior in pagan temples in 1 Corinthians 8–10, it would seem likely that here *pornoi* has its root sense of "prostitute," and especially when coupled with idol worshiper, the sense of "temple prostitute." Paul has grouped several related sexual sins together here, and *moichoi* must surely mean "adulterers." This could lead to the conclusion that *malakoi*, which literally means "soft" and refers to an effeminate male homosexual, and perhaps to a male prostitute, might also be found in the pagan temple.[12] *In any event, nothing in the Pauline use of the term encourages us to think that* moicheia *and* porneia, *especially when coupled together or occurring in the same context, refer to the exact same sexual sin.* Porneia in Paul's letters refers either to sexual sin in general or, when it is more specific, refers to having sex with a prostitute or incest. When it refers to a single sexual sin, there is no evidence in the entire NT that it refers to adultery or marital unfaithfulness.

If we were to work through the references in Revelation 2:21, 9:21, 14:8, 17:2, 4, 18:3, and 19:2, we would discover as well the regular association of this term with prostitution, even when it is used in a more figurative and spiritual sense. In Revelation as well, the term *porneia* is never used to refer to adultery. For that sin, the NT reserves the term *moicheia*.

While much more could be said along these lines, this discussion suffices to show that we were surely on the right track in dealing with the exception clauses in Matthew 5 and 19. It is very unlikely that either of them refers to adultery or marital unfaithfulness. It is far more likely that they refer to a specific sexual sin, such as incest or prostitution, which made the relationship not a proper marriage to begin with. While it is perhaps barely possible that *porneia* in those clauses in Matthew 5 and 19 is used as an umbrella term to refer to a wide array of sexual sins, the context does not at all favor such a conclusion, especially the context in Matthew 19 where the disciples react with surprise. If that was Jesus' view, it hardly differed from what some other early Jewish teachers had said. And we must bear in mind that the social context for Jesus' discussion of the matter was in Galilee and in the wake of what Herod Antipas had done not only with Herodias, but to John the Baptizer, Jesus' relative. A text without a context is just a pretext for whatever the interpreter wants to make it mean. In this case, the social context strongly favors the idea that *porneia* in Matthew 5 and 19, as in 1 Corinthians 5:1, refers to incest and thus to an illegal, immoral, and not divinely sanctioned relationship that should not be graced with the term *marriage*.

9

What's in a Phrase?

"No Male and Female" (Galatians 3:28)

Galatians 3.28 is the Magna Carta of Humanity.

—Krister Stendahl[1]

Unfortunately, Galatians 3:28 has become the perfect example of the problems with reader-response criticism—namely, that overly active readers often read their own meanings into texts, at the expense of what the author was trying to convey. Some scholars have urged that this text is a sort of emancipation proclamation for women, while others just as strongly have urged that it only deals with one's status in the eyes of God, not one's social status on earth. Galatians 3:28 has thus become a long-standing battleground in New Testament discussions about the role of women in Paul.[2] This text has even been the basis for arguing that Paul either saw the original Adam as androgynous or that he is conjuring up an androgynous Christ here![3]

FRAMING THE DISCUSSION

In my judgment, what is more important for understanding this text than the history of religious discussions about an androgynous ancestor or savior is the intertexual echo of the Genesis story here, seen in the phrase "no male and female," and also the parallels in Pauline literature to the formula here, which has been widely regarded as a pre-Pauline baptismal formula. There are, for example, close parallels of thought and structure between 1 Corinthians 12:13, Colossians 3:10-11, and Galatians 3:28, suggesting this construction might be about some sort of rite of passage, involving a contrasting of opposites. What these three texts have in common is (1) the language of baptism or its accompanying rituals (putting off the robe, putting on the robe); (2) contrasting pairs; and (3) unity in Christ thereafter, whether that is expressed as being part of one body, one person, or all being filled with one Christ. One may suspect that what the formula indicates is what one is leaving behind when one becomes a new creature in Christ. It would be meaningful to compare for example 2 Corinthians 5:17, which says "therefore if anyone is in Christ, there is a new creation [or he is a new creature, it could be read either way], the old has passed away, the new has come!" Paul is referring here to how the old self has passed away, and the new person has come into being in Christ; notice that the verb tense there is quite clear. Paul is not saying the old is in the process of passing away, but rather that the old has passed away. He is not saying that the new is in the process of showing up, but rather that the new is here. This has direct relevance to the way we read the baptismal formulae in the Pauline texts listed above. It strongly suggests that when one converted to Christ and was baptized, it was believed that that person had left his or her old condition behind, which had not only spiritual ramifications but also social ones. We shall say more on this presently. Here, it is sufficient to note that gender, generation, and geography were thought to be the major determinants of identity in antiquity. One's sex, one's ethnic extraction and more particular ancestral heritage, and where one came from was thought to most determine one's identity. In addition, what social situation one was born into (patrician, plebeian, slavery) was also seen as a major determinant. It would appear on the surface that Paul himself thinks that conversion to Christ changes the core of one's identity; put another way, the new birth supersedes some of the aspects and implications of the original physical birth and original social location.

SAYINGS ABOUT IMPARTIALITY

Sometimes in the discussion of Galatians 3:28, texts, both biblical and otherwise, are trotted out to show that God is impartial or "no respecter of persons." For example, *Seder Eliyahu Rabbah* 7 says, "I call heaven and earth to witness that whether Gentile or Israelite, man or woman, slave or handmaiden reads this verse . . . the Holy One blessed be He, remembers the binding of Isaac." This saying is of relevance because it uses the same triad of ethnic, sexual, and social binary opposites that we find in Galatians 3:28. The gist of the saying, however, is about God's being no respecter of persons. The same can be said about the saying of R. Judah ben Shalom in *Exodus Rabbah Beshallah* 21.4. In discussing who gets listened to on earth, Judah says that few pay any attention to what the poor say, but the rich always have a listening audience. By contrast, he says about God, "Before God, however, all are equal: women, slaves, poor and rich." The point is that God is impartial and listens to all. Yalkut Lek Leka sec. 76 is even more directly to the point:

"God said to Moses: Is their respect of persons with me? Whether it be Israelite or Gentile, man or woman, slave or handmaiden, whoever does a good deed shall find the reward at its side." These sayings are, however, not about the condition of humans but about the attitude of God, an attitude of impartiality, and we could point to NT texts to the same effect (Rom 2:11; Acts 10:34).[4]

Of a very different sort are the sayings, both Jewish and Greco-Roman, about being glad one was born in a certain condition. For example, there is the famous (or infamous) threefold blessing in J. T. Ber. 13b attributed to R. Meir (but in B. T. Ber. 7.18 to R. Judah b. Elai): "Blessed be He that he did not make me a Gentile; blessed be He that He did not make me a slave (or ignorant peasant); blessed be He that he did not make me a woman." This can be compared to Diogenes Laertius' expression of gratitude to Thales and Socrates "that I was born a human being and not a beast, next a man and not a woman, thirdly a Greek, and not a barbarian (*Vit. Phil.* 1.33). These texts refer to what a person is by way of birth and original social location, but Galatians 3:28 surely is about what a person is by rebirth and resocialization, which is a different matter.

What these sayings do further underscore is that it is likely that Galatians 3:28 is commenting on actual social change involved with the spiritual change that happens at conversion and baptism. The basic social divisions in society, whether seen through the eyes of a Greek or a Jew, are assumed in some way and to some degree to be overcome in Christ. This is perhaps why in one version of the Pauline saying, it seems closer to the Jewish triad of binary opposites, but in a social location where the earlier saying of Diogenes Laertius could well be known, Colossians 3:11 refers as well to barbarians and Scythians. The assumption that biology or birth state is destiny is reflected in the Jewish and Greek sayings, but it seems to be rejected by Paul in all three of the sayings listed above. I suggest that Paul is using these sayings to help construct what is called today a *conversionist sect*, a sect created by conversion, and certainly is believing that conversion was a possibility by means of the work of the Spirit of God. Pauline Christianity was a sect that had its own rites, rules, routines, beliefs, and definitions of who were and were not the people of God, based on their relationship with Christ. As J. Dunn rightly stresses, Galatians 3:28 "implies a radically reshaped social world as viewed from a Christian perspective."[5] What Paul is certainly not doing here is reflecting on an androgynous Christ, body of Christ, or androgynous individuals within the body of Christ, as ought to be quite clear from the use of the masculine term *eis* here to refer to this "body," as well as the fact that Paul says here "no male *and* female" and then says all are one person (*eis*) in Christ (cf. Eph 2:15; Justin *Dial.* 116).

Paul's basic sectarian message, summed up in these formulae, particularly in Galatians is clear enough: (1) the boundaries of the community are crossed by conversion and initiation, and no other boundaries need to be crossed (e.g., into Judaism by means of circumcision). The Galatians are already "in"; (2) the benefits of salvation have already been obtained through faith by the Galatians, including the inheritance or blessing promised to Abraham; (3) the time for submission to the Mosaic law is passed; and (4) the body of Christ is an egalitarian body with universal scope where social, sexual, and ethnic differences do not determine entrance or status and are not the basis for unity and cohesion of the group. We should compare this to the inscription from the Temple of Artemis in Ephesus recited by Philostratus: "Your temple is thrown open to all who offer sacrifice, or offer prayers, or sing hymns to suppliants, to Hellenes, barbarians, free persons, to slaves" (*Vita Apoll.* Letter 67).

THE RHETORICAL LOGIC OF GALATIANS 3:26-28

The thrust of Galatians 3:26-27, which immediately precedes our key verse, seems to be as follows—"All are sons and daughters of God through faith in Christ *for* as many as have been baptized into Christ have put on Christ." Here we should compare the close parallel in 1 Corinthians 12:13, where it is the Spirit, not the apostle, who baptized a person into the one body of Christ. Paul does not make clear in Galatians 3:26-27 whether he is talking about water baptism, baptism by the Spirit (as in 1 Cor 12:13), or some assumed conjunction of the two. Before we too quickly assume that Paul is suggesting some sort of magical view such that the rite of water baptism "saves," we must bear in mind 1 Corinthians 1:14, where Paul says he is glad he did not baptize more of the Corinthians, even various of them who were converted, lest they have a magical view of baptism.[6] Paul certainly could never have said, "I thank God I did not convert more of you," but he does say this about water baptism. This should give us pause before we assume too quickly that Galatians 3:27 is a description of what happens spiritually when one receives Christian baptism at initiation. Conversion and initiation are distinguishable for Paul, and clearly the former is more crucial. Conversion happens by grace and through faith, while baptism depicts and provides a formal means of recognizing who is "in the community." That is the function of a rite of passage. Because Paul does not in Galatians spend time contrasting the merits of water baptism with circumcision but rather contrasts conversion to Christ with the benefits of circumcision and keeping the Law, it follows that we should likely see Galatians 3:27-28 as referring to spiritual transformation in verse 27 and to its social consequences in verse 28. Those who have been truly converted to Christ have been truly and spiritually united not only to him, but to his people—his body. This could not help but have social consequences if indeed the converts were forsaking what was past and holding on to what had come to be. This brings us to Galatians 3:28 itself.

Set in this context, Galatians 3:28 spells out the social implications of being in Christ and his body. It needs to be emphasized that Paul is not merely talking about how God views matters, as in the impartiality sayings cited above. What Paul is trying to do with his fledgling converts in Galatia is to convince them not to listen to the rhetoric of the Judaizers about their needing to be circumcised and keep the whole Mosaic law in order to be full-fledged Christians. Paul's argument for concord in the body of Christ is based on a strong belief that unity in Christ transcends and transforms the ethnic, social, and sexual categories that separate and distinguish human beings. What really matters to Paul, as he makes evident not only in 2 Corinthians 5 but in Galatians itself, at Galatians 6:15, is when he says, "neither circumcision nor uncircumcision is anything, but rather a new creation." Paul was indeed a quite sectarian person, and he drew clear boundary lines around the people of Christ. What mattered was conversion. There is something, however, we have not considered thus far. Why exactly does Paul break up the nice parallelism with the triad of binary opposites in Galatians 3:28? Why does the segment about male and female read differently in the Greek, despite the attempt of various modern translations to obscure this difference? We need to explore these questions at some length.

WHY "NO MALE AND FEMALE"?

Perhaps the first question to be raised about Galatians 3:28, is why is it only here that Paul mentions male and female but not in the parallel formulae in 1 Corinthians 12:13 and Colossians 3:10-11. What was there about the Galatian situation that led to this way of framing the discussion? One plausible suggestion is that Paul is adding here to the preexisting baptismal formula in order to deal with a specific issue in Galatia. But what could that issue be? Some scholars have tried to deflect the issue by saying that Paul is simply alluding to the Genesis 1:27 LXX text and cites it "as is."[7] Elsewhere, Paul is not loathe to tailor a citation to suit his purposes, so it is hard to believe he would not feel compelled to do so here. After all, he makes nothing of the intertextual echo here and does not expand or expound on the meaning of Galatians 3:28 in what follows. From a rhetorical point of view, this would seem to be an inept way of citing a text if he wanted actually to use it as an authoritative or authentic proof to help him make his point.

Here is where I stress that *arsen* and *thēlu* are not the Greek words for "man" and "woman" but specifically focus on the gender distinctiveness of the sexes. This suggests that Paul is saying something fundamental about how the combination of male and female is in some sense overcome in Christ. But how? I suggest we consider closely the fact that the Galatians apparently are in danger of getting themselves circumcised and keeping the entire Mosaic law. It was indeed a traditional way of reading the creation story in Genesis 1–2 to come to the conclusion that to "be fruitful and multiply," and thus the coupling of male and female, was an obligation, not merely an option, for God's people. Call it the reproduction mandate or something else, but the evidence is clear that early Jewish teaching affirmed such an idea, except in the case of those who were disabled or unable to fulfill such a mandate.[8]

It will be noted however, that Matthew 19:10-12 indicates that Jesus actually suggested something novel in this regard. He suggested that being single for the sake of the kingdom was a legitimate second option for his followers. Furthermore, we know that Paul himself took up this ball and ran with it a long way, as 1 Corinthians 7 shows. There Paul argues at length that there are two callings—or as he puts it, two *charismas* or grace gifts—to be married in the Lord or to be single for the Lord, and clearly he prefers the latter at that juncture in his life and wishes more of his audience did as well.[9] It is thus perfectly believable that he would have taught his Galatian converts that they did not need to be married to be in Christ. The relevant phrase then in Galatians 3:28 would mean that while Christians know about the creation order mandate from Genesis, to which the phrase alludes, nevertheless in Christ there is not simply a recapitulation of the creation order, but rather as Paul repeatedly says "a new creation." This being so, neither women nor men in Christ need feel compelled to get married and have children. This had become a blessed option but not an obligation in light of the Christ event and the changed eschatological situation. But there is more to ponder.

Why is Paul so adamantly opposed to his audience being circumcised? Circumcision was a covenant sign, a sign of true and total commitment to the Mosaic covenant, and the audience had already undergone a different, more gender-inclusive covenant sign—namely, Christian baptism. The signs of the respective covenants speak about the differences between the covenants and the character of their communities. Judaism was a patriarchal religion, and only males bore its covenant sign. It propagated its faith by simple procreation, not by evangelizing propaganda, by and large. Christianity by contrast was an evangelistic movement and a conversionist sect. It had a very different ethos and character in key respects. For the Galatians to get circumcised and take on the yoke of the Law would be to go backward, not forward, and furthermore it would be a repudiation of the new creation and its implications, spelled out in miniature in Galatians 3:28.

It is possible, though we cannot be sure, that the Judaizers' rhetoric in Galatia went something like this: "Because women cannot bear the Mosaic covenant sign, in order to be full participants in their new messianic Jewish faith in Jesus, they need to fulfill the other major commandment incumbent on Jews—namely, the creation order mandate. This in turn means that women have to be married to circumcised Christian men to be in compliance with the keeping of the Mosaic law." This would be a reinscribing of the patriarchal order of things. Paul did not want that, because it would deny the new creation and place women as well as men back under the old patriarchal system. To counter such a move he says that in Christ there is no male and female, by which he meant no necessary coupling of male and female. A woman as well as a man in Christ could remain single for the sake of the kingdom. Bear in mind that the creation order mandate about propagating comes immediately after the statement about God making them male and female (see Gen 1:27-28).

Strongly in favor of their being a social thrust to what Paul says in Galatians 3:28 is the fact that we know elsewhere Paul affirms the social implications of their being no Jews or Gentiles in Christ. Indeed, he even says he himself is able to be the Jew to the Jew and the Gentile to the Gentile, while viewing himself largely on the basis of a Christian paradigm, not an ethnic one (see, e.g., 1 Corinthians 9; Phil 3:4-9).[10] Furthermore, Paul also, when he has a chance, not only tries to ameliorate the various negative social effects of slavery on his converts (see Colossians 3–4; Ephesians 5–6), but when he is able to do so, he appeals to Philemon to manumit his runaway slave, Onesimus, and to treat him "no longer as a slave, but as a brother in Christ."[11] There are levels to Paul's social discourse, and he tries to deal with human fallenness in a way that recognizes where the audience is in their progress in growth in Christ, but it is clear enough that Paul's remarks elsewhere about Jew and Gentile, about slave and free, have clear social implications. We would not expect it to be otherwise when he discussed male and female in the light of being one in Christ and in the light of the new creation, which he believed wholeheartedly already existed in part. R. Loewe long ago made these very perceptive remarks about early Christianity: "The sociological basis on which Christianity rests is not on ties of kinship, as in the case of Judaism, but that of fellowship—fellowship in Christ. . . . Such fellowship may acknowledge kinship as a potential ally; it may regard it indifferently, as consisting of an equivocal force; or it may repudiate it, as being a distracting encumbrance. Whichever position it adopts, the ties of kinship are, for Christianity, in the last resort, expendable."[12] To this I must add that Paul is not suggesting that these three sorts of distinctions simply disappear in Christ. Men and women do not cease to be men and women. But what he does believe is that in the new creation the old is transformed and transfigured. The ethnic, social, and sexual distinctions continue to exist in Christ, but they do not determine one's soteriological, spiritual, or social standing in the body of Christ, nor do they determine the ministerial roles one can play in Christ. That is a matter of who is called and who is gifted by the Spirit to do certain tasks in the church.

Here at the heart of his discourse, and in the middle of a whole series of rhetorical arguments, at Galatians 3:28, Paul articulates a vision of humankind and human unity that still challenges us today. It explains a good deal of why Paul is so vocal about rejecting the appeal that his converts should take up the yoke of the Mosaic law. Why should they do that when, as Galatians 3:29 goes on to say, they inherit the heritage and blessings of Abraham simply by being "in Christ"? Gentiles do not need to become Jews in order to be Christians. Slaves do not need to become free persons (though it would be a good thing; see 1 Corinthians 7) to be in Christ. And women do not need to be linked to men to either be in Christ or to play important roles in Christ. Being a part of the one new person in Christ by grace and through faith is the one thing all Christians must share. Any other categories than this one-person identity must be sub-categories that serve, not sever, the body of Christ. The new creation has happened, and there are new creatures in Christ. Perhaps in the end it is true that Galatians 3:28 is the Magna Carta not merely of true humanity but of Christian freedom.

"Christianity in the Making"

Oral Mystery or Eyewitness History?

When Thou hast done, Thou hast not done, For I have more.
—John Donne, "A Hymn to God the Father"

The very long and notable tradition at the University of Durham in England of having world-class New Testament scholars stretches back now some one hundred fifty years and includes the likes of J. B. Lightfoot, B. F. Westcott, A. Plummer, H. E. W. Turner, C. Cranfield, C. K. Barrett, J. D. G. Dunn, and now J. Barclay, F. Watson, L. Stuckenbroeck, and others. It is a notable and rich heritage, and in the early 1980s, Dunn succeeded Barrett (my own mentor) in the Lightfoot Chair there.

When we look back now at the body of work that Dunn has given us since he assumed the Lightfoot Chair, it is clear that although his work before the early 1980s was important and noteworthy, it was but a harbinger of bigger things to come. Who could have foreseen two such massive and important works as his *Theology of Paul* and now *Jesus Remembered*? Clearly the remark of that other Donne, John Donne the English cleric, is appropriate here: "when thou hast done, thou hast not done, for I have more." And indeed, much more, to judge from the fact that *Christianity in the Making* involves two more volumes beyond the 900 pages of *Jesus Remembered*!

It is precisely the issue of eyewitnesses, an issue largely neglected in *Jesus Remembered*, in favor of talking about the developments of oral traditions that I want to raise in this chapter. In order to do that, however, it is important to lay out how Dunn differentiates the methodology of his project from the previous efforts to analyze the Jesus tradition largely on the basis of form and redaction criticism. I shall demonstrate that I am in full agreement with much of his critique of the use of both these tools in the study of Jesus and his words and deeds.[1] The paradigm shift Dunn is urging, based on recent gains in orality studies, is welcome, but I shall argue that not a folk version of oral tradition (à la K. Bailey) but a version of the oral history theory best explains the data we are discussing.

ORAL TRADITIONS OR REDACTION HISTORY?

The scope of Dunn's project is breathtaking, but equally impressive are the critical rigor applied to the data and the compelling sequential logic of his argument. It takes some three-hundred-plus pages to get to the point of actually discussing *Jesus Remembered*, and, unlike some books of this nature and length, the preliminary discussion is hardly pro forma or boring. Indeed, it is so well written and interesting that one forgets about being impatient to hear what Dunn will say about what was remembered about Jesus and simply enjoys the ground-clearing and stage-setting exercises done with the efficiency and panache of a well-seasoned, highly learned scholar. What becomes clear throughout the first three hundred pages of this study is that Dunn actually wants to change some of the paradigm and the methodological assumptions by which we evaluate the Jesus tradition and the Gospels. No, he is not rejecting Markan priority or even the reality of the Q tradition, nor does he reject the concept of redactional activity of a literary sort being applied by Matthew or Luke on the earlier Markan and Q material and other sources.

What Dunn does want to argue for, however, long and hard, is that such redactional activities do not account for a vast amount of what we find in the Jesus tradition—we need a more "oral" and less "literary" way of evaluating these things, including the way we evaluate what happened between the time Jesus actually spoke and acted and the time when the Gospels were written down. Let us consider some particulars of how he argues his case.

At the very beginning of his study Dunn informs us all that "the most distinctive feature of the present study will be to attempt to assess freshly the importance of the oral tradition of Jesus' mission and the suggestion that the Synoptic Gospels bear testimony to a pattern and technique of oral transmission which has endured a greater stability and continuity in the Jesus tradition than has thus far been generally appreciated."[2] This places him between the form critics of old and those who stress the close connection of the tradition with eyewitnesses. Drawing on recent studies of orality by W. Kelber and, more importantly, the now-somewhat-dated studies of Bailey, Dunn finds fault with the attempts to treat the Gospels and their sources as literary texts in the modern sense rather than oral texts in the ancient sense. Dunn urges that both Jesus and the Gospel writers lived in largely oral cultures, which he is certainly correct about, and therefore he argues that we need to be examining how largely oral cultures passed on their sacred traditions and what the function of sacred texts would be in such a setting. This is exactly right in my judgment.

Dunn believes that various modern forms of literary criticism, including form, redaction, and narrative criticism, approach the text in thoroughly modern, not to mention ahistorical, ways. For example, read his critique of narrative criticism:

> [N]arrative criticism has attempted in effect to narrow the hermeneutical circle of the whole and parts, by limiting the whole to the text itself. In narrative criticism, in order to make sense of a part, verse, or passage of the Gospel, the hermeneutical circle need only take in the whole of the Gospel itself. . . . The reality is that the historical text draws on (and its communication potential depends on) wider linguistic usage of the time; it makes references and allusions to characters and customs which are not explained within 'the closed universe' of the text; it cannot be adequately understood without some awareness of the society of the time. For example, without knowledge of the extra-textual social tensions between Jews and Samaritans, a central thrust of the parable of the Good Samaritan (Luke 10) will be lost.[3]

Dunn is no ally to those who say "all we have is texts." In other words, a more historical and less anachronistic approach to the Gospels is necessary if we are to understand them properly. In this, Dunn sounds much like a traditional historian or linguist. It is precisely for this same reason that Dunn will go on to caution against using models of tradition development that are entirely too modern, such as analyzing Balkan folklore, as a tool to explain the permutations and variations we find in the gospel traditions.

He is not happy either with what can only be called the vicious circle of the hermeneutics of reader-response criticism, another form of modern literary criticism. There must be interplay between the text and the reader such that "the text reacts back upon the pre-understanding, both sharpening it and requiring of it revision at one or another point, and thus enabling a fresh scrutiny of the text. . . . To conceive the hermeneutical process as an infinitely regressive intertextuality is a counsel of despair which quickly reduces all meaningful communication to impossibility and all communication to a game of Trivial Pursuit."[4]

Thus far, Dunn sounds both traditional in his use of the historical method and rather conservative. But he warns repeatedly that we do not have "the Jesus papers" in the Gospels. We do not have Jesus directly or the exact words of Jesus in the sayings collections. Jesus probably did not speak Greek to his disciples, much less King James' English! We have then, as the subtitle of his book implies, a mediated Jesus—Jesus as he was remembered by various disciples. This does not mean that

Dunn thinks that we are not in touch with the historical Jesus through such material. What he is wanting to stress is the mediated character of the portraits, reflecting in his view traditions passed down over a couple of generations orally before reaching a somewhat-fixed written form.

What is interesting is that he does not apply a hermeneutic of suspicion to these traditions in the same way some would, such as the Jesus seminar. For example, he urges, "The idea that a Jesus reconstructed from the Gospel traditions (the so-called historical Jesus), *yet significantly different from the Jesus of the Gospels*, is the Jesus who taught in Galilee (the historical Jesus!) is an illusion. The idea that we can see through the faith perspective of the NT writings to a Jesus who did *not* inspire faith or who inspired faith in a *different* way is an illusion."[5] What is the original impetus and impulse behind the Gospel record? In Dunn's view, it is the sayings and deeds of Jesus himself as witnessed, heard, seen, and retained in the memory of his disciples. We have the impact crater, not the meteor that made the impact, in the Gospels; we do not have Jesus in all his fullness but rather the remembered Jesus. For example, the sayings and deeds of Jesus reported are the ones remembered over the course of time and eventually recorded. As John 20:30 and 21:25 says, there were many other things Jesus said and did that were not remembered and not passed on orally, or in writing for that matter.

In chronicling the process that led to the Gospels, Dunn goes on to argue that various gospel traditions reflect the pre-Easter impact of Jesus' creating faith even then. Peter and the other disciples did not first become disciples after Easter, nor did they first begin to learn, remember, think about, and appropriate in faith the words and deeds of Jesus only after Easter. The "actual Synoptic tradition, with its record of things Jesus did and said, bears witness to a continuity between pre-Easter memory and post-Easter proclamation, a continuity of faith. However great the shock of Good Friday and Easter for the first disciples, it would be unjustified to assume that these events marked a discontinuity with their initial disciple-response."[6] Just so, and thus we might expect Dunn to go on and elaborate at length as to whether we have, at least in Mark and Q, eyewitness memory, but this he does not do. Rather, in a lengthy chapter 8, Dunn lays out his theories about oral gospel tradition, oral texts, and their development over time. It is to this material that we need to pay especially close attention, and here in particular Dunn's indebtedness to Bailey is very apparent.

Let us start with the spectrum of possibilities he sets up for how the Jesus tradition was passed on: formally controlled tradition (à la B. Gerhardsson), informally controlled tradition (à la Bailey), and informaly uncontrolled tradition (à la various of the form critics, including recent ones in the Jesus seminar—R. Funk, J. D. Crossan, and so forth).

Against R. Bultmann, Dunn thinks the handling of the Jesus tradition as a sacred tradition, while not like the latter rabbinic models of memorization and passing on of tradition, nonetheless was rather conservative. There was community control of a pedagogical sort. Dunn is working then with a sociological model of community control and formation of the oral tradition.

Dunn is not convinced by the argument of E. Boring and others that new sayings of the risen Jesus were retrojected back into the Gospels alongside the authentic sayings of the historical Jesus. Christian prophets are not depicted as speaking with the voice of Jesus or for Jesus in the Christian assemblies in Corinth and elsewhere, so it is unlikely that they were the tradents shaping the tradition: "Bultmann and Boring are overeager to find evidence of prophetic activity in the Synoptic tradition. The broader evidence suggests rather that such utterances were the exceptions rather than the rule."[7] Dunn adds that any prophecy claiming to come from the exalted Lord would have been tested against what was already known of what Jesus said and did, and thus in a surprising conclusion he urges, "the less closely a saying or motif within the Jesus tradition coheres with the rest of the Jesus tradition, the more likely is it that the saying or motif goes back to Jesus himself!"[8] This is because an alleged prophetic saying of the exalted Jesus would be subject to a criteria of coherence with previous tradition.

Bultmann had wanted to suggest that there were "laws of style" that determined how traditions were transmitted, in what forms, and how they would be elaborated. Basically, he argued a "from the simple and pure, to the complex and prolix" sort of case, drawing on a literary model of accretions, additions, and editing: "The image is drawn from the literary process of editing, where each successive edition (layer) is an edited version [for Bultmann an elaborated and expanded version] of the previous edition (layer). But is such a conceptualisation really appropriate to a process of oral retellings of traditional material?"[9]

If one is going to dethrone a dominant theory, then one has to have something to put in its place. What Dunn draws on largely, as we have said, are the insights of Bailey. Dunn is right to find it amazing that the old form critics (Bultmann and M. Dibelius) and even more recent ones never bothered actually to investigate, if possible, the original first-century techniques of oral transmission. Gerhardsson tried to remedy this oversight by proposing formally controlled tradition along the lines of the later rabbinic model, with memorization being the basic technique of all such early Jewish education. Thus Gerhardsson, in reacting to Bultmann, insisted that Jesus taught his disciples to memorize his teachings, and therefore the Synoptic Gospel writers had a fixed tradition to work with when they wrote their Gospels.[10]

Against this sort of view, there were several objections: (1) the Gospels do not depict Jesus teaching his disciples to rehearse things by repetition; (2) the post–A.D. 70 situation in Israel and elsewhere changed how Jews handled tradition, and the later Mishnaic model of traditioning should not be retrojected back into Jesus' day; and (3) most importantly, all the variants we find in the parallel versions of Jesus' words and deeds suggest a less formal or rigid handling of the gospel traditions. In other words, Gerhardsson is accused of anachronism, just in a less gross or remote form than Bultmann.

What then could be the bridge between Jesus and the Gospels, or the original disciples and the Gospel writers, and what sort of tradition transmission was there? Dunn opts for oral transmission, a

> "mid-state between fixed and free." Oral transmission exhibits 'an insistent conservative urge for preservation' of essential information, while it borders on carelessness in its predisposition to abandon features that are not met with social approval. Variability and stability, conservatism and creativity, evanescence and unpredictability all mark the pattern of oral transmission—the oral principle of variation within the same.[11]

On this theory, variations on a story or a saying are more likely to reflect multiple tellings of the tradition not redactional or other literary work at the juncture when Gospel writers were editing their sources.

Dunn is certainly right that ancient texts were meant to be heard and are by nature "oral texts."[12] They were not meant to be read silently, and they partake of all the oral and aural devices one would expect (rhythm, rhyme, alliteration, assonance, and so forth). What Dunn does not say is that it is precisely these oral features that make the material memorable, indeed even memorizable, as C. F. Burney long ago pointed out.[13]

It is interesting that Dunn does not seriously engage with or pause to refute an alternate theory to his own by S. Byrskog (a student of Gerhardsson)—namely, the theory of oral history. He only says of Byrskog's model, "But this model assumes later historians (like Luke) seeking out and inquiring of those like Peter, the women at the cross and tomb, and the family of Jesus, who could remember the original events and exchanges (cf. Luke 1:1-4). Byrskog, in fact, has no real conception of or indeed role for oral transmission as itself the bridging process."[14] In other words, this theory is dismissed without refutation. And furthermore, this comment is buried in a footnote.

Dunn then does not bother to rebut the theory of oral history; he basically just ignores it, practicing benign neglect, in favor of the notion that there was a generation or more during which time there was oral transmission of this gospel material that involved a good deal of flexibility except for the central features or sayings of a tradition. This is problematic not simply because a viable alternative theory is not dealt with, much less refuted. It is problematic because it does not explain some crucial things about the Synoptic tradition. For example, Dunn's theory hardly explains why it is that 95 percent of Mark's material is found in Matthew, and of that material 52 percent is verbatim. This hardly seems like a case in which there is considerable flux around the edges except when it comes to central motifs or crucial sayings or events. The differences in the shared material between Mark and Matthew, perhaps our two earliest Gospels, are much more easily explained on the whole in terms of Matthew's redactional tendencies than on the basis of oral variations on a theme. For example, where Mark tends to raise questions about the disciples' having no faith, in Matthew they are regularly called "you of little faith." Consistent tendencies of variation in Matthew compared to Mark seem purposeful and the result of a particular kind of editing of source material.

To his credit, Dunn does not deny there has been redaction of gospel source material by later Gospel writers. He simply wants to maintain that a good deal of the differences in the accounts can be best explained as reflecting orality and oral transmission. It is a shame that Dunn's masterwork came out prior to the publication of the equally masterful work of R. Bauckham, titled *Jesus and the Eyewitnesses*, in which Bauckham draws on and expands upon the argument of Byrskog, dealing with the issue of eyewitnesses more seriously and in depth. We shall have occasion to draw on Bauckham in critiquing Dunn's approach in the next section of this chapter.

Here, however, we need to get to the heart of the matter—the reliance on the suggestion of Bailey of "informally controlled tradition" in the Gospels based on an assumed analogy with what he, Bailey, observed for many years in Middle Eastern villages in the earlier twentieth century. First, note that Bailey, unlike Gerhardsson, draws on illustrative situations that are hardly from antiquity. In this respect, Bailey could equally be accused of the same sort of anachronism that Bultmann is accused of. The assumption is that village life in the Middle East in the twentieth century must be much the same as village life in Jesus' day when it comes to the matter of orality, oral tradition, and most importantly oral transmission of key or sacred traditions.[15] It must be said that this is an enormous assumption that needs substantiation.

Dunn freely admits that Bailey's evidence is anecdotal and is not the subject of systematic or scientific research.[16] We do not become more assured about Dunn's reliance on Bailey's observations when he adds, "the character of oral tradition which it illustrates accords well with the findings of other investigations of oral tradition and *is self evidently far closer to the sort of oral traditioning which must be posited for the Jesus tradition*."[17] Beware when scholars tell you something is self-evident or that a particular theory *must* be posited for the Jesus tradition. This last remark is all the more stunning when one turns to the next page and then reads: "We certainly do not know enough about oral traditioning in the ancient world to draw from that knowledge clear guidelines for our understanding of how the Jesus tradition was passed down in its oral stage."[18]

But if we do not know such things about antiquity, then we also *do not know* that the analogy with oral traditioning in twentieth-century village life in and around Palestine is apt. One needs knowledge on both sides of the comparison. Even more specifically, should we really assume that Palestinian nomads and their traditioning processes are a good point of analogy for what could be said about Jesus and his disciples and the processes they used?

It takes a considerable leap of faith, not to mention a leap over all sorts of cultural differences, to accept this analogy with much confidence. First, Jesus and his disciples grew up in a Jewish culture or subculture as people of the Hebrew Scriptures. These nomads did not. Second, the issue is not how just any sort of oral traditions, stories, parables, or proverbs might be handled or handed down, but how those considered "sacred traditions" were handled. But Bailey does not really make this sort of necessary distinction. He simply thinks that orality works the same way, regardless of what sort of stories and sayings one is relaying and retelling to others.

Dunn seeks to bolster his case by providing core samples from the NT of places where oral transmission and retelling of stories seems best to explain things. Oddly, his first example is the threefold telling of Saul's conversion in Acts—not a part of the gospel tradition at all! If we compare side by side the three accounts in Acts 9, 22, and 26, and at the same time compare the way Dunn analyzes the data with the way, for example, R. Tannehill analyzes the three accounts as examples where Luke cumulatively informs his audience about Saul's conversion by adding fresh and different details as the narrative goes on, it must be said that Tannehill is more convincing in explaining the differences in the accounts. They are purposeful, and they reflect various Lukan tendencies in his editing and overall presentation of his material over his two volumes, not oral tendencies.[19] Luke is following the rhetorical rules about varying an account when it is repeated and amplifying or adding new details to the later accounts so we do not have simple redundancy. In other words, the variations here do not reflect multiple oral retellings by later Christians; they reflect in the first instance the fact that Luke is drawing on both first-person accounts, one of which he heard, and then is composing a third-person account that we find in Acts 9, composing each with attention to the rhetorical rules about such speech material. I have dealt with this at length elsewhere and have shown how we can learn much about what is going on in Acts from the way Luke edits his Markan and Q source material in his Gospel.[20]

What is most surprising to me is that despite all his emphasis on orality, Dunn does not discuss at all the issue of rhetoric, the oral art of persuasion in the Greco-Roman Empire, even though Luke has been shown at length and by numerous commentators to be using rhetoric, especially in the presentation of his speech material in Luke–Acts,[21] even though we have long known there was even a school of rhetoric in Jerusalem in Jesus' era and afterward, and even though Christianity was an evangelistic movement seeking to persuade others about Jesus.

If one is going to deal with the orality of early followers of Jesus, including the Gospel writers who wrote in Greek, Paul, and others, then one has to come to grips with the nature of a rhetoric-saturated culture and how oral traditions and sacred traditions function in a rhetorical culture. When you do assess the data in light of rhetorical conventions and tendencies, rhetorically purposeful variation, rather than just flexible oral storytelling and traditioning, better explains most of the data.

Dunn analyzes briefly the two accounts of the healing of the centurion's servant (Matt 8:5-13; Luke 7:1-10) and raises the point that the differences between these two versions of the story (and also from John 4:46-54) are better explained by the theory of oral transmission, which has stability in the central saying and skeletal narrative elements but flexibility in the rest of the pericope, than by positing two different editions of Q, one used by Matthew, one by Luke. I agree with this critique about Q, but is this explanation also more plausible than assuming considerable amplification of the story by Luke himself or recasting of the story by John? Dunn thinks so, and I must say that here his argument seems stronger. Whatever one makes of the differences in these three accounts, they need to be explained in some fashion, and they do not seem to submit easily to the theory of mere redactional change or augmentation or recasting. It must be said, however, that because we obviously do not know what the oral tradition looked like independent of its frozen form in our actual Gospels, there is less control that can be exercised by positing this theory than when one explains the differences on the basis of redaction of earlier traditions, at least when we are dealing with a use of Mark by Matthew and Luke. With Q, because we do not have it independently of its inclusion in Matthew and Luke, obviously there is much less certainty about earlier forms or redaction, despite the confidence of those who find multiple layers in a Q document we do not have on hand to examine. There is the further problem that in an oral culture, what we call Q may well have not been a document or documents but rather streams of memorized oral tradition, which both Matthew and Luke dip into from time to time in various ways and places.

Dunn also discusses the triple tradition story of the stilling of the storm (Mark 4:35-41; Matt 8:23-27; Luke 8:22-25). He asserts at the outset, "Here again we have the characteristic features of different retellings of a single story about Jesus."[22] It would have been more reassuring if he had actually analyzed the details of the three accounts and explained why his theory works better than a more literary theory here.

What he does point to is that there are inconsequential variations of synonymous verbs, little varying details about Jesus sleeping and the like, and he thinks this is best explained by independent retellings of the story orally. This overlooks that there were specific rhetorical rules the Gospel writers could have followed when it came to the matters of repetition and amplification of written or oral source material. One of the key rules was that one would deliberately use differing terms that conveyed the same meaning to make the material one's own.[23] In any case, there are clear editorial tendencies evident when one compares the presentation of the disciples in Mark and in Matthew. In the former presentation, the disciples say, "Lord don't you care we are perishing?" and Jesus responds, "Have you still no faith?" The phrase "Lord don't you care" and the reference to no faith, which reflect badly on the disciples, are missing in Matthew. Luke also ameliorates the harshness of the Markan account with Jesus simply asking, "Where is your faith?" which seems to suggest that Jesus thinks they have some but are not exhibiting it. Dunn wishes to argue for spontaneous multiple variations on a theme rather than different versions of the story or different editing of a story.

After presenting several more examples, especially choosing those where there is a wide degree of variation between the different forms of the story or passage, Dunn then argues that we need to free ourselves from thinking of these traditions in a purely literary way, as if the differences could only be explained in terms of differing source texts or redaction of texts. I agree with this. Dunn also, however, admits that many of the differences can be explained on the basis of Luke's or Matthew's editing Mark or Q, and again I must agree.

On more than one occasion, Dunn cites the material in Eusebius where he is quoting from the earlier writings by Bishop Papias of Hierapolis about the composition of Mark: "but Peter adapted/gave his teaching with a view to the *chreias* but not as making an orderly account of the Lord's sayings, so that Mark did no wrong in thus writing down some things as he recalled them" (*Hist. eccl.* 3.39.15). Here Dunn translates *chreia* in its mundane sense of needs (needs of whom?) and does not even consider the possibility that Papias is telling us that Mark composed his work following the rhetorical rules about forming *chreia* (short stories usually climaxing with a pithy memorable saying of the central figure). Elsewhere, I have demonstrated at length that this is precisely how Papias' quote ought to be read and is precisely what Mark was doing.[24]

Mark follows the elementary rules for composing brief narratives in a rhetorically effective manner. Luke does the same thing. What is in play here is not mere oral flexibility or variation on a theme but a purposeful editing or modifying of a tradition, whether oral or written, so that it adds to the persuasiveness of the material in Greek. It is only Matthew who seems to have other tendencies and aims in the way he handles the tradition, doing so in what I would call a far more Jewish, even halakic or haggadic, manner. Thus, while I agree that the variations in shared traditions do not at all reflect a cavalier attitude about history or a lack of historical interest, it is a shame that Dunn does not see that rhetoric is one of the keys to analyzing how the tradition was handled, shaped, and handed on, early and late. He is, however, right that these traditions are not traditions freely composed nor, for that matter, traditions seen as inviolable and frozen into a sort of textual rigor mortis either.[25] The actual differences in the parallel accounts must be given their due and not glossed over. The question is, how are the differences most adequately explained?

What Dunn wants to insist on in the end is the corporate or group formation of the tradition through repeated tellings rather than the theory of mainly key apostolic individuals shaping the tradition. Striving for some balance, he puts it this way after a long lobbying for the communal and oral nature of the tradition:

> Nor should we forget the continuing role of eyewitness tradents, of those recognized from the first as apostles or otherwise authoritative bearers of the Jesus tradition. . . . Such indications as there are from the pre-Pauline and early Pauline period suggest already fairly extensive outreach by such figures, both establishing and linking new churches, and a general concern to ensure that a foundation of authoritative tradition was well laid in each case. In focusing particular attention on the communal character of the early traditioning process we should not discount the more traditional emphasis on the individual figure of authority respected for his or her own association with Jesus during the days of his mission.[26]

And now we get to the real heart of the matter. Dunn thinks there is a need for a considerably long bridge between Jesus and the Gospel writers, and his theory of a rather lengthy oral stage in the process is the bridge he provides between A and B. This is why he rejects Byrskog's theory about oral history. That theory makes the eyewitnesses not some kind of supplement to the communal shaping of the tradition over considerable time but rather makes them much more central in positing a theory of how we get from Jesus to the Gospels.[27]

In actuality, Dunn is looking for a middle way, a *via media*, between the theory of memorization and close contact of the Gospel writers with eyewitnesses on the one hand or free-flowing, freely amplified tradition in a literary mode based on little shards of historical information going back ultimately to Jesus on the other hand.[28] He is to be commended for this, but one must ask whether the evidence we have—not only from Papias, but also from Luke's preface in Luke 1:1-4 and from what Paul tells us about traditions handed down to him, apparently by eyewitnesses—needs to be given a bit more credence and careful attention. One must ask whether Byrskog actually has the better of the argument on this point. At this juncture, we shall take time to interact first with Byrskog and then with Bauckham and his use of Byrskog and see what further light this sheds on Dunn's approach.

JESUS, THE EYEWITNESSES, AND ORAL HISTORY

It is to the credit of Byrskog that, despite the neglect in recent orality studies by Kelber and others of the theory of oral history that is grounded in the actual examination of oral testimony and oral informants in antiquity, he has continued to pursue the matter. And it has borne good fruit in Bauckham's recent masterful study. As Byrskog points out, the alleged polarity between orality and written texts, overplayed repeatedly by Kelber and his disciples, has skewed the discussion of the gospel traditions in various ways and even has led to a romanticizing of orality and oral performance over "textual rigor mortis."[29] The basis of Byrskog's study is the examination of the actual practices and also what is said by ancient historians ranging from Herodotus to Luke about the handling of eyewitness testimony. To his credit, Byrskog is aware of the way rhetoric and ancient philosophy affected these matters, so he also takes into account what is to be learned from rhetoricians and philosophers about eyewitness testimony and oral history.

Byrskog focuses on the historians, because they were the ones who systematically and consistently tried to search out the past: "They are the prime representatives of ancient people who related in a more or less conscious way to past events. Their writings are most clearly reflective of the dynamics of story and history, present and past, in the sociocultural setting of the gospel tradition."[30] Byrskog goes to some lengths to make clear that orality and writing should not be set over against one another, as if the latter was seen as a dead medium and the former as a living, in some sort of dramatic contrast. It is true, there was a preference for the living voice over the written record in many contexts, but the texts we have in the NT are by and large "oral texts," texts that not merely come out of an oral environment but are meant to be read out loud and heard, and even in various cases meant to be performed, in a rhetorically effective manner. When texts are but surrogates for or transcripts of oral speech, there can be no hard and fast division between the oral and the written or a pitting of one over against the other.

Byrskog is right on target in saying that in a culture of about 10 percent to 15 percent literacy, what is remarkable about the NT documents is the level of literacy, knowledge, and rhetorical skill reflected in them. He puts it this way:

> The majority of the authors of the New Testament, as we realize today, were highly literate, and not, it seems, all that reluctant to employ rather refined forms of the written medium as a means of communication. Not only the rich 'bibliographical substructure' but also the advanced literary level of the New Testament contradict, on the face of it, our insistence that in antiquity writing was after all inferior to the oral medium.[31]

For our purposes, what the New Testament exclaims to us by its very features is that early Christianity was led to a large extent by a socially more elite group of persons than we are sometimes led to think, persons who not only could read and write, but persons who also could write sophisticated biographies, historical monographs, sermons, or letters in ways that would be effective in a culture that was awash with rhetoric, both in the form of avid producers and consumers of rhetoric.

In his criticism of the old form critics and their views of orality and aurality, Byrskog makes some telling points. First, they assumed that it did not matter who passed on or who received the oral tradition, "because the individuality of each informer and listener was entirely swallowed up by the collective identity and the common hearing of the larger community. The challenge of oral history to take seriously the uniqueness as well as the representativeness of each narration is nowhere to be found in Bultmann's approach."[32] What is ironic about Dunn's study is that although he is very critical of the old form critical approach, he still ends up with a more collectivistic view of the formation and passing on of the oral tradition, and he stresses the oral dimension to the neglect of the eyewitness dimension of things. Second, however, there is an emphasis in the ancient tradition on actual seeing and being in contact with those who have seen the events and the oral performances of Jesus. In other words, the neglect of the "autopsy" factor is everywhere apparent in the old form critical approach but also in Dunn's work: "Discipleship was always the matrix of a double activity; it was a way of learning that including hearing as well as seeing."[33]

When we hear in the Gospel of John "the man who saw it has given testimony and we know his testimony is true" (John 19:35), the connection between eyewitness and oral testimony becomes clear and is seen as very important, even in the latest canonical Gospel to be produced.

Or, again in the preface to 1 John, when we hear "that which was from the beginning which he heard, which we have seen with our eyes, which we have looked at and our hands have touched" (1 John 1:1), we are not encouraged to think of a process of the passing on of tradition that was both strictly oral and anonymous. As Luke says, the tradition was handed down by "those who were from the first eyewitnesses and servants of the word" (Luke 1:2). We neglect these deliberate assertions about eyewitnesses to our peril if we want to understand the bridge between Jesus and the Gospels.

What we find in Byrskog, which is missing in Dunn, is a serious discussion of the eyewitnesses of Jesus' ministry. Byrskog puts it this way: "The historical Jesus event was experienced through their [i.e., the earliest disciples] eyes and their ears and soon became historic by entering into the present, oral currencies of observers such as Peter, the women, James, and Mary; it became their own oral history which they proclaimed to others. One needed their eyes as well as their ears."[34] This is because what Jesus did included what he said. Speaking was an action not divided from other deeds in the memory of the eyewitnesses. The narratives or stories told included words and deeds from the first, which should not be radically separated, as if we can only get back to the historical Jesus by treating him as a talking head.

Oral history is the testimony of eyewitnesses in the first place, and this is the bridge between past and present that is being actually mentioned in the NT itself, not an anonymous passing on of oral traditions in general between countless generations and voices. When the material is written down, it is written down for oral performance, what Byrskog calls *reoralization*, such that the Gospels are oral texts that are grounded in the testimony of eyewitnesses, not merely later earwitnesses of the story. The ancient model was history and story in constant interaction, such that the story was corrected by the history and by the eyewitnesses and the retelling was normalized by those who were the original eyewitnesses and the faithful servants of the Word who heard them.

Byrskog argues that we must not view the memory of ancient witnesses as a sort of fuzzy and entirely fluid collection of reminiscences. This is not only because memorization was an essential part of all education, especially the education of persons who learned to read and write, persons such as the Gospel writers themselves, but also because in oral cultures there were times, places, and rewards for recitation for what one had correctly stored in one's memory. The sophist Hipias tells us of how Plato was able to repeat fifty names after hearing them only once (*Hi. Maior* 285e), and Seneca tells us that as a youth not only could he repeat two thousand names read to him, but he was able to recite back in reverse order two hundred verses of some text read to him (*Contr.* 1, V.2). Even allowing for rhetorical exaggeration here, one gets the point that oral memory was cultivated and praised and prized in antiquity. What helped this process was the use of mnemonic devices and rhetorical devices to make things lodge in one's memory.

"The oral history approach takes very seriously the fact that accurate memory depends on social interest and need. A person involved remembers better than a disinterested observer."[35] This is not to say that eyewitnesses did not have their biases and points of view—of course they did. Yet ancient historians and biographers rightly preferred the testimonies of those actually and actively involved in the events for the very good reason that they were fully engaged mentally in what was happening and were more likely to remember substantial details of what was said and done, though undoubtedly their reports had to be carefully and critically sifted.

Notice again that Luke says that he observed and carefully investigated things over a period of time before he sat down to write out an orderly account for Theophilus (Luke 1:1-4). In this, he is not acting any differently from other ancient historians who placed a premium on eyewitness testimony. Ancient historians were wiser than many modern ones in understanding that "the historical reliability of an eyewitness has little or nothing to do with passive transmission or detachment from the event. Engaged interpretation is part of the process from the very beginning; to see is to interpret with one's own frame of mind; the present is always a part of the past; and this is an asset not a drawback, even insofar as we are concerned with historical reliability."[36] Byrskog then has presented a cogent and plausible case for seeing oral history and the way oral history was dealt with by the ancients as the proper model for viewing both the orality and literacy that lead to the Gospels we have. At this juncture, we need to turn to the application of the model by Bauckham in his book *Jesus and the Eyewitnesses*.

BAUCKHAM AND THE GOSPEL TRADITION

I was given the privilege of reading the proofs of *Jesus and the Eyewitnesses* while staying with Bauckham in St. Andrews in the summer of 2006, and I realized at once that this was a landmark study, just as *Jesus Remembered* is. Bauckham argues from the outset that the model for evaluating the Gospels properly is the model of testimony. They are the sort of historiography that the term *testimony* best describes: "Testimony offers us, I wish to suggest, both a reputable historiographic category for reading the Gospels as history, and also a theological model for understanding the Gospels as the entirely appropriate means of access to the historical reality of Jesus."[37] What Bauckham is arguing, and I would also stress, is that the Gospels are not the result of a long process of anonymous oral transmission of traditions that went through umpteen permutations and combinations. On the contrary, the Gospels were all written while there was still living memory of eyewitnesses to be consulted about the events. Furthermore, those eyewitnesses did not suddenly retire to a nice beach-side condo and never speak about the matter after they first told the tales. For "at least a generation they moved among the young Palestinian communities, and through preaching and fellowship their recollections were at the disposal of those who sought information."[38]

Thus, Bauckham emphasizes, "the period between the 'historical' Jesus and the Gospels was actually spanned, not by anonymous community transmission, but by the continuing presence and testimony of the eyewitnesses, who remained the authoritative sources of their traditions until their deaths."[39] This does not mean of course that many others did not tell these tales in worship and fellowship meetings. What it does mean is that the ones on whom the Gospel writers relied for their information were the eyewitness, not later tradents. What prompted the writing of the Gospels was precisely that the eyewitnesses were dying out and their testimonies needed to be preserved, in this case in writing. The method that the Gospel writers followed when it came to collecting and editing their source material was to seek out the eyewitnesses and those who were in contact with the eyewitnesses and listen closely to their testimonies. Oral testimony from such persons was much preferred over anonymous written records. These ancient writers heard and responded to the cry "*ad fontes*," which was the preferred and normal modus operandi of ancient historians and biographers of the age.

Bauckham is well aware of some of the criticisms leveled against the work of Byrskog and sees it as his task to answer them or fill in the gaps where Byrskog did not adequately deal with possible objections. In order to do so, Bauckham turns to the report of the early second-century bishop Papias of Hierapolis and what he says about the origins of the gospel tradition. Besides the internal data of the Gospels themselves, this account, coming from the early second century from someone who was actually in touch with at least one eyewitness and another person or two who seems to have known some eyewitnesses, is extremely valuable, and unfortunately Dunn is only one of the most recent in a long line of scholars who neglects to interact seriously and in detail with the Papias traditions. Bauckham makes up for such an oversight in the balance of his study, which goes on for some five hundred additional pages. Here we can only give a précis of some of the crucial highlights.

Bauckham points out that we should not simply derive from Papias the preference for the living voice over the written book, for what Papias is mainly saying in Eusebius' account in *Hist. eccl.* 3.39.3-4 is that he wanted to hear from the eyewitnesses or those who were in contact with them.[40] As Bauckham argues, this passage calls Aristion and John the elder disciples of the Lord, which is to say eyewitnesses of Jesus, and Papias apparently claims to have had personal conversation with them, which means probably no later than in the A.D. 80s.[41] The text may, however, mean he had personally met those who had had personal contact with these two men. Papias also seems to have been in direct contact with the prophesying daughters of Philip mentioned in Acts 21:9 (*Hist. eccl.* 3.39.9). In any case, this testimony must be put alongside what Luke 1:1-4 says; both seem to be commenting on a period in the 80s when eyewitnesses were still alive and could be consulted, which was during the time when all the Synoptic Gospels seem to have been written.

What is important about this portion of Papias' testimony, as Bauckham stresses, is that Papias is speaking about oral testimony that is connected to specific named eyewitnesses, not an anonymous community. Furthermore, what Papias means when he refers to his preference for "the living voice" is not merely a preference for oral over written but, as he says, for the "living *and surviving* voice." He is referring to "the voice of an informant—someone who has personal memories of the words and deeds of Jesus and who is still alive." The "saying about the superiority of the 'living voice' to books refers not to oral tradition as superior to books, but to direct experience of an instructor, informant, or orator as superior to written sources."[42] Bauckham profitably compares this to 1 Corinthians 15:6, where Paul refers to numerous witnesses of the risen Lord "who are still alive, though some have died."[43] The point is simple: whether we begin with Paul or move to Luke, on to the Fourth Gospel, or finally to Papias, all these writers are concerned with being in touch not with merely the oral tradition but with the autopsy of eyewitnesses. The distinction between oral history and oral tradition becomes clear—the former necessarily involves the testimony of eyewitnesses, and the latter does not. Oral tradition may have passed from mouth to ear many times and is typically collective and anonymous; oral history is not. Papias had no interest in simply reflecting on the collective memory of early Christian communities. He wanted to hear from, preferably directly, the eyewitnesses; failing that, he relied on those who had heard the eyewitnesses.

In an article that appeared after *Jesus Remembered*, Dunn quite specifically and more directly critiques Byrskog. Here his tone is more strident:

> I simply do not believe that Peter, Mary of Magdala and the like stored up many memories of Jesus' mission, which were only jerked into remembrance by "oral history" inquiries of a Luke or a Matthew. They had

already fed those memories into the living tradition of the churches, as major contributory elements in the forming and shaping of that tradition. No doubt other memories were brought to the surface by inquiries of a Luke or a Matthew, but these would be supplementary to what was already known and performed in the various assemblies week by week. I guess the same was true of Papias and Irenaeus.[44]

As Bauckham laments, Dunn simply assumes here that the Gospels are the product of community tradition, but this is not at all what Luke says in Luke 1:2 about his modus operandi and who he consulted. Bauckham further complains, rightly, that it was not a case of prying information out of eyewitnesses who heretofore had remained silent. They had shared, probably many times, their testimonies, and those testimonies had become common coin in various communities. This is not the point. The issue is, *who did the Gospel writers consult when they wrote their Gospels*? Luke tells us he consulted eyewitnesses, and he implies he knows previous attempts to write an account of the gospel events. Similarly, Paul tells us in Galatians 1 that he went up to Jerusalem to learn the *historia* from Peter, James, and John, and we may be sure they did not spend two weeks discussing the weather on Zion's heights. Thus, when Paul tells us that he passed on what he had received in 1 Corinthians 11 or 15, we should take this to mean he got it from the horse's mouth. He consulted the eyewitnesses when he was able to do so. We should also take seriously what was said in Acts 1 about the criteria for who could become the replacement for Judas among the Twelve—namely, someone who had been a participant in the ministry of Jesus from the baptism of John onward. Why this criteria? Because they wanted eyewitnesses of as much of the story as possible if the Twelve were to continue to be the agents for and representatives of Jesus in Israel.

What about the Gospel of Mark? After pointing out the interesting *inclusio* in Mark 1 and Mark 16 where Peter is the first named disciple of Jesus, and then learning in Mark 16:7 that the women must go tell the disciples and Peter that Jesus is going before them into Galilee, and after noting that Mark's Gospel has the highest frequency of mentions of Peter of any canonical Gospel (Matthew included), Bauckham turns once more to the tradition of Papias about the composition of Mark's Gospel, our earliest and in some ways most important Gospel for the purposes of this discussion.[45] I will say here in advance that the explanation as to why Luke or the First Evangelist would have used Mark so extensively, especially when it was known that Mark was not an eyewitness and Luke professes to consult such people, will become less of a mystery in a moment. In short, it is because it is the testimony of Peter.

Here is the crucial passage from Papias, as translated and helpfully clarified and amplified by Bauckham:

> The Elder used to say: Mark, in his capacity as Peter's *hermeneutes*, wrote down accurately as many things as he [Peter?] recalled from memory—though not in an ordered form—of the things either said or done by the Lord. For he [Mark] never heard the Lord nor accompanied him but later, as I said, [he heard and accompanied] Peter, who used to give his teachings in the form of *chreiai* but had no intention of providing an orderly arrangement of the *logia* of the Lord. Consequently Mark did nothing wrong when he wrote down some individual items just as he [Peter?] related them from memory. For he made it his one concern not to omit anything or falsify anything. (Eusebius *Hist. eccl.* 3.39.14-16)

This passage, whose historical significance is too often dismissed or ignored, Bauckham elaborates on at length. Here are some of the key points. While *hermeneutes* could certainly mean "interpreter" here, it can also mean "translator." As Bauckham says, what Papias goes on to add suggests that he means "translator" by the use of this term. Mark's job was to omit nothing and add nothing so as to avoid falsifying Peter's eyewitness testimony. Thus, Mark does not even assume the authority to arrange the material in a best order; he simply reproduces exactly what he heard from Peter just as he recalled it. In other words, this is not about Mark's being Peter's interpreter when the oral word was shared by Peter. This is a reference to how the Gospel of Mark came to be composed as it was. And it may also explain why Luke stresses that he (unlike his Markan source) will indeed offer up a rhetorically and historically effective ordering of the material.

This brings us to a third important point. At various junctures in Mark, we have brief quotations of Aramaic from Jesus that are then rendered telegraphically into Greek. This presupposes Mark's audience does not know Aramaic, but it shows that the Evangelist is bilingual, at a minimum (he may know some Latin as well). M. Casey has shown at great length that a considerable portion of our earliest Gospel is quite readily retrojected back into Aramaic.[46] He suggests that some of the awkwardness we find in Mark's Greek is due to translation issues, which is more than just the issue of Semitic interference (a person thinking first in a Semitic language and then attempting to compose in Greek but often still carrying over the structures or earmarks of the primary language).

This brings us to an important point. Casey's insights favor the suggestion of Bauckham that Mark translated Peter's Aramaic recollections into his Gospel. Peter spoke in Aramaic and perhaps some wooden Greek, remembering various things Jesus did and said, and

Mark wrote it down in better Greek. As Bauckham argues, the second verb for memory in the passage above from Papias means "relate or record from memory." But this verb is much more naturally applied to Peter, whose testimony Papias is interested in, than to Mark. Thus, we see Mark as the scribe for Peter, taking down what Peter recalled and then related from memory. And, as Bauckham goes on to stress, this very language is the language used in Greek of *Memoirs* by Xenephon, and more importantly by Justin Martyr to refer to the Gospels as the "memoirs of the Apostles" (*1 Apol.* 66.3, 67.3; *Dial.* 107-17).[47]

Bauckham goes on to urge that the translation of *chreia* here as "according to needs," which Dunn favors, has largely and rightly been abandoned by Markan scholars.[48] As a rhetorical term, it makes very good sense with regard to what we find in our earliest Gospel—short narratives that contain actions and sayings, or actions or sayings often climaxing with a pithy memorable remark. The English word *anecdote* is perhaps the closest parallel. *Chreia* was a form of rhetorical composition found at every level of education and was used to teach reading and writing. To say Peter related and Mark composed these tales in the form of *chreia* is not to claim a sophisticated knowledge of rhetoric, such as we find in Paul or in the author of Hebrews, only an elementary knowledge of it.

But if this Gospel was written for an audience in Rome, such a form of composition would have been not merely helpful but almost required—for Rome was rhetoric central in the A.D. mid-first century, and no persuasion was likely to happen, particularly of any educated persons, without the use of it. What the use of *chreia* implies is the evangelistic intentions of Peter, Mark, or both. They wanted the relaying of the Jesus tradition to convince people about "the Good News of Jesus the Christ, the Son of God." There is much more in Bauckham's rich treatment of Byrskog's theory and his amplification and justification of the approach of oral history to the formation of the gospel tradition, but this must suffice for now—he seems to have shored up all the gaps and weaknesses in Byrskog's presentation and made a compelling case for this sort of approach to our canonical Gospels. It is time now for us to draw this discussion to a close and assess what all this means for evaluating Dunn's *Jesus Remembered*.

AND SO?

What are the implications for this study? The actual historical evidence in the Gospels and elsewhere in the NT, and in the testimony of Papias, strongly suggests that the proper model for evaluating the gospel traditions is the model of oral history, not the model proposed by Dunn of informally controlled oral tradition that percolated for a long time in communities and was subject to anonymous collective control from Christian community to community. This does not mean Dunn is wrong and I am right. He may well be right. But he must demonstrate why the case laid out in full by Bauckham is in error at crucial junctures. This he has not yet done, and so his work is not done.

In the crucial sections of Dunn's work in which he deals with sources and traditions, one wishes for a much more detailed justification for the view that the gospel traditions, especially when there are notable differences in the parallels, support the view of considerable flexibility in the oral tradition, only an informal control at most, rather than support the view of editing and amplification by the Gospel writers themselves. The flexibility itself speaks against the view of a more formal control as envisioned by Byrskog's mentor, Gerhardsson. Dunn is right that the evidence for some sort of strict formal control, such as later Mishnaic practice, is lacking in the actual data we have in the Gospels themselves when closely examined.

And it is the great merit of Dunn's methodological discussion that he shows the fatal weaknesses in the old form critical approaches to the gospel data, which were based on no well-known ancient analogies at all as to how oral tradition was handled. As we have seen in this chapter, however, I am doubtful that the modern materials produced and drawn upon by Bailey are much more helpful in allowing us to deal with this material. But the detailed work of Byrskog and Bauckham on ancient historians, rhetoricians, and biographers helps remedy this problem with the proper sort of ancient Greek analogies.

But here is the irony in this discussion. The parallel accounts in the Synoptics say what they say, whatever our theories about the origins and transmission of these traditions. Any theory of origins and transmission must make sense of and allow for the actual differences we find there. As Dunn stresses, they cannot be ignored, they cannot be finessed, and they cannot be dismissed, so they must be dealt with. And at the end of the day, even if one was only sure that Matthew used quite a lot of Mark and Luke used some of it and one claims nothing else, it is quite clear and evident that there was some flexibility in the handling of even the sayings of Jesus, although they were more conservatively passed on than some of the narrative material, it would appear.

It seems to me that although this flexibility may in some minority of incidences reflect a flexibility at the oral stage of things, the repeated patterns of Matthew's and Luke's use of Mark (and perhaps of Q) suggest that most of the differences we find are purposeful and important and are the result of the evangelists' handling of the material themselves. Indeed, most of them can be explained in terms of the evangelists' following either their own agendas and interests or following the guidance of the rhetorical rules of how to make a narrative an effective act of persuasion and keep the audience interested, even when one is sometimes repeating material.

Let me emphasize once more, the evidence both internal and external about the Gospels suggests to me that the theory of oral history rather than somewhat flexible informally controlled oral transmission better explains what we find in the canonical Gospels. We have here in these Gospels "Jesus remembered," not just by anyone or everyman but by those who knew him best, those who were eyewitnesses or in touch with the eyewitnesses and original heralds of the Word.[49] The communities did not create these traditions—the eyewitnesses did.

What the communities did do was validate the tradition's veracity and use their contents mightily to lead many to become followers of Jesus. The final words of the Fourth Gospel encapsulate very well the roles of community and eyewitnesses. The community said, pointing beyond itself, "this is the disciple who testifies to these things and has written them down. We know his testimony is true" (John 21:25). Herein lies the roles of both laid bare, explaining why, as Dunn so rightly stresses, the historical Jesus is indeed the Jesus of the Gospels, the Jesus lodged in the minds and hearts of his earliest disciples and eyewitnesses and enshrined in our canonical Gospels.

11

The Rise of Canon Consciousness and the Formation of the New Testament

It is the simple truth to say that the New Testament books became canonical because no one could stop them doing so.

—William Barclay[1]

Put another way, instead of suggesting that certain books were accidentally included and others were accidentally excluded from the New Testament canon—whether the exclusion be defined in terms of the activity of individuals, or synods, or councils—it is more accurate to say that certain books excluded themselves from the canon . . . it is a clear case of survival of the fittest.

—Bruce M. Metzger[2]

One of the notable trends in New Testament studies over the last couple of decades is the revision of what many, perhaps most, scholars think is the case about the development and closing of the NT canon. This sea change in opinion is clearly reflected in what is perhaps the best of all recent books on the canon, L. McDonald's *The Biblical Canon*.[3] What has largely prompted this revision in the received wisdom—which now states that there were likely no canon lists in the second century A.D., but rather that kind of activity and attempt to define and delimit the NT canon did not transpire until the fourth century—is the work of G. Hahneman, who in turn has drawn on the earlier suggestions from the 1960s and 1970s of A. C. Sundberg.[4] Whereas before these two scholars weighed in on canon lists, and particularly on the Muratorian Canon list, the large majority of NT scholars have argued that the Muratorian list, however anomalous, dates to the end of the second century, now many if not most are suggesting the fourth-century date of the Muratorian Fragment is very likely, if not virtually certain.

It is the mark of a good thesis that it changes minds and sometimes even paradigms, and Hahneman's thesis, done as a doctoral thesis

143

under M. Wiles at Oxford, has had an influence out of all proportion to the normal impact of doctoral theses on the guild. Part of the problem is that one must be polymath to assess a good deal of Hahneman's case properly, and most NT scholars these days are such specialists that they shy away from dealing with arguments that require a wide range of expertise, particularly when we are talking about expertise in early church history, Latin, and patristics and not just in the NT. Nevertheless, it is important now to assess the Hahneman hypothesis further, because at this juncture it is too often taken as a "proved" hypothesis and therefore not needing to be reargued or further argued. I do not agree with this attitude about the Hahneman case; in this essay, I shall first critique the arguments of Hahneman and then secondly provide a constructive alternative to the Hahneman model in a brief outline that will need to be further developed on a future occasion.

RED HERRINGS—THE HAHNEMAN HYPOTHESIS REDUX

One of the things that often happens in scholarly works is that quite naturally scholars like to display their erudition in detail, which has the rhetorical effect of stunning at least some of the audience into silence, because they do not share the level of expertise the particular scholar in question demonstrates in that particular field. I have noticed this often happens with NT scholars who do not know Latin when they are in the presence of someone who knows it very well.

Such a person is Hahneman, and thus the opening of his study in chapter 1 is more than a little daunting because of the detailed argument about the Latin text of the Muratorian Fragment. This argument is of some merit, because it shows that the long form of the Muratorian Fragment found in Milan reflects some poor Latin and worse copying by a careless scribe. I grant from the outset that this particular Latin copy of the Fragment may well date to the fourth or fifth century, and I also grant that the fragments found at Monte Cassino, which reflect better Latin, demonstrate just how poor the Latin text really is of the major Muratorian Fragment. Furthermore, the orthographic studies on the text of the Muratorian Fragment from Milan do indeed provide some useful evidence for the fourth-century or later dating of this particular copy of the list.

All of this, however, and I do mean all of it, is rather irrelevant because even Hahneman readily grants what has been argued from the time of this discovery—namely, that the list was *originally in Greek, not Latin*. In fact, Hahneman concedes that some of the howlers in the Latin text of the Muratorian Fragment are readily explained when one recognizes they are rather poor attempts at translating the Greek original.

Thus, in the end, the value of the lengthy discussion of the Latin of the Muratorian Canon list is that it demonstrates that the original text *was not likely in Latin.* This being the case, all the orthographic arguments about the fourth- or fifth-century Latin copy are irrelevant in assessing the date or provenance of the Greek original, which was reconstructed already more than one hundred twenty years ago by J. B. Lightfoot in a classic work that has even been reprinted yet again in 2007.[5]

The second major red herring, or irrelevant argument, is Hahneman's discussion of the seventh-century codex that contains the Muratorian Canon. This codex contains a variety of patristic documents, including various ones from the fourth century. No one disputes this. But because Hahneman finds mostly fourth-century documents copied in this codex, he then concludes that this suggests a fourth-century date for the Muratorian list as well. Alas, even a brief study of other major Christian codexes shows how specious this sort of reasoning is. Take, for example, Codex Claremontus. Along with various NT books, there is in addition the Revelation of Peter included in this book. Should we conclude that the Revelation of Peter therefore is a first-century document? No scholar that I know of thinks so. Or consider Codex Sinaiticus—it includes the *Shepherd of Hermas* along with various NT books in it. Does this provide a warrant for our concluding that Hermas thus *must* or *is likely to be* a first-century document? Certainly not, and most scholars date Hermas to sometime in the second century. This kind of argument I shall dub "dating by association or proximity." It is a specious argument.[6]

Christian codexes included a variety of Christian documents and were composed for a variety of reasons and purposes. And while we are discussing this matter, it needs to be said that *a table of contents of a codex is by no means the same thing as a canon list,* whether open or closed. Inclusion in a codex simply demonstrates that these Christian documents were highly valued, often copied, and were considered important Christian resources. Now if one could demonstrate that all the contents of this or that codex were read out in Christian worship somewhere as a scriptural text, that might provide some support for such a case. But because we know that codexes were mostly *not* used as pulpit Bibles, certainly not in the fourth century and earlier, we must assume that they came from the scriptorium and stayed in the scriptorium— they were used for study and reflection of various sorts, not for worship. There is already evidence in the second and third centuries (see the case of Bishop Serapion)[7] of a distinction being made between Christian books that may be read and studied and what amounts to Scripture that should be read in the worship service.[8] This distinction still existed in the late patristic period and early Middle Ages, when many of the great codexes were produced. We cannot conclude therefore that what was copied and read in private or in the scriptorium and that made it into a Christian codex was necessarily seen as Scripture and suitable for reading in worship. For it to be seen as Scripture suitable for use in worship, it had to pass more stringent tests of apostolicity, historical antiquity, and truth and not just be a text of general usefulness or relevance.

A third red herring is the whole discussion of the Peshitta in Hahneman's study. It is implied that the Peshitta must be dated now to the fourth century, perhaps the late fourth century, and that therefore it provides no parallel with the Muratorian Fragment as an early canon list of a sort. First, the Peshitta is a Bible, unlike the Muratorian Canon, and so the two are not really comparable. Second, at least the Old Testament portion of the Peshitta dates to the second century A.D., and the NT portion surely must date from before the fourth century, not least because it is widely used by various of the Antiochean and Syriac Fathers in the fourth century—for example, it is used liberally by Ephrem of Syria.[9] The dating of the Peshitta in any case does not impinge on the dating of the Muratorian Canon because there is no textual connection between the two, but this can be said—the Peshitta probably does provide pre-fourth-century evidence for some sort of closed canon of NT Scriptures in the Syrian church.

An excellent example of assuming what one has to prove comes early in Hahneman's study, where he argues that because the original of the Muratorian Canon was probably in Greek, *its provenance is likely to be from the eastern part of the empire because Greek ceased to be used in the West sometime during the second century.*[10] This is a truly amazing non sequitur—he first assumes that the Muratorian list must be from the fourth century, and then he argues that fourth-century conditions in regard to Greek must apply to this document. If, however, the Muratorian Canon dates to the end of the second century, then it is perfectly plausible that it may have come to us from the western end of the empire, including from Rome. Hahneman also did not pause to demonstrate that Greek was not used in the West in the third and fourth centuries, at least in some contexts. But a minute's reflection will show that this assumption is problematic, especially if we are talking about Christian documents copied by scribes. Tutors and scribes in the West continued to teach and use Greek well beyond the second century,[11] even though Latin was the official language of the empire. If the Muratorian Fragment was originally composed by a scribe, it could have been composed at any time during the three centuries of church history that followed the NT era, and almost anywhere.

ARGUMENTS FROM WHAT'S INCLUDED
AND WHAT'S MISSING

Hahneman spends some time pondering why James, Hebrews, and 1 Peter are missing from the Muratorian Canon, while Revelation is included. He seems to think this favors the notion of an eastern provenance for the document rather than a western one. Again, we are dealing with the author's *assuming* what he needs to *show*, because the vast majority of scholars before Hahneman believed the Muratorian list came from the end of the second century. He argues that the eastern provenance is more likely because of these exclusions and inclusions, *based on how these documents were viewed in the church of the fourth century*. But then he is forced to admit that the Muratorian Fragment is a mutilated manuscript and that that other nineteenth-century Durham denizen (other than Lightfoot) B. F. Westcott long ago had pointed out that the full form of this document may well have included these books in the list. We have only part of the Muratorian list, not the whole list, and, more to the point, *absence of evidence does not provide one with a warrant to assume evidence of absence*. But, furthermore, if the Muratorian Fragment does date to well before the fourth century, there is no reason why it could not have come from the West as well as the East, because various Catholic epistles and Revelation were still being debated in that era; Eusebius in the fourth century says some from various parts of the empire were still debating these books.

Though I do not put a lot of weight on this sort of evidence, the fact that the Muratorian Fragment lists second-century heretics and *not* later ones is consistent with a second-century provenance of this document. My point is that there are not any tell-tale signs of anachronism in what is said in this document about such matters, signs that might tip us off that it actually comes from a later century although it openly presents itself as a second-century document.

HAHNEMAN ON HERMAS

The *Shepherd of Hermas* was certainly a very popular early Christian document, and most scholars are convinced it comes from the first half of the second century, although a few have dated it to the end of the first century. Hahneman expends no little ink on his discussion of the reference to Hermas in this document, because in his view the heart of the case for a second-century date for the Muratorian Fragment is based on the analysis of what is said about Hermas. It will be useful at this point to provide a translation of the relevant lines of the Muratorian Fragment, beginning with line 73: "But Hermas wrote the *Shepherd* quite recently, in our times, in the city of Rome (*urbs Roma*) while Pius, his brother, was occupying the chair of the church of the city of Rome. And therefore it ought indeed to be read, but it cannot be read publicly to the people in church either as among the prophets whose number is complete or among the apostles, for it is after [their] time."

This very interesting discussion of Hermas comes toward the end of the Fragment and after the listing of the NT books, which remarkably concludes with the listing of the Wisdom of Solomon and both the Apocalypse of John and of Peter! Now what is immediately noticeable is that this author has no hesitation in endorsing the Wisdom of Solomon or these two apocalypses for reading in church, but *not* Hermas. The quotation also makes clear that what is decisive for this author in regard to Christian books to be read in worship at least is that they be apostolic in character. Now one has to ask, when it comes to reading them in church, do these last accepted and unaccepted books favor a fourth-century date, when we do indeed have fourth-century canon lists—*none of which include Revelation of Peter but at least one of which (Rufinus' list) includes Hermas* as an apostolic work—or would an earlier date be more plausible, *before* there were more definitive lists in the East and the West? One can argue both ways, but on the whole these anomalies compared to various fourth-century lists suggest an earlier date.

Let us consider in some detail Hahneman's arguments about Hermas itself. Hahneman in chapter 2 attempts to argue that the *Shepherd of Hermas* could not date from as late as the middle of the second century but must come from at least thirty years prior. Few if any scholars would date Hermas later than the middle of the second century in any case, because there is papyri evidence to support a second-century date, but the issue is, is there internal evidence to suggest it comes from as early as 110 or even earlier, and thus well before the reign of Bishop Pius?

There *is* internal evidence in the *Shepherd* that Hermas seems to have lost his job (20.2) at some point due to some persecution of Christians. One suggestion of Hahneman is that this happened under Domitian in the 90s. One of the major problems with this suggestion is that Hermas seems to know the book of Revelation and, in addition, disagrees with its eschatology, just as he disagrees with the strong language in Hebrews about no second chances 'if one commits apostasy. Also, he seems to know Clement, who wrote in Rome in the 90s. This likely places him in the second century, not the first, and one must also ask how soon such a document as Revelation written for churches in Asia in the mid- to late 90s reached Rome and received Hermas' attention.

In any case, losing a job or property is not the same as prosecution, much less execution, during a full-scale persecution of Christians.

Consider, for example, what Hebrews 10:32-34 says, referring to loss of property, harassment, mockery, and even imprisonment but falling short of drawing blood. We might expect Hermas to react to his situation more like the author of Revelation if he were enduring the same things at the same time as John and his audiences were in Asia.

A second and better option would be that Hermas lost his job during the crackdown under Trajan (see Pliny *Ep.* 96–97, which dates to A.D. 112) or Hadrian. Trajan reigned as emperor 98–117 and Hadrian, his adopted son, reigned 117–138 and continued his policies. Furthermore, there was severe persecution of Jews during this time. One can mention the Bar Kokhba defeat in A.D. 135. In Roman eyes, the Christian cult was still closely associated with Judaism and the Jewish people, who suffered in the aftermath of what was a third Jewish revolt (i.e., 66–70, 115–117, and finally 132–135).

Hermas may well reflect a time around 140 just after another round of persecutions of Jews that may have affected Christians in Rome. How so? Because Christians were still viewed largely as a despised split-off sect of Judaism, and because the emperor had ordered the attack on the Jews in the East, things could not have been good for those in Rome who had associations with Jews or synagogues, for Romans were famously anti-Semitic and all the more so when they were at war with Jews in Israel.

It needs to be stressed that the emperors of the late first and early second centuries all saw Christianity as a *superstitio* and as such subject to harassment, being an illicit and unsanctioned religion. This was the view not only in the provenances but also in Rome itself of most Romans.

It is important to add that Hermas refers to this loss of job as something in the past, perhaps considerably in the past, as he also refers to events that happened to him thereafter. There is then no reason, based on the reference to persecution, why the *Shepherd* could not have been written close to A.D. 140, and the differences in Hermas from the eschatological and ecclesiological views expressed in earlier Christian literature written in the 90s suggest a later date for this work.

Hahneman then offers the argument that Hermas, apparently an ex-slave, could not have been the brother of Pius, a bishop. This is nonsense. Bishop Onesimus himself had been a former slave, as had various other Christian leaders in the early part of the Christian era. Hermas may in any case not be the author's given name but simply a nickname, such as slaves acquired. What is said about Hermas in the *Shepherd* is that he had been a prosperous businessman as well before the harassment or persecution. Freed men were capable of having considerable wealth, prominence, and importance in Roman society, and there is no reason why he could not have a brother who became a bishop of an "illicit" religion! While the name *Pius*, a Latin name, could be the brother's given name, it could also be a name taken when he converted or assumed the episcopacy, an especially appropriate name to indicate his new faith. And this brings us to what we know about Bishop Pius himself, a real bishop in Rome in the second century.

Bishop Pius and his episcopacy date to the middle of the second century, around 140–155, so it is perfectly possible for a writer at or near the end of the second century who knew this man and his brother to have written in the fashion he does in the Muratorian Fragment. He uses the term *nuperrime*, which in Latin means "recently" or, if it is used in its superlative sense, "quite recently." Apparently the point of the use of term, however, is not so much to date Hermas close to the time of the author, but rather to make clear that the book was written closer to the time of the author than to the time of the apostolic age, *because the author is contrasting the status of Hermas with the status of earlier apostolic documents, not with his own situation and status.*

Hahneman objects to the use of the phrase *urbs Roma* in line 76 of the fragment, suggesting that proper Latin would have read *hic in urbe Roma*. Again, what he is objecting to is translation Latin and not very good translation Latin at that; but purely from a grammatical point of view, *urbs Roma* is perfectly acceptable Latin. More importantly, it does refer to the eternal city of Rome, and here we have a clue to provenance.

Even if the bare reference to *urbs* in line 38 (which alludes to Paul's going to Rome on the way to Spain) is not relevant to deciding the issue of provenance of the Muratorian Fragment, the *only document* that has a clear provenance in this whole list is Hermas' document! What is said about it is that it was written "very recently in our time in Rome." The phrase "very recently" suggests at a minimum that the author lives in the same century as the one that produced Hermas, and he is cognizant that he and the author of Hermas live in a time *after* the apostolic age. One must ask why the city of Rome is mentioned no less than three times in the Muratorian Fragment when *no other cities are mentioned in this way at all in this Fragment*. Especially extraneous to a list of this sort, if the provenance of this document is not Rome, is the reference to Bishop Pius, who held the episcopal chair in Rome at the time when Hermas was written. In short, the repeated references to Rome cry out for an explanation. The most obvious one is that they tip us off to the document's provenance. It was written in Rome after the time of Bishop Pius.

Hahneman further makes the argument that because Hermas is not placed in the category of apostolic documents, this reflects the later view of Hermas in subsequent centuries and not the view in the second century. In regard to the first half of the second century, we have no evidence of reactions to the book. Later, Irenaeus and Clement of Alexandria approve of the book, and it is possible Irenaeus even sees it as Scripture, but Tertullian clearly enough rejects the book.

It is insufficient to say of Tertullian, as Hahneman does, that Tertullian rejects it simply because he has joined a sect, for Tertullian says it was rejected in his day *"by 'every' synod even of the non-Montanists!"* (Pud.). Now even allowing for a certain amount of rhetorical hyperbole, it is unlikely that Tertullian is simply telling a lie here about considerable rejection of the document even by non-Montanists. This means that there was a divided view of Hermas at the turn of the third century or a bit before, in which case the remarks in the Muratorian Fragment are in line with the views of some other important Christians of that era.

The suggestion by Hahneman that the rejection of the apostolicity of Hermas in the Muratorian Fragment reflects knowledge of the tradition of apostolic authorship of the document reflected in Origen and other later writers is simply mirror reading of the Fragment. You assume that because the Fragment says X, the author must be reacting to others claiming Y. Furthermore, the remark about Pius seems innocent of polemics, as does the remark about Hermas. Indeed, association with the bishop would have improved Hermas' honor rating! It is just that the author of the Fragment, whoever he is (Hippolytus, as Lightfoot suggested, is a possibility), does not see Hermas as an apostolic document. That is not a criticism, just honesty. It was not an apostolic document.

The heart of Hahneman's case is his argument about the reference to Hermas and his book in the Muratorian Fragment, but as we have shown, it is a very dubious argument at best and can be countered with even better arguments for a second-century western provenance for the Muratorian Fragment. There is no good reason why the reference to Hermas' loss of job could not reflect conditions under Trajan or Hadrian, and thus no good reason why the book could not have been penned about A.D. 140 when Pius assumed the episcopacy.[12]

THE ARGUMENT FROM SILENCE

One of the arguments that is repeated ad infinitum not merely by Hahneman but by later canon scholars, such as McDonald, is that if the Muratorian Fragment is a turn-of-the-third-century document, it is an anomaly or stands alone. This is an argument entirely from silence. It is a way of saying, "we know of no other such lists in the period." The issue is that because we have not yet found a comparable list from the second century, there must not have been any! In other words, once again, *absence of evidence is taken as evidence of absence.* But you cannot logically jump from saying "we know of no other such lists" to

"therefore it is unlikely there were any such lists in the second century."
In any case, someone had to be first, and it might as well have been the
author of the Muratorian Fragment.[13] Furthermore, there was plenty
of incentive to make such a list and check it twice during the latter half
of the second century, and this *historical incentive is hinted at toward
the end of the Muratorian Fragment itself—namely, Marcionites and
Gnostics.*

There was continual influence of the Marcionites beyond the time
of Marcion himself to the end of the second century. And call it what
you will, Marcion did have a very limited list of books he considered
viable as sacred Christian texts. The Gnostics, on the other hand, had
too many sacred books, and more importantly some of them falsely
claimed apostolic authorship. In such a situation, we can not only
explain the natural reaction of Irenaeus at the end of the century to
such non-orthodox thinking, but also explain what would prompt
some orthodox Christian to produce the Muratorian list as well. The
Muratorian list does not reflect concern about heresies that sprang up
after the second century, but it clearly has an axe to grind about those
arising in the second century. And this brings me back to the Peshitta.
It appears likely that the whole Peshitta does not date from much later
than the Muratorian Fragment—that is, from sometime in the third
century. As such, it presents us with a complete Bible of sorts that arose
before the canon lists of the fourth century and before the period of the
great codexes we now have, including the Muratorian Codex.[14]

J. Verheyden, after refuting at length the Hahneman hypothesis and
demonstrating that it is far more likely that the Muratorian list is from
the second century and from the West, concludes as follows:

> The author who composed the Canon Muratori in the West at the end
> of the second or the beginning of the third century probably would never
> have imagined that his work would be mistaken for a fourth-century
> eastern product. After the Fragment was composed, it seems to have been
> largely forgotten for many decades, until it was recovered, translated,
> and employed in the fourth century. After it was copied in the eight cen-
> tury, it was again buried, this time for a thousand years. I am afraid I
> have to conclude that the suggestion of a fourth-century eastern origin
> for the Fragment should be put to rest not for a thousand years, but for
> eternity.[15]

While H. Gamble is likely right to assert that we cannot see Marcion
as the *ultimate* stimulus that produced canon consciousness among
the orthodox,[16] nevertheless, it is clear enough from the late second-
century Christian writers that he provided one of the wake-up calls
that led to a more clearly delineated way of thinking about apostolic

documents. This way of thinking is reflected not only in Irenaeus, but also in Tertullian and Hippolytus, the great figures of the end of the second century. There is no reason why the author of the Muratorian Fragment should not be another example of the same sort of dawning awareness; Lightfoot might after all be right that Hippolytus was the author of the Muratorian list. But we have begun to wander into the part of our discussion that is better reserved for the second half of this chapter—a historical reconstruction of the rise of canon consciousness and the eventual closing of the canon.

CANON CONSCIOUSNESS AND THE FORMATION OF THE NEW TESTAMENT

The canonizing process seems to have begun, in regard to what we call the OT, before the time of Jesus. This is reflected not only in the traditions surrounding the various stages of the translation of the Hebrew texts that became the LXX or Old Greek Scriptures. It is also reflected in the preface to Sirach written around 130 B.C. that counts as Jewish Scriptures the Law, Prophets, and Writings, whatever the latter two categories may contain. Around 130 B.C., Sirach's grandson, upon the translation of Sirach into Greek, wrote in the foreword, "For what is said in Hebrew does not have the same force when translated into another tongue. Not only the present work but even the Law itself, as well as the prophets and the other writings are not a little different when spoken in the original." He seems to know already a threefold division of Tanak. This means at least in some quarters, particularly perhaps in the Diaspora, there was already the beginning of a canon consciousness and a concern about it. We must add to this the coming of Hillel from Babylon to Jerusalem, bringing with him his own version and vision of what the sacred texts were and were not. His collection as well seems to be rather less than may have been the case at Qumran.

The evidence at Qumran needs to be sifted very carefully. We find every OT book, with the (probable) exception of Esther, among the Qumran Scrolls. We also find books that may or may not have had scriptural authority, such as the well-attested books of Jubilees and Enoch, which supported teachings very dear to the men of Qumran (touching law, calendar, antediluvian stories). But were these books "canonical," or were they auxiliary writings treasured because they supplemented and interpreted Genesis and the Law in ways amenable to Qumran beliefs? We find at Qumran other parallel versions of the Pentateuch (e.g., so-called 4QRewritten Pentateuch), but there is no compelling reason to believe these writings were also regarded as Scripture. These writings midrashically elaborated on the Law, as the men of Qumran understood it. Jubilees and Enoch may well have served a similar purpose.[17]

Sociological studies of sectarian groups ranging from ancient ones, such as the Essenes, or the Christian sect or the later Gnostic sect have shown the propensity of such groups *to have their own consciousness of what sacred texts were and to engage in the process of creating their own sacred texts to add to previous ones. This is particularly true of millenarian sects, such as that at Qumran and the Jesus movement.*[18] The degree to which a millenarian sect truly believes it is "the people of God" and that God is now intervening in human history affects the way they think about such things as Scripture and its importance and fulfillment. Particularly the fulfillment mentality presses such a person to define what are true oracles or Words of God, especially when he or she believes that such prophecies and other texts are being fulfilled in his or her founder and his people. This clearly enough describes the mentality of the early Christians who wrote the NT books. They believed they were living in the age of fulfillment and that the end of the eschatological events might be close at hand. This sort of belief changes the way one looks at Scripture and indeed ups the ante when it comes to canon consciousness.

Clearly enough, the most prominent and influential of the subsets of early Judaism was Pharisaism, and we would expect their views on sacred texts to be the predominant one, not only after the fall of the temple but also before, because they and their scribes were so influential in the synagogues, and, as Josephus tells us, even the Sadducees followed the Pharisaic views of how the sacrifices should be done. But the dominant Pharisaic tradition in the time of Jesus was the Hillel/ Gamaliel tradition, which is important because this is the tradition in which Saul of Tarsus and many other Jews were trained in Jerusalem. It was a tradition that valued and used a wide array of ancient Jewish texts but only treated as Scripture a subset of the texts that eventually became fully codified as the First Testament.

Whatever else one can say about Luke 24's reference to the Law, the Prophets, and Psalms, it must be noted that such books as Wisdom of Solomon and Sirach were considered Wisdom literature in their own time and thereafter, not prophetic literature, so it is highly unlikely that such sources would be included under the rubric of "the prophets." And certainly they could not be called "the psalms." My point is this—this Lukan phrase refers to some sort of bounded collection the author and audience are already familiar with. If it goes back to Jesus, which I suspect ultimately it does, it is quite telling. Jesus suggested to his followers that there is a bound collection of scriptures they should study and in which they should find the messianic story about him. And the interesting thing about this is that he mentions all three parts of what came to be called Tanak. Probably, however, the Greek favors the notion that Law and Psalms are being placed under one heading, so this single bit of evidence should not be overpressed. In any case, it is typical of the eschatological mentality that sees *all* the sacred texts as having prophetic potential. Even if we owe the reference in Luke 24 only to Luke himself, it still provides us with evidence of a canon consciousness that had at least begun to think in terms of definite boundaries.

What Jesus says in Luke 24 may be compared to what we find in Josephus' *Apion* 1.37-43, written in the last decade of the first century, which says:

> We *do not have innumerable writings that disagree and contradict, but only 22 books which are truly reliable and contain the account of the whole period* [i.e., of Jewish history]. Of these, the first five books of Moses contain the laws in addition to the tradition of the origin of humanity up to Moses' death. This period encompasses almost 3,000 years. From Moses' death to Artaxerxes, the Persian king after Xerxes, the prophets have recorded the events of their times in thirteen books. The remaining four books contain hymns to God and didactic poems for human life." (emphasis mine)

Here we not only see the threefold division of the OT, but we have a specific number of books mentioned, which again bespeaks a closed or closing canon, according to the thinking of Josephus. Here is where I say that his thinking on such subjects is likely to have been most informed by his connections with the Pharisees and his admiration of them. At 1.42, he stresses that what is in these Scriptures are "the decrees of God." What would have been included in the thirteen books of prophets? This may be debated, and it is also not clear whether he would have considered 1–2 Samuel, 1–2 Kings, 1–2 Chronicles, and Ezra-Nehemiah as single books or not. Were Esther, Ruth, and Daniel included as well, because he is thinking of prophetic books that chronicle history? It is hard to say. What is not hard to say is that he thought there *was* a threefold division and a definite limit to the OT canon. It was a closed rather than an open collection for him, and this was well before the second-century list in Baba Batra. Furthermore, Josephus never claimed to be a theologian or an expert in the Hebrew Scriptures. He must have gotten the notion of a twenty-two-book collection from someone else. My suggestion would be it came from the Pharisees.

The list we find in B. Bat. 14b-15a has traditionally been dated somewhere between A.D. 70–200. This list clearly identifies the twenty-four books that today make up the Hebrew Bible and also presents us with the threefold division of Tanak. McDonald, in his discussion of this list, says the following: "*Baba Batra* is very important to canonical studies since it is the first listing of the twenty-four books that eventually formed the contents and groupings of the HB. That this tradition comes from Babylon fits with Cross' suggestion that Hillel, who came from Babylon, heavily influenced the scope of the biblical canon for Pharisaic Judaism."[19] F. Cross is right to emphasize this point, and in my view it is likely that this tradition dates to sometime early in the second century A.D., but McDonald fails to see its import for the formation of the Christian canon. That Christians did take some of their cues on such matters from the rabbis is clear from the case of Melito of Sardis.

Melito of Sardis in about A.D. 180 (see Eusebius *Hist. eccl.* 4.26.13-14) made a pilgrimage from Asia to the Holy Land to find out which were the books in the Hebrew Bible. He lists them clearly and completely, leaving out only Nehemiah (but that maybe included under the mention of Ezra) and Esther and adding only Wisdom of Solomon. What is interesting about this is that if Nehemiah is included under the heading of Ezra, this list comports very nicely with the list in *B. Bat.* 14b-15a, with the exception of Wisdom of Solomon. That is to say, both in Judaism and in the case of the Christian Bishop Melito, we now have a reflection of a canon identical with the Hebrew Bible we know today, and as things turned out it was accepted both by the rabbis of old (and new) and later by the Protestants, again with the exception of Wisdom of Solomon. This suggests that in the Holy Land and in some Christian quarters, the canonical issues in regard to the OT canon were basically a resolved matter by the late second century A.D. This must be taken quite seriously in view of the fact that such seminal figures as Jerome and Eusebius, who both had much to do with the closing of the canon, spent their most important scholarly time in the fourth century and efforts in the Holy Land itself, in consultation with the rabbis.

Let us say a bit more about the growing Christian movement of the first four centuries of the common era. Where do their ideas of what Scripture is come from? Why do they cite some books and not others? Because all such historical arguments are based on a weighing of probabilities, all such arguments fill in gaps in one way or another, because the evidence is not exhaustive, sadly. Arguments from evidence are necessary, as opposed to arguments from silence. But it is not an argument from silence to say that the threefold division we find in Sirach, perhaps in the NT with Jesus, and on into the second century in *B. Bat.* is consistent with the hypothesis that there was a reasonably clearly defined and mostly bounded concept of what constituted the Scriptures and what did not for some Jews in that period. We have this threefold division in each of these three centuries. It does not crop up for the first time in the second century and well after A.D. 70.

Therefore, it is not adequate simply to say we do not know what was in those groupings. Actually we probably do know what was there for the most part. We simply catalog what was cited or used as scriptural authority. And lo and behold, in the NT, with one possible exception, there is no evidence of the "citation" of any extracanonical literature as Scripture (by which, I mean no quoting of such texts and no use of such formulae as "Scripture says," "God says," or "it is written"). This is truly remarkable—I would say astounding if the OT canon were wide open for debate—and many things were in doubt, and many extra books were in play, at least for the early Christian movement. In other words, the first-century evidence from the NT itself, which is the Christian starting point, reflects far less diversity than the next two centuries and far less diversity than found at Qumran. Why is this?

One suggestion is because all the writers of the NT were Jews, with the possible exceptions of Luke (whose knowledge of the LXX suggests he was at least a God-fearer) and the author of 2 Peter. I would suggest that there was a legacy from Jesus and also from Paul in regard to what counted as sacred text—perhaps not an approved or exhaustive reading list, but nonetheless a tradition. I suggest the legacy reflects the influence of Hillel/Gamaliel and the Diaspora tradition. One has to explain the lack of diversity in what is used *as Scripture* in the NT, not merely the presence of more speculation later when the church was overwhelmingly Gentile.

At this point, some scholars will object and say, "What about the evidence of Jude verse 14?" I am referring to the much-debated reference to an Enochian text in Jude. Does this not provide clear evidence of at least one early Christian who had a broader canon of Scripture than what eventually made it into the Hebrew Bible? Observe how the quotation of the Enochian text reads: "Enoch, the seventh from Adam, prophesied about them: 'See the Lord is coming. . . .'" This verse does not say it is quoting a sacred *text* but rather a holy prophet who, as the seventh from Adam, spoke a prophetic word. It is the *person*, not some text of 1 Enoch, to whom authority is ascribed and presumed in this verse. For all we know, Jude is quoting some oral tradition he knows. And notice that we do not find the formula "it is written" here, which would refer to a sacred text. But even if he is quoting this line out of a copy of 1 Enoch, this does not mean he sees the whole of 1 Enoch as having some scriptural authority any more than Paul's quoting of Greek poets from time to time does. It simply means that he thinks this bit of prophecy is true, but notice he is careful not to use a scriptural formula to introduce it. In other words, this single exception to the rule that NT writers only quote as Scripture books that were later viewed as part of the Hebrew Canon proves not likely to be an exception to the rule.[20] But what about what we will call NT canon consciousness?

In the first chapter of this study, I pointed out that at least some NT authors, such as Paul, are aware that they are both speaking and writing the Word of God, by which phrase they are referring to their tellings of the story of Jesus.[21] It is, however, one thing to have an awareness of writing God's Word, but canon consciousness is something else. By *canon consciousness*, I mean an awareness not only that what you say is God's Word but that it needs to be written down and put together with other samples of the Word of God, thus forming a sacred corpus, a Scripture, a canon. In a seminal essay by my old mentor, C. K. Barrett reflects on what it was that Luke, the author of Luke–Acts, saw himself as doing with his two-volume work. After ruling out various options, including the view that Acts should be seen as a stand-alone work of apologetics, Barrett suggests the following:

> The author accepts the OT and provides to accompany it an explanatory and interpretive parallel book that we may call, though Luke did not, a NT. It was the only NT Luke's church had, and this was the first church to have one. Throughout the development of the NT canon, NTs (including Marcion's; his gospel and apostle must have made it very difficult for those who wished to beat him at his own game to use any other form, and it was intrinsically right) had the same basic form: gospel and apostle. In his first volume, Luke supplied the teaching and action of Jesus, which provided the foundation on which the whole Christian movement rested, and he was careful to show at the beginning of the book that Jesus was born within Judaism and in fulfillment of prophecy and to underline the same point at the beginning of Jesus' ministry: "Today has this scripture been fulfilled in your ears" (Luke 4:21). His second volume provides the guarantee that what followed was the intended and valid outcome of what had been narrated in the first and also contained specimens of the teaching of the apostles—sufficient to show (to the satisfaction of an author who was not a profound historian) the content of the Gospel and the unity of representative leaders in preaching it. What more did a church such as Luke's need? This was their NT, and, as far as we know, it was the first.[22]

From a historical point of view, it would be hard to exaggerate the significance of these remarks if Barrett is correct. It would mean that not only was there an awareness of writing the Word of God on the part of some NT writers, there was also a canon consciousness, not just about the OT but, in the case of Luke, about the beginnings of a NT as well. This development did not begin after and in reaction to Marcion. It began in the first century A.D., even while some of the eyewitnesses and original apostles were still alive.

Let us turn to the end of the NT era. The discussion of the understanding of inspiration in early Judaism and early Christianity, particularly in eschatological/prophetic/messianic sects, should be broached at this point. What determined whether something should be seen as sacred text was whether it was believed to be an inscripturated form of the Word of God—in this case, the Word of God proclaimed and then written down in the first century. This belief is crucial to understanding why there was so much emphasis on the apostolic source documents, viewing them in a more hallowed light than that in which a second-century figure, such as Bishop Papias or Bishop Ignatius, viewed his own writings. They understood the crucial nature of apostolic and eye-witness testimony[23] long before there were any canon lists at all, so far as we know.

But where do we find the origins of the idea that what the earliest Christians were proclaiming and writing was itself the Word of God and thus suitable to be viewed as Scripture if written down? Remember once more that 1 Thessalonians 2:13 is in perhaps the earliest of all Christian documents and already presents us with evidence that Paul's proclamation of the gospel was considered inspired, indeed considered to be the Word of God by Paul himself, and not merely the opinions of a human being.[24]

In other words, the issue was not just whether Paul had the Spirit, which was true of all early Christians—the issue was whether he was an apostle of Jesus Christ commissioned for proclaiming the living Word of God to various people. Not all Christians were given such a gift or a task, as the gift lists in the Pauline Epistles make clear. Apostles are seen as gifts to the church distinguishable from other inspired figures, such as prophets (see 1 Corinthians 12). First Corinthians 14:36-37 makes clear Paul's own thinking about this sort of matter, for in one and the same breath he affirms he has the Spirit, that he is authorized to give his converts the command of the Lord (which refers to what he is writing at that moment in 1 Corinthians 14), and that he speaks the Word of God, and it did not originate with the Corinthians. In other words, we already see a mentality here that affirms not only that the apostle proclaimed the Word of God orally but that what he wrote as well was "the Lord's command" for that audience, not distinguishing his own teaching from that of Jesus in terms of inspiration or authority. Therefore, we already see in our earliest Christian writer the beginnings not only of Scripture consciousness when it comes to Christian writings of the apostles and their co-workers but a connection between that idea and the apostolic proclamation.

The process of collecting and circulating apostolic documents in groupings had already begun by the end of the NT era if not before, as is evidenced by 2 Peter 3, which most commentators on that document

do think comes from the turn of the era, not much later.[25] Not surprisingly, the earliest NT documents were the first ones to make it into a
circulating collection—Paul's letters. More importantly, we learn from
2 Peter 3:16 that the letters of Paul could be ranked with "the other
Scriptures." Now this implies not only that the author is thinking of a
collection of Paul's letters as a known entity but also that he assumes
the audience will know what "the other Scriptures are" as well. We
are thus dealing with the beginnings of Christian canon consciousness
here, and Paul's letters are already seen, despite their difficulties, as
part of the collection of sacred texts for Christians. One would not
refer to "the other Scriptures" unless one was implying that Paul's letters were considered as that by at least this author and his Christian
audience.[26]

I am among those who agree with G. Stanton and M. Hengel that
the labels "according to Matthew" (et al.) did not become widely used
until there was a grouping of these documents together, no later than
early in the second century.[27] If these documents had been previously
anonymous, which is not clear, they certainly were not by Papias' day,
because he calls them by their canonical names in A.D. 125 or so. It
seems likely that there was already a codex of gospels, perhaps the
canonical four, already early in the second century. We thus have in
play, perhaps as early as A.D. 125, collections of texts, the large majority of which was to become the NT, collections made well before the
end of the second century.

How were these texts viewed? Were they viewed as being like the
writings of Ignatius or Justin Martyr or Papias? There is absolutely no
evidence they were. Those three writers all cite the earlier apostolic
documents in ways that distinguish their own efforts from them, even
when *they see their own writings as in some sense inspired*, as Ignatius
seems to have done. Why? Because although there may not have been
what could be called a full canon consciousness on their parts, there
was a strong apostolic writings consciousness as the source documents
of the movement. This is already evident in the 90s, in the way Clement
of Rome treats Paul's letters.

Thus when we get to the Muratorian Fragment and Irenaeus at the
end of the second century, they should not be seen as anomalies out of
due season prior to the fourth century. They are rather reflecting this
earlier apostolic tradition and even canon consciousness, if I can put it
that way. The argument that the Muratorian list is anachronistic in the
second century is questionable at best, especially when *this list does not
match up with later canon lists*. Were it a later list, we might expect
it to be more like one or another of the fourth-century lists surely,
and perhaps we have shortchanged the impetus Marcion provided in
the direction of composing such a list. Clearly, Irenaeus is reacting to

Marcion and the Gnostics. There is no reason why the composer of that Muratorian list might not have done so as well.

By the end of the second century, the church was not only overwhelmingly Gentile, but it had largely begun to adopt the LXX as its OT Bible, for better or for worse. As the Gnostic movement was to show, there was a growing anti-Semitism in early Christianity and in its fringe or split-off sects, witnessed both by Marcion and the Gnostic literature. This brings us to the so-called canon debate about the Catholic epistles and Revelation. The real problem with such documents as Jude or James is that they were far too Jewish and too unlike the favored Pauline collection. The same was especially the case with Revelation. Eusebius can hardly contain his animus against the "chilasts" and Judaizers within Christianity. The same is sadly true of other church fathers. Second Peter comes under the same rubric, because it cites so much of Jude. And even Hebrews is suspected by some not merely because it is anonymous, but because it is too Jewish. Probably 2–3 John, especially if bundled with some of these other documents, raised problems for the same reason.

If we ask the question of why it was so difficult to see these documents as genuine and apostolic in the third and fourth centuries (and even beyond), the answer is not hard to figure out. They are too unlike the more Gentile documents. They thus had an uphill climb into the hearts of many Christians in those centuries. In other words, it is not hard to figure out why the church of postapostolic times took so long to figure out what was already known by some in the first century—the general apostolic limits of their sacred texts. The truth is the church had a different character and mentality, a largely non-Jewish one, by the end of the second century. This is why the recognition of some of the apostolic documents took so long in various quarters in the church.

We do not need here to retell the tale of Athanasius and his Festal Letter mentioning just twenty-seven NT books, the concurrence of Pope Innocent with that limitation, or the Africa councils of the late fourth century, nor do we need to rehearse the canon lists themselves. What we need to note is that from at least three very different segments of the church, the word went out that there were definite boundaries not only to the OT but to the NT at that point in time. That the lists composed are not identical is not surprising, because the church was not united. What is remarkable is that both in the East and in the West, there was an ecclesiastical voice that said the NT had these twenty-seven books and not others.

What all such lists were saying is that the canon was closed, even if different segments of the church had lists with slightly different contents for the closed canon of the Bible as a whole. In all of this, it was not a matter of the church's defining but rather of the church's recognizing what were and were not the apostolic books. This process of recognition inherently ruled out gnostic and other later books, even books written by orthodox postapostolic Christian figures.

In my judgment, it is a mistake to take the great codexes and their contents as canon lists. Nowhere in those documents is there a preface or addendum that says, "these are our Christian Scriptures." What we may assume is that these books present in the great codexes were all viewed as important and valuable Christian texts, and thus where there was room in the codex, more might be included than just the apostolic ones. The codexes might even go backward and include favorite earlier works, such as Wisdom of Solomon. These were approved books for Christian study. We do not know that such codexes were taken out of the scriptorium and used as pulpit Bibles, so to speak.

What closed the canon was not the church but rather the dying of the apostolic and eyewitness figures whose pens were laid down once and for all, and this happened in the first century. It took a growing and increasingly Gentile church an additional three centuries to recognize fully the importance of what had happened in the first century, not just in terms of the *regula fidei*, but also the *regula canona*. The issue was not merely whether a writer had the Spirit. The church continued to have the Spirit. This was not the sole or whole basis for what was to be considered Scripture. What was also required was proximity to the Christ event and its first eyewitnesses and apostles. What was required was being part of the earliest and most ancient apostolic circles of Peter, Paul, James, and others.[28]

Even secondary figures, such as Luke or Mark, who had direct contact with and had learned from the apostles and eyewitnesses were able to write these new Christian source documents, something later generations, not privy to interviewing or being eyewitnesses, could not do. Luke 1:1-4 makes quite clear what the mentality was, particularly of those in the wider apostolic circle. The eyewitnesses and original preachers of the Word had to be sought out and consulted. If earlier accounts had been written, they had to be consulted by the likes of Luke. Papias reflects this whole attitude very clearly. He wanted to hear what the apostles had said, at least from those of the second and third generation who had met and heard them. The apostolic testimony was all important, and in the end its pedigree would be the decisive issue. Why?

Christianity, like early Judaism, was a historical religion, and in historical matters antiquity, eyewitness testimony, and authoritative original witnesses were crucial.[29] Even in Paul's day, this was understood. He tells us, writing in about A.D. 52, that he passed on to his Corinthian converts what he had already received of the gospel story of the passion, burial, and resurrection, which had happened "according to the Scriptures" (1 Cor 15:1-4)—not according to one or another text of Scripture or one or another prophetic scroll. The Scriptures were all seen as testifying to Jesus. Paul had received this testimony as a sacred trust and tradition handed on to him probably, as Galatians 1–2 suggests, from Peter himself, who helped him get the *historia* straight. Early Jews handled their sacred traditions with care and reverence. Paul was no different in handing on the gospel tradition.

M. Mitchell, in a seminal essay on the "Emergence of the Written Record," says,

> The earliest gospel message had texts in it as central to it—in this case the holy scriptures of Israel. The first followers of Jesus of Nazareth had turned to their 'scriptures,' the sacred texts of Judaism in the Hebrew and Greek languages, and sought to explain the Jesus whom they had come to know by what they found there. Paul could only have confidently summarized the message that these things were 'according to the scriptures' if he was certain his audience was already familiar with the key supporting texts.[30]

Just so, and this implies there was an enormous reason for the earliest Christians to have in hand and be sure about what their sacred texts were and what they contained. They after all had to demonstrate some remarkable things from Scripture, including the idea of a crucified messiah, which would have seemed sheer folly to early Jews not expecting such.

I am thus understandably dubious that there was not considerable clarity about the general boundaries of the sacred Scriptures of Israel for early Christians like Paul. If even such texts as Job, Malachi, Ezekiel, Zechariah, Jeremiah, Isaiah, and Daniel could be seen as crucial sources for explaining the Christ event, then it is clear that the corpus of sacred texts was viewed as much more than the Torah alone or even the Torah plus the former prophets and the later preexilic ones. And most remarkably, neither those who relied on the Hebrew text nor those who relied on the Greek text cite as Scripture anything that does not eventually end up in the Hebrew Canon—not once. This speaks volumes, and it needs to be taken into account by those who want to see the earliest period of the canonizing process as nothing but flux and great uncertainty.

What did the author of 2 Timothy 3:16 mean when he says, "every passage of Scripture (or all Scripture) is God-breathed and profitable"? Notice the use of the singular for Scripture. It reflects an assumption of a bound collection that has plenary inspiration. Yes, there was already in the NT era a reasonably clear sense on the part of some Christians of what counted as the OT Scriptures and what did not.

So, once more with feeling, let me reiterate: The canonizing process not only began before the first century for the OT and in the first century for the NT (as witnessed by Luke and 2 Peter 3), but its limits were de facto defined by the nature of the historical reality of early Christianity in the first century, with its reliance on the apostolic and eyewitness testimony to provide it with its sacred tradition.

Canon consciousness is not the same as apostolic consciousness or awareness of writing Scripture. Canon consciousness, when it comes to the NT as a full collection, is something that was a matter of the later recognition by the church of final limitations or hard boundaries of the whole collection. It is possible, and many would say probable, that some of the writers of the NT may well have been unaware they were writing "canonical" documents, documents meant for a specific collection, but to judge from the case of our earliest Christian writer, Paul, they *were* aware that they were speaking "the Word of God" when they spoke the gospel and not merely the words of human beings, as that very early document 1 Thessalonians already tells us (1 Thess 2:11-12). They were aware of speaking inspired speech, and the written residue of such speech was likewise seen as inspired, authoritative, important, and true. In the case of Luke, he was also aware that a "new testament" would include some combination of gospel plus apostle— the stories and teachings of Jesus and of his immediate apostolic followers and successors. There was no reality or cognizance of a full NT in the NT era as a collection. Such a full collection would come at a later time. For the very earliest Christians, there was the OT (see 2 Tim 3:16) and the apostolic tradition. As things turned out with regard to the NT books, apostolic documents were all that were to end up in the Christian canon as well, three hundred years later.[31]

The recognition and final definition of the canon took centuries. It is thus all the more remarkable that only apostolic books and not those of the worthies of later centuries were included in the NT canon. In the end, even the highly Gentile fourth-century church did not want to break faith with their Jewish Christian apostolic forebears, and so both *regula fidei* and *regula canona* were grounded in the earliest, apostolic testimonies, which became the NT. Canon lists are only the after-the-fact residue of this affirmation of faith in the original apostolic witness. They should not be the main focus or *bête noir* of canonical criticism or canon studies today.

12

Signposts along the Way

On Taking the Less-Traveled Path

. . . Two roads diverged in a wood, and I—
I took the one less traveled by,
And that has made all the difference.

—Robert Frost "The Road Not Taken" (1915)[1]

In the powerful movie *Gone Baby Gone*, the narrator begins to tell the listening audience that sometimes people feel that the choices they do not make are what most determine who they are—where they were born, which family they were born into, their house and neighborhood and neighbors where they were born. There is some truth in the assertion that much of human identity is formed by forces and factors beyond the individual's control. We have talked a bit about this view of reality in a couple of places in this study and have gone on to say that actually what transforms and transfigures those factors may define a person even more. And then, as Robert Frost's poem suggests, there is also the element of human choice, not to be underestimated, although too often in our culture it is overestimated.

Nearly twenty years ago, I began to have conversations with Duane Watson and other friends about rhetoric and the ancient social world. I remember Watson's telling me about his experience at Duke when he submitted his doctoral work on the rhetoric of Jude and 2 Peter, based on his careful rhetorical study of these documents under the guidance of George Kennedy, then at the University of North Carolina. Father Roland Murphy was stunned by the thesis, because it used such a different methodology to study the NT text, one he himself had not used and perhaps had not considered using, so he had trouble knowing what to make of this thesis.

Was the New Testament really written according to the dictates of Greco-Roman rhetoric? Could it really be studied and interpreted in that way? My study of the Greek and Latin classics, going all the way back to the eighth grade when I began Latin, told me that not only could the Greek NT be read this way—it should! Not to the exclusion of numerous other valid methodologies, but this method showed great promise because, as I said in the opening chapter of this book, the world in which the NT was written was a rhetorically saturated environment and an oral culture, beyond cavil. One of the things I have tried to show, especially in the chapter on Romans 7, is that *it is necessary to study the NT in light of Greco-Roman rhetoric, because numerous NT writers, all literate persons, were also rhetorically skilled persons. They wrote knowing and using rhetorical conventions.*

This should hardly surprise us because early Christianity was a movement of preachers, teachers, evangelists, and missionaries, and they sought to persuade all imaginable sorts of persons about the importance of Jesus Christ. To accomplish this end, they not only used the language that was the lingua franca of the empire—Greek—but they used the modes of communication in that language that were considered to be the most effective arts of persuasion. Never again should it be optional whether we study the NT, especially its so-called epistolary literature, and Acts in the light of ancient rhetoric. Such studies provide us with insights into the meaning of ancient texts that we could not get in any other fashion. Adam's tale in Romans 7:7-25 has been treated in all sorts of bad, misleading, and inappropriate ways due to the neglect of the rhetorical signals. The ever-burgeoning literature on the rhetoric of the NT cries out for such mishandling to stop.

I honestly did not know what I was getting myself into when I began to write socio-rhetorical commentaries in the very early 1990s. Now, looking back on the process that led to socio-rhetorical commentaries on every book of the NT, with the exception of two of the Gospels, I can only say that the road less traveled certainly led to some wonderful and fruitful and beautiful and interesting places. It led to a revamping of my view of the NT and its literature as well as a reenvisioning of the nature of early Christianity. What are some of the main things that I have learned from such studies?

First, I have learned not to underestimate the rhetorical skill and finesse of most of the NT writers. And once that skill is properly recognized and assessed, it changes the way one views the leadership of early Christianity. Although it might be romantic to think of early Christianity as being led by a group of humble peasants, illiterate fishermen, or bucolic farmers, this view I think must be abandoned altogether. I do not doubt that there were many persons from the lower social orders of society involved in the rise of early Christianity. They, however, did not write, nor did they cause to have written, the NT literature. As Edwin Judge said to me and many others a long time ago, early Christianity was led by a socially pretentious group of persons who were not only literate, they were rhetorically skilled, which made evangelism all the more possible and effective in a rhetorically saturated milieu. Rhetoric in the NT in itself implies much about the social level of the leaders of early Christianity. It implies much about the great desire to persuade the Roman world about Jesus.

Second, I have learned that atomizing the NT text into "McNuggets" is not the best way to get at the meaning and significance of these texts. Unfortunately, modern ways of preaching and teaching the Bible have furthered this atomizing process, and we need look no further than some of the truly bad word-study sermons we have heard, where it is assumed that one can simply connect some or all the texts that use the same word. Often such homileticians are oblivious to the fact that the word in question has differing nuances in differing contexts, not least because the semantic range of many words, such as key terms *eidolothuton* or *porneia*, is broad, and only the immediate context provides clues as to what particular meaning is being conveyed in a particular text. More to the point, not just the immediate literary context but the social world and social context conjured up by the NT text must provide clues and guidance as to what the meaning of the term is in this or that text. Unless one understands that the Apostolic Decree in Acts 15 is more a banning of going to a particular social and religious venue rather than an attempt to enforce a particular menu on Gentiles, one will not get the point of the Decree. The nexus of social world and religious text is tight in an oral and rhetorical culture. One cannot simply study the NT as literary artifacts without realizing that they are socio-historical artifacts as well, and if one wants to get at the intended meaning of the texts, due attention must be given to the social world in which they were created and the social context for which they were created.

A good illustration of how social world and literary or even rhetorical studies of the NT are intertwined was impressed upon me last summer when I climbed Mount Nimrud in eastern Turkey. Here were the great monoliths of King Antiochus, the king of the Commagenes, and for his own benefit he had erected an enormous stele full of Asiatic epideictic rhetoric, lauding the king himself. As it turns out, the Greek and rhetoric on the Nimrud-Dag stele is closer in style and substance to the rhetoric we find in 2 Peter and also in bits of Ephesians than either Ephesians or 2 Peter is to the rest of the NT.

Without the work of the archaeologists, we would not have the philological and rhetorical data to do the meaningful comparison of inscriptions with the inscribed texts we have in the NT. Lexicons are mute testimonies to the enormous work of recovering ancient data— texts, inscriptions, and the like. Our grasp of NT Greek depends in considerable measure on our grasp of the Greek of the larger culture in that era. The same can be said of the rhetoric of the NT. It is a mistake to study the NT as if all we have are texts, and in particular these texts. This is not only myopic, it is simply untrue. The reason for a socio-rhetorical approach that takes history and archaeology seriously is because many different kinds of data can better inform us about the nature and meaning of texts in an ancient oral culture. We need all the help we can get.

I have also learned that social readings of NT texts provide us with a necessary corrective to overly spiritualized readings of such texts. A good example of this was my examination of Galatians 3:28. This is not merely a nice little saying about how God regards all as equal. It is rather a social manifesto, for Paul was working against the flow of the culture when it came to Jew-Gentile relationships and prejudices, the treatment of slaves, and the religious roles of women. Such texts need to be judged not merely on the basis of their position but also their direction, their trajectory. If it was not required for women to marry and have children, then all sorts of possible roles could be open to them "in Christ." Paul had to deal with a de facto patriarchal culture and the reality of an economy largely dependant on slave labor. He had to deal with anti-Semitism and Jewish suspicions about Gentiles. In such a world, what is remarkable is how much Paul sought to deconstruct the dominant paradigm and reconstruct a more Christian one in his house churches.

Then, too, a study of ancient social history confirms that the cultures of the NT era were indeed oral cultures, and the Jewish ones especially were cultures of sacred stories, sacred traditions, and sacred texts. The careful social historian will recognize that modern anachronistic models of how the early Christian documents were formed will not help much when he or she is investigating either the bridge between Jesus and the written Gospels or the rise of canon consciousness among the earliest Christians. An oral history approach, grounded in the actual clues in the NT, in Papias, and in our knowledge of how sacred Jewish traditions were likely to be learned and passed on in the NT era, provides us with a strong reason for seeing the main bridge between Jesus and the Gospels not as anonymous communities but named and known eyewitnesses and apostles. It is not an accident that in our latest NT book, 2 Peter, we also find that canon consciousness, now being applied to Christian documents, thinks in terms of collections of sacred Christian texts *attributed to named apostolic writers, such as Paul.* Having been led astray by R. Bultmann and his successors, we may hope to be led back on the right track by S. Byrskog and R. Bauckham when we think of the social phenomena of oral history and the rise of canon consciousness.

Once one understands the workings of an oral culture, one realizes that texts are mostly surrogates for oral communication that could not be made in person, and this is especially the case with texts written at a distance from their intended audiences, which were to be taken to those audiences and "delivered" orally, not merely handed over. In such an environment, documents with epistolary frameworks are mainly speeches waiting to be delivered, sermons waiting to be proclaimed, discourses waiting to persuade. They are not texts in the modern sense at all, meant for silent reading and private consumption.

The orality of the world of the Bible was emphasized at some length in the discussion of scribal culture, aided and abetted by the recent seminal work of K. van der Toorn. His thesis about scribes' playing a crucial role in the formation of the Hebrew Bible has much to commend it and stands against recent "open canon" theories that I discussed at some length in the penultimate chapter in this book.

All the studies in this volume can indeed be subsumed under the heading of socio-rhetorical studies, some focusing more on the first part of the term and some more on the latter part of the term, but all are informed by the perspective that oral cultures and their texts must be viewed differently than we view texts in our postmodern Internet age. If this volume has provided a little further impetus to reexamine our paradigms for NT studies using socio-rhetorical methods, I am content. After all, ancient crafts, like NT studies, cannot be steered in a new direction on a moment's notice. It requires gradual changing of course, recognizing where the shoals and the rocks of the past have led to shipwreck or to smooth sailing. Having been on the journey for a while now, I can say that it is well worth the trip. Here is the reader's invitation to join me on the voyage.

Notes

INVITATION TO THE DANCE

1   There is a powerful and useful critique of those who bandy about the phrase
     "intentional fallacy" when scholars bring up an author and text-centered
     approach to meaning by P. Esler in his *New Testament Theology: Communion
     and Community* (Minneapolis: Augsburg Fortress, 2005).

2   James D. G. Dunn, *Christianity in the Making* , vol. 1: *Jesus Remembered*
     (Grand Rapids: Eerdmans, 2003), 114.

3   Here I am echoing and paraphrasing some of the concerns of one of my doc-
     toral students, David Schreiner, which he recently shared with me in an e-mail
     dated December 15, 2007, after one of our doctoral seminars.

4   Here I am following the lead long suggested by E. A. Judge. See his seminal
     essays, now gathered and edited by my old mentor, David M. Scholer, in *Social
     Distinctives of the Christians in the First Century: Pivotal Essays by E. A.
     Judge* (Peabody, Mass.: Hendrickson, 2007).

CHAPTER I

1   Averil Cameron, *Christianity and the Rhetoric of Empire: The Development
     of Christian Discourse* (Berkeley: University of California Press, 1991), 15.

2   On levels of literacy and the creation of ancient texts, see Harry Y. Gamble,
     Books and Readers in the Early Church: A History of Early Christian Texts
     (New Haven: Yale University Press, 1995), 1–41.

3   We know for a fact that John is addressing various churches in Asia Minor (see
     Revelation 2–3), so it is quite impossible to argue that the reference to "the
     reader" (singular) in Revelation 1:3 refers to the audience. It must refer to the
     rhetor or lector who will orally deliver this discourse to the audience of hear-
     ers. I suggest that we must draw the same conclusion about the parenthetical
     remark in Mark 13:14, which in turn means that not even the Gospel of Mark
     should be viewed as a text meant for private reading, much less the first real
     modern "text" or "book." Rather Mark is reminding the lector, who will be
     orally delivering the Gospel in some or several venues near the time when this
     "abomination" would be or was already arising, that he needed to help the

audience understand the nature of what was happening when the temple in Jerusalem was being destroyed. Oral texts often include such reminders for the ones delivering the discourse in question.

4   Cameron, 24–25.

5   Cameron, 20.

6   See Ben Witherington III, *The Living Word of God: Rethinking the Theology of the Bible* (Waco, Tex.: Baylor University Press, 2008).

7   See Kim Haines-Etzen, *Guardians of Letters: Literacy, Power, and the Transmitters of Early Christian Literature* (Oxford: Oxford University Press, 2000).

8   It is interesting that such an important literate figure as Papias of Hierapolis, who lived at the end of the NT era, repeatedly said that he preferred the living voice of the apostle or one who had heard the eyewitnesses to a written document. In this, he simply reflected the normal attitude of ancient peoples, literate or not.

9   A good place to begin reading about this whole subject and its various practitioners is Stanley Porter, ed., *Handbook of Classical Rhetoric in the Hellenistic Period, 330 B.C.–A.D. 400* (Leiden: Brill Academic, 1997), especially the essays by George Kennedy.

10   See, e.g., Vernon Robbins, *Exploring the Texture of Texts: A Guide to Socio-Rhetorical Interpretation* (Harrisburg, Penn.: Trinity International, 1996).

11   See Bruce W. Longenecker, *Rhetoric at the Boundaries: The Art and Theology of New Testament Chain-Link Transitions* (Waco, Tex.: Baylor University Press, 2005).

12   See Ben Witherington III, *Letters and Homilies for Hellenized Christians,* vol. 1: *A Socio-Rhetorical Commentary on Titus, 1–2 Timothy and 1–3 John* (Downers Grove, Ill.: InterVarsity, 2006). See the discussion of the enthymemes in the Pastoral Epistles.

13   See the discussion in Ben Witherington III, *The Letters to Philemon, the Colossians, and the Ephesians: A Socio-Rhetorical Commentary on the Captivity Epistles* (Grand Rapids: Eerdmans, 2007).

14   We will discuss this more in a later chapter; see pages 61–76, below. See also Ben Witherington III and Darlene Hyatt, *Paul's Letter to the Romans: A Socio-Rhetorical Commentary* (Grand Rapids: Eerdmans, 2004).

15   See the more detailed explanation in Ben Witherington III, *1 and 2 Thessalonians: A Socio-Rhetorical Commentary* (Grand Rapids: Eerdmans, 2006).

CHAPTER 2

1   James M. Robinson and Helmut Koester, *Trajectories Through Early Christianity* (Philadelphia: Fortress, 1971), 269. This chapter is a revision and amplification of my previous discussion of this in *Letters and Homilies for Hellenized Christians*, vol. 1.

2   Documents with a false attribution of authorship.

3   See the helpful discussion in David deSilva, *An Introduction to the New Testament: Contexts, Methods & Ministry Formation* (Downers Grove, Ill.: InterVarsity, 2004), 685–89.

4   See the Introduction to 2 Thessalonians, in Witherington, *1 and 2 Thessalonians*, and the Introduction in Witherington, *Letters to Philemon, the Colossians, and the Ephesians*.

5   We shall discuss at some length the relationship between Jude and 2 Peter in volume 2 of this study. At this juncture, one may consult my article "A Petrine Source in 2nd Peter," in *SBL Seminar Papers 1985*, 187–92.

6   See the Introduction to Ben Witherington III, *Matthew*, Smyth & Helwys Bible Commentary (Macon, Ga.: Smyth & Helwys, 2006).

7   One should, however, consider the careful study of E. Randolph Richards, *Paul and First-Century Letter Writing: Secretaries, Composition and Collection* (Downers Grove, Ill.: InterVarsity, 2004).

8   I owe this helpful supplemental point to my friend, Dr. Jan van der Watt.

9   The issue of pseudepigraphy does not arise for the Johannine Epistles, for the very good reason that they are formally anonymous, attributed to one called either the Old Man or the Elder, depending on what one makes of *ho presbuteros* in 2 and 3 John.

10 Sometimes the Epistle to Barnabas is singled out as a pseudepigraphical letter, but this is actually a treatise, not a letter, as pointed out in David Aune, ed., "Barnabas, Letter of," in *The Westminster Dictionary of New Testament & Early Christian Literature & Rhetoric* (Louisville: Westminster John Knox, 2003), 71–73. It is a polemical Christian document from sometime after A.D. 70 and probably as late as the first quarter of the second century.

11 4 Ezra is probably from the late first century A.D., but it would appear that the OT canon was not really closed until about that time, and it could have been included under the third section of that canon—the Writings. See Martin Hengel, *The Septuagint as Christian Scripture: Its Prehistory and the Problem of Its Canon* (Edinburgh: T&T Clark, 2001).

12 R. J. Bauckham, "Pseudo-Apostolic Letters," *JBL* 107, no. 3 (1988): 469–94, here 475.

13 Bauckham, "Pseudo-Apostolic Letters," 475.

14 I. H. Marshall, "The Problem of Non-Apostolic Authorship of the Pastoral Epistles," (paper presented at Tyndale Fellowship Cambridge, England, 1985), 1–6, here 1.

15 David G. Meade, *Pseudonymity and Canon: An Investigation into the Relationship of Authorship and Authority in Jewish and Earliest Christian Tradition* (Grand Rapids: Eerdmans, 1987). This study can profitably be compared and contrasted with Terry L. Wilder, *Pseudonymity, the New Testament, and Deception: An Inquiry into Intention and Reception* (Lanham, Md.: University Press of America, 2004). More bibliography can be found below.

16 See Witherington and Hyatt, *Letter to the Romans*.

17 See Wilder, 3.

18 In a work called *The Dissonance of the Four Generally Received Evangelists*. See Wilder, 4.

19 See, for example, the discussion in Lewis R. Donelson, *Pseudepigraphy and Ethical Argument in the Pastoral Epistles* (Tübingen: J. C. B. Mohr, 1986), 24–55; and deSilva, *Introduction to the New Testament*, 686–87.

20 Here we must reject the attempt to lump together anonymous and pseudonymous documents by K. Aland, "The Problem of Anonymity and Pseudonymity
in Christian Literature of the First Two Centuries," *JTS* n.s. 12 (1961): 39–49.
The former sort of documents does not appear to be part of an attempt to
deceive anyone about their provenance. For a pseudonymous document to be
successful, to be believed, and to have its intended effect of being a word of its
reputed author, it must successfully deceive its intended audience. Otherwise,
it was seen as disreputable or of lesser value, as the older study of F. Torm on
Greco-Roman, Jewish, and Christian literature showed. Torm is helpful and
correct about the psychological dynamics involved. See his *Die Psychologie der
Pseudonymitat im Himblick auf die Literatur des Urchristentums* (Guterloh:
Bertelsmann, 1932). He rightly points out that in antiquity, the defense of "rhetorical impersonation" is never used to justify creating such a document. The
older discussion in Donald Guthrie, *New Testament Introduction* (Downer's
Grove, Ill.: InterVarsity, 1990), 1011–28, is also still helpful.

Equally unconvincing is the argument of Aland that if a person were
speaking in the Spirit, it did not matter who he claimed to be or who others later claimed he was, so long as the voice was from God. There were, no
doubt, oracles of the risen Lord spoken, such as in Revelation through John
of Patmos. But they are presented as exactly that: oracles of the risen Lord
spoken by John, not words of the historical Jesus during his ministry. In other
words, one should not claim that the pneumatic nature of early Christianity
led to a blurring of the concern about who said what and when and then
extend that reasoning to provide a justification or explanation for pseudepigrapha. Even more amazingly improbable is the argument of K. Koch that
Paul in heaven was speaking through his disciples in the pseudepigrapha; see
his "Pseudonymous Writing," in *The Interpreter's Dictionary of the Bible:
An Illustrated Encyclopedia, Supplementary Volume*, ed. K. Crim (Nashville:
Abingdon, 1976), 713.

21 See James D. G. Dunn, *Unity and Diversity in the New Testament* (London:
SCM Press, 1977); and idem, *The Living Word* (London: SCM Press, 1987),
83–84.

22 It should be noted that letters in general are not included in the OT canon at all
as discreet documents, although there are some letters within OT documents,
particularly historical ones, such as 2 Chronicles. All the Jewish pseudepigrapha
that Bauckham discusses as discreet documents are extracanonical, which is
very interesting indeed. See Bauckham, "Pseudo-Apostolic Letters," 478–87.
The Baruch correspondence, the letter of Jeremiah, or the epistle of Enoch do
not really help us much, and we may think that there were good reasons why
such documents were omitted from the OT canon. Bauckham can point to 2
Chronicles 21:12-15 and Daniel 4 as examples of probable pseudepigraphical
letters, but even this can be debated. The truth is, the OT canon provides very
little evidence of relevance and very little precedent for this phenomena being
seen as acceptable as part of some sacred text by early Jews.

23 See E. E. Ellis, "Pseudonymity and Canonicity of New Testament Documents,"
in *Worship, Theology and Ministry in the Early Church: Essays in Honor of
Ralph P. Martin*, eds. M. J. Wilkins and T. Paige (Sheffield: Sheffield Academic,
1992), 212–24.

24 Bauckham, 488.

25 Bauckham, 489.

26 On which, see pp. 143–63, below.

27 At least Seneca lived during the time of Paul and in a city Paul likely visited!

28 See K. K. Hulley, "Principles of Textual Criticism Known to St. Jerome," *Harvard Studies in Classical Philology* 55 (1944): 104–9.

29 Salvian offered in his defense the claim of modesty—that is, he was avoiding pretence or trying to make some honor claim for himself. See B. M. Metzger, "Literary Forgeries and Canonical Pseudepigrapha," *JBL* 91 (1972): 3–24, here 8–9.

30 Cf. Metzger, "Literary Forgeries," 3–24; Wilder, 35–73.

31 Metzger, "Literary Forgeries," 6.

32 See Wilder, 42–44.

33 Metzger, "Literary Forgeries," 12–13. We must give up the myth that ancient persons were not capable of using critical judgment in such matters. This is just a modern prejudice held by too many scholars.

34 Wilder, 42.

35 See his *Die literarische Falschung* (München: Beck, 1971).

36 See Wilder, 45–46.

37 Torm, 19.

38 Donelson, 24, 55.

39 Ellis, 220–23.

40 Ellis, 223–24.

41 C. J. Classen, *Rhetorical Criticism of the New Testament* (Tübingen: Paul Mohr Verlag, 2000), 46.

CHAPTER 3

1 Karel van der Toorn, *Scribal Culture and the Making of the Hebrew Bible* (Cambridge, Mass.: Harvard University Press, 2007), 47–48.

2 See, e.g., Richards, and cf. Jerome Murphy-O'Connor, *Paul the Letter-Writer: His World, His Options, His Skills* (Wilmington, Del.: Michael Glazier Books, 1995).

3 Van der Toorn, 2.

4 Van der Toorn, 2.

5 Van der Toorn, 5.

6 Van der Toorn, 5, states boldly there was no concept of intellectual property in the OT era, but if one thinks some of those books were produced during the Hellenistic era, a certain revision of these ideas would be warranted. For example, what one thinks about Sirach could well be affected.

7 Van der Toorn, 6.

8 Van der Toorn, 9.

9 On which, see pp. 21–32, above.

10 Van der Toorn, 10.

11 Van der Toorn, 10.

12 Van der Toorn, 12.

13 Van der Toorn, 12.
14 Van der Toorn, 14.
15 See Van der Toorn, 15.
16 Van der Toorn, 19.
17 See Gamble, *Books and Readers in the Early Church*.
18 Van der Toorn, 19–20.
19 Van der Toorn, 20.
20 Van der Toorn, 24.
21 Van der Toorn, 31.
22 Van der Toorn, 38.
23 Van der Toorn, 45–46.
24 Van der Toorn, 33.
25 Van der Toorn, 35.
26 Cited in Van der Toorn, 56.
27 Van der Toorn, 56.
28 Van der Toorn, 57.
29 See Van der Toorn, 68.
30 See Van der Toorn, 90.
31 Van der Toorn, 90.
32 Van der Toorn, 100.
33 On these six, see Van der Toorn, 110.
34 Van der Toorn, 126.
35 Van der Toorn, 234.
36 Van der Toorn, 234.
37 Van der Toorn, 241.
38 Van der Toorn, 247.
39 Van der Toorn, 252.
40 See the discussion in van der Toorn, 255–56.
41 Van der Toorn, 263–64.

CHAPTER 4

1 See J. A. Overman, "Homily Form (Christian and Early Hellenistic)," *ABD* 3: 280–82. Some of the material in this chapter is an expansion and attenuation of material found in Ben Witherington III, *Letters and Homilies for Jewish Christians: A Socio-Rhetorical Commentary on Hebrews, James and Jude* (Downers Grove, Ill.: InterVarsity, 2007).
2 On the debate about the existence of synagogues in the first century A.D., see Ben Witherington III, *The Acts of the Apostles: A Socio-Rhetorical Commentary* (Grand Rapids: Eerdmans, 1997), 255–57.
3 R. Riesner, "Synagogues in Jerusalem," in *The Book of Acts in Its Palestinian Setting: Acts in Its First Century Settings*, vol. 4, ed. Richard Bauckham (Grand Rapids: Eerdmans, 1995), 179–210.

4   See L. I. Levine, "The Nature and Origin of the Palestinian Synagogue Reconsidered," *JBL* 115 (1996): 425–48, here 431–32, 439–41.

5   See the discussion of P. H. Davids, "Homily, Ancient," in *Dictionary of New Testament Background*, ed. Craig A. Evans and Stanley E. Porter (Downers Grove, Ill.: InterVarsity, 2000), 515–18, esp. 515–16.

6   It is clear from Saul of Tarsus' zealous activities against Jewish Christians that orthodoxy was of some concern as well—see Galatians 1.

7   F. Wills, "The Form of the Sermon in Hellenistic Judaism and Early Christianity," *HTR* 77 (1984): 75–99.

8   See C. C. Black, "The Rhetorical Form of the Hellenistic Jewish and Early Christian Sermon: A Response to Lawrence Wills," *HTR* 81 (1988): 1–18; and Witherington, *Acts of the Apostles*, 406–7, on Acts 13.

9   On this matter, see Ben Witherington III, *The Paul Quest: The Renewed Search for the Jew of Tarsus* (Downers Grove, Ill.: InterVarsity, 1998), 90–98; and Martin Hengel, *The Pre-Christian Paul* (Valley Forge, Pa.: SCM Press, 1991), 54–60. On the whole issue of Judaism and Hellenism, the classic study is Hengel's *Judaism and Hellenism: Studies in Their Encounter in Palestine During the Early Hellenistic Period*, 2 vols. (Philadelphia: Fortress, 1975), to which one must add the supplement of his *The "Hellenization" of Judaea in the First Century After Christ* (Philadelphia: Trinity International, 1990).

10 See Witherington, *Acts of the Apostles*, 39–51.

11 Larry Hurtado, *Lord Jesus Christ: Devotion to Jesus in Earliest Christianity* (Grand Rapids: Eerdmans, 2003).

12 Cameron, 19–20.

13 Overman, "Homily Form," 281.

14 Cameron, 41.

15 See Witherington, *1 and 2 Thessalonians*.

16 See rightly Donald A. Hagner, *Encountering the Book of Hebrews: An Exposition* (Grand Rapids: Baker Academic, 2002), 29.

17 Daniel J. Harrington, *What Are They Saying About the Letter to the Hebrews?* (New York: Paulist, 2005), 1.

18 H. Thyen, *Der Stil der judisch-hellenistichen Homilie* (Göttingen: Vandenhoeck and Ruprecht, 1955), 106. One should compare the more recent discussion in F. Seigert, *Drei hellenistich-judische Predigten* (Tübingen: Mohr, 1992). On Hebrews as a homily, see J. Swetnam, "On the Literary Genre of the 'Epistle' to the Hebrews," *NovT* 11 (1969): 261–69; J. C. McCullough, "Some Recent Developments in Research on the Epistle to the Hebrews," *IBS* 2 (1980): 141–65.

19 Thomas Long, *Hebrews* (Louisville: Westminster John Knox, 1997), 6.

20 See Ben Witherington III, *Jesus the Sage: The Pilgrimage of Wisdom* (Minneapolis: Augsburg Fortress, 1994).

CHAPTER 5

1   This goes against several of the essayists in Stanley L. Porter, Dennis L. Stamps, and Thomas H. Olbricht, eds., *Rhetorical Criticism and the Bible* (Sheffield:

Sheffield University Press, 2002), who continue to misjudge Paul in this regard, as has rightly also been noticed by M. M. Mitchell in several publications. See, e.g., *The Heavenly Trumpet: John Chrysostom and the Art of Pauline Interpretation* (Louisville: Westminster John Knox, 2002).

2   For an earlier and simplified version of this discussion, see Witherington and Hyatt, *Paul's Letter to the Romans*.

3   "Impersonation" was a rhetorical device used to train those learning to write letters (see Theon 2.1125.22).

4   See W. G. Kümmel, *Romer 7 und das Bild des Menschen im Neuen Testament* (München: Kaiser, 1974).

5   Stanley Stowers, *A Rereading of Romans: Justice, Jews, & Gentiles* (New Haven: Yale University Press, 1994), 264–69.

6   Unfortunately, we have only fragments of Origen's Romans commentary. See the careful discussion by Stowers, 266–67. Origen rightly notes that (1) Jews such as Paul do not speak of a time when they lived before or without the law, and (2) what Paul says elsewhere about himself (cf. 1 Cor 6:19-20; Gal 3:13 and 2:20) does not fit this description of life outside Christ in Romans 7.

7   See Stowers, 268–69.

8   It appears that the better a commentator knew both Greek and rhetoric, the more likely he or she was to read Romans 7 as an example of impersonation.

9   See Witherington and Hyatt, *Paul's Letter to the Romans*, Introduction.

10 See Quintilian, *Inst. Or.* 9.2.30-31: "By this means we display the inner thoughts of our adversaries as though they were talking with themselves . . . or without sacrifice of credibility we may offer conversations between ourselves and others, or of others among themselves, and put words of advice, reproach, complaint, praise or pity into the mouths of appropriate persons."

11 The sensitive analysis by J. N. Aletti, "The Rhetoric of Romans 5–8," in *The Rhetorical Analysis of Scripture: Essays from the 1995 London Conference*, eds. Stanley E. Porter and Thomas H. Olbricht (Sheffield: Sheffield Academic, 1997), 294–308, here 300, deserves to be consulted. He makes clear that Paul is not talking about Christians here.

12 In what follows, I am indebted to T. J. Deidun for pointing me in the right direction. See especially his helpful summary of the data, "Romans," in *A Dictionary of Biblical Interpretation*, eds. R. J. Coggins and J. L. Houlden (Philadelphia: Trinity International, 1990), 601–4. Also helpful is J. Godsey, "The Interpretation of Romans in the History of the Christian Faith," *Interpretation* 34 (1980): 3–16.

13 Philip Melanchthon, *Commentary on Romans*, trans. F. Kramer (St. Louis, Mo.: Concordia, 1992), 156.

14 The discussion by P. W. Meyer, "The Worm at the Core of the Apple: Exegetical Reflections on Romans 7," in *The Conversation Continues: Studies in Paul and John in Honor of J. Louis Martyn*, eds. R. T. Fortna and B. R. Gaventa (Nashville: Abingdon, 1990), 66–69, of Augustine Luther and Melanchthon is helpful.

15 Erasmus, it should be noted, rejected altogether Augustine's view.

16 Deidun, 601.

17 Deidun, 601.

18 Deidun, 602.

19 See the lengthy discussion by Gerd Theissen, *Psychological Aspects of Pauline Theology* (Philadelphia: Fortress, 1987), 177–269.

20 On Adam in Romans, see R. Hammerton-Kelly, "Sacred Violence and Sinful Desire: Paul's Interpretation of Adam's Sin in the Letter to the Romans," in Fortna and Gaventa, *Conversation Continues*, 35–54. See Witherington and Hyatt, *Paul's Letter to the Romans*, 141–53.

21 It is telling that some of the most thorough recent treatments of Romans 7, even from the Reformed tradition, have concluded that Paul cannot be describing the Christian experience here; cf. D. Moo, *Romans* (Grand Rapids: Eerdmans, 1996), 443–50; N. T. Wright, "Romans," in *New Interpreters Bible*, vol. 10, ed. Leander Keck (Nashville: Abingdon, 2002), 551–55 (who changed his mind from his earlier view that Christians were in view in Romans 7:14-25); Brendan Byrne, *Romans* (Collegeville, Minn.: Liturgical, 1996), 216–26; cf. Joseph A. Fitzmyer, *Romans* (New Haven: Yale University Press, 1993), 465–73; Talbert, *Romans*, 185–209. See also Meyer, 62–84; Jan Lambrecht, *The Wretched "I" and Its Liberation: Paul in Romans 7 and 8* (Louvain: Peeters, 1992).

22 See Ben Witherington III, *Paul's Narrative Thought World: The Tapestry of Tragedy and Triumph* (Louisville: Westminster John Knox, 1994), 14–15.

23 It is not surprising that some early Jews saw the commandment given to Adam and Eve as a form of one of the Ten Commandments, specifically the one having to do with coveting. See Witherington, *Paul's Narrative Thought World*, 14.

24 See now the very helpful treatment of Paul's rhetorical use of "I" here by J. N. Aletti, "Romans 7:7-25 encore une fois: enjeux et propositions," *NTS* 48 (2002): 358–76. He is also right that Paul reflects some understanding of both Jewish and Greco-Roman anthropology in this passage.

25 Stowers, 269–70.

26 As even C. E. B. Cranfield, *Romans*, vol. 1 (Edinburgh: T&T Clark, 1975), 337, has to admit, Paul in Romans 7:6 and in 8:8-9 uses the phrase "in the flesh" to denote a condition that for the Christian now belongs to the past. It is thus hopelessly contradictory to say on the one hand, "We no longer have the basic direction of our lives controlled and determined by the flesh" (p. 337), and then turn around and maintain that Romans 7:14-25 describes the normal or even best Christian life, even though 7:14 says, "we are fleshly, sold under sin," which comports only with the description of pre-Christian life in 7:6 and 8:8-9. This contradicts the notion that the believer has been released from the flesh in a moral sense.

27 Ernst Kasemann, *Commentary on Romans* (Grand Rapids: Eerdmans, 1980), 192–212.

28 Peter Gorday, *Principles of Patristic Exegesis: Romans 9–11 in Origen, John Chrysostom, and Augustine* (New York: Edwin Mellen, 1983), 164.

29 Notice that it was a Latin, rather than a Greek, church father who made this identification and only after he felt the strong influence of Manicheanism. It does not appear to me that Augustine was all that aware of rhetorical devices and techniques in the Greek tradition.

30 See the famous essay by Krister Stendahl with this title in *Paul Among Jews and Gentiles and Other Essays* (Philadelphia: Augsburg Fortress, 1977).

31 Note that Paul's frequent expressions of pathos in his letters, including in Romans, have regularly to do with his concern for his converts or his fellow Jews and not with his own personal moral struggles as a Christian. The absence of expressions of guilt about his current conduct, unless Romans 7 is an exception, is noteworthy. Furthermore, Philippians 3:6 strongly indicates that Paul did not have a guilt-laden conscience when he was a non-Christian Jew, either.

32 Some commentators, such as C. K. Barrett, *Romans* (Peabody, Mass.: Hendrickson, 1990), 134–35, attempt a combination interpretation. Barrett avers the text is about Adam and also autobiographically about Paul. The rhetorical conventions suggest otherwise, but Paul is retelling the story of Adam because of its relevance for his audience's understanding of themselves. They are not to go back down the Adamic road.

33 See 4 Ezra 7:11; B. T. San. 56b; and on the identification of Torah with the preexisting Wisdom of God, see Sirach 24:23 and Baruch 3:36–4:1.

34 See Kasemann, 196: "Methodologically the starting point should be that a story is told in verses 9-11 and that the event depicted can refer strictly only to Adam. . . . There is nothing in the passage which does not fit Adam, and everything fits Adam alone."

35 But see Barrett, *Romans*, 134.

36 Barrett, *Romans*, 132, points out the difference between here and Romans 3:20, where Paul uses the term *epignosis* to refer to the recognition of sin. Here, he simply says, "know."

37 See the earlier discussion of this view at some length by S. Lyonnet, "L'histoire du salut selon le ch. 7 de l'epitre aux Romains," *Bib* 43 (1962): 117–51; and the helpful discussion of Neil Elliott, *The Rhetoric of Romans* (Sheffield: Sheffield University Press, 1990), 246–50, who comes to the same Adamic conclusion on the basis of rhetorical considerations.

38 Barrett, *Romans*, 132, puts it vividly: "The law is not simply a reagent by which the presence of sin is detected: it is a catalyst which aids or even initiates the action of sin upon man."

39 See Stowers, 271–72. He suggests the tragic figure of Medea might be conjured up by what Paul says, but surely Adam is a more likely candidate to have come to Paul's mind and those of his audience as well.

40 It simply complicates and confuses the matter to suggest Paul is also talking about Israel as well as Adam here. Paul is addressing a largely Gentile audience that did not identify with Israel but could understand and identify with the progenitor of the whole human race. That Israel might be included in the discussion of those who are "in Adam" in 7:14-25 is certainly possible, but even there Paul has already described earlier in Romans 2 the dilemma of a Gentile caught between the law and a hard place. My point would be that even in verses 14-25, he is not specifically focusing on Jewish experience or the experience of Israel.

41 This has confused those who are unaware of this rhetorical convention and have taken the outburst "Thanks be to God in Jesus Christ" to be a cry only a Christian would make, assuming therefore that Romans 7:14-25 must be

about Christian experience. However, if 7:14-25 is meant to be a narrative of a person in Adam who is led to the end of himself and to the point of conviction and conversion, then this outburst should be taken as Paul's interjected reply or response with the gospel to the heartfelt cry of the lost person, a response that prepares for and signals the coming of the following argument in Romans 8 about life in Christ.

42 Cranfield, 351–52.

43 As we shall see, there is also nothing in Romans 7:14-25 to suggest that his complaint is specifically with Jews. It is sin and death, their effects on humankind, and the law's effect, whether on Gentiles or Jews, that is critiqued. Furthermore, Paul, despite Luther's insistence, is not critiquing here the self-righteousness of Jews or others caught between a rock and a hard place when they know what they ought to do but are unable to do it. Sometimes, in order to hear the text without the baggage of later interpretations, one has to deconstruct the later interpretations first.

44 Barrett, *Romans*, 136: "Sin in its deceitful use of the law and commandment, is revealed not merely in its true colors but in the worst possible light."

45 Kasemann, 200.

46 Gerald Bray, ed., *Romans* (Downers Grove, Ill.: InterVarsity, 1998), 189–90.

47 See Bruce Longenecker, *Rhetoric at the Boundaries* (Waco, Tex.: Baylor University Press, 2005).

48 Longenecker, 88–93, shows in great detail how this works in Romans 7:14-25, and his argument answers every question or possible objection to this view of this passage.

49 Longenecker, 92. On the frequency of use and popularity of this rhetorical device, see 11–42 in this same study.

50 The key essay can be found in Stendahl, *Paul Among Jews and Gentiles*, but it originally was written in 1963 and caused an explosion when it first appeared in print.

CHAPTER 6

1 See pp. 7–17, above.

2 M. M. Mitchell, "Rhetorical Shorthand in Pauline Argumentation: The Function of the Gospel in the Corinthian Correspondence," in *Gospel in Paul: Studies on Corinthians, Galatians and Romans for Richard N. Longenecker*, eds. L. Ann Jervis and Peter Richardson (Sheffield: Sheffield University Press, 1996), 63–88, here 88.

3 One of the clear clues that we are dealing with oral stories that were written down separately and then later combined in a full gospel narrative meant to be delivered orally is the pericope about the woman caught in adultery, which appears not to have made the original cut of what would be included in this gospel narrative, but nonetheless was viewed as a beloved and valid part of the testimony of the Beloved Disciple and so became a text looking for a home, which led to its inclusion in various places in John (including at 7:53–8:11) and even in one Lukan manuscript.

4 On which, see p. 188 above and note 27.

5   On this entire matter, and on the reliability of Papias, see now Richard Bauckham, *Jesus and the Eyewitnesses: The Gospels as Eyewitness Testimony* (Grand Rapids: Eerdmans, 2006).

6   See, e.g., the *ABD* article on Papias.

7   Martin Hengel, *The Johannine Question* (Harrisburg, Penn.: Trinity International, 1990).

8   M. Oberweis, "Das Papias-Zeugnis vom Tode des Johannis Zebedai" *NovT* 38 (1996): 277–95.

9   Andrew T. Lincoln, *The Gospel According to Saint John* (Peabody, Mass.: Hendrickson, 2005), 22.

10   Think for a moment of the highly schematized nature and arrangement of the Gospel such that we have seven sign miracles climaxing in the grandest one, the raising of Lazarus; seven "I am" sayings; and seven discourses linked to the "I am" sayings in one way or another. Clearly, schematization and internal signals by key word or phrase is a major rhetorical trait of this Gospel.

11   It has been asked, when I gave this lecture, would Lazarus not have known about the threat against his life by these very people and would that not have prevented him from going to the high priest's house? This is a reasonable question, but one must realize that Lazarus in the story has just been raised from the dead. What had he to fear from further death threats? He was instead concerned about the danger his beloved friend Jesus was in. Another question asked is, if Lazarus had been ill and then dead, would he have not been unclean and not allowed into the high priest's home? The text of John 18:15 actually only mentions his coming into the courtyard, but, more importantly, Lazarus would have likely gone through the mikveh rituals prescribed by the priest after his raising in order to be considered no longer ritually unclean, and the priests would likely have known of this fact. See, for example, what Jesus says in Mark 1:44: "Go present yourself to the priest, and offer for your cleansing what Moses commanded."

12   Ben Witherington III, *John's Wisdom: A Commentary on the Fourth Gospel* (Louisville: Westminster John Knox, 1995).

Chapter 7

1   On which, see Witherington, *Letters and Homilies for Jewish Christians*.

2   What follows here is an expansion of an earlier study I have done: Ben Witherington, "Not So Idle Thoughts about *Eidolothuton*," *TynBul* 44, no. 2 (1993): 237–54.

3   See, for example, Hans Conzelmann, *1 Corinthians* (Philadelphia: Augsburg Fortress, 1975), 139; Gordon D. Fee, *The First Epistle to the Corinthians* (Grand Rapids: Eerdmans, 1987), 357 n. 1.

4   See Pieter van der Horst, *The Sentences of Pseudo-Phocylides* (Leiden: Brill Academic, 1978), 135–36; and cf. Douglas Young, ed., *Theognis, Ps-Pythagoras, Ps-Phocylides* (Leipzig: Teubner, 1961).

5   Cf. H. Anderson, "4 Maccabees," in *The Old Testament Pseudepigrapha*, vol. 2, ed. James H. Charlesworth (New Haven: Yale University Press, 1985), 533–34.

6   Anderson, 539–41. See now David A. deSilva, *4 Maccabees* (Leiden: Brill, 2006), xlv–xv.

7   See Witherington, *Acts of the Apostles.*

8   On this whole matter of *Corban*, see Ben Witherington III, *Women in the Ministry of Jesus* (Cambridge: Cambridge University Press, 1984), 12–13.

9   But see John Collins' remarks in *Old Testament Pseudepigrapha*, vol. 1, ed. James H. Charlesworth (New York: Doubleday, 1983), 347. The way he divides the text assumes that 2:95 is the close of the previous section, but there is actually no good reason not to connect it to what follows.

10   See W. Burkett, *Greek Religion* (Cambridge, Mass.: Harvard University Press, 1985), 55–60.

11   See R. M. Ogilvie, *The Romans and Their Gods in the Age of Augustus* (New York: Norton, 1969), 44ff.

12   Ogilvie, 49.

13   G. H. R. Horsley, ed., *New Documents Illustrating Early Christianity*, vol. 1 (Grand Rapids: Eerdmans 2001), 5–8.

14   This goes against Wendell Willis, *Idol Meat in Corinth: The Pauline Argument in 1 Corinthians 8 and 10* (Chico: Scholars Press, 1985), 63.

15   While it is true that sometimes *peri de* can be just a topic marker (see Margaret M. Mitchell, *Paul and the Rhetoric of Reconciliation* [Tübingen: Mohr, 1991], 3 and n. 7; and her article "Concerning *PERI DE* in 1 Corinthians," *NovT* 31 [1989]: 229–56), here it surely is introducing a subject the Corinthians raised with Paul in light of what follows where there are further quotes on the subject.

16   For much more discussion on all this, see Ben Witherington III, *Conflict and Community in Corinth: A Socio-Rhetorical Commentary on 1 and 2 Corinthians* (Grand Rapids: Eerdmans, 1995).

17   On meat as a luxury item, see Ramsay MacMullen, *Paganism in the Roman Empire* (New Haven: Yale University Press, 1981), 34–42 and the notes.

18   On the textual issues, see Witherington, *Acts of the Apostles*, 455–68.

19   On which, see Witherington, *Conflict and Community in Corinth*, 186–230.

20   See Ben Witherington III, *Revelation* (Cambridge: Cambridge University Press, 2003), 103–4.

21   See Ben Witherington III, *What Have They Done with Jesus? Beyond Strange Theories and Bad History—Why We Can Trust the Bible* (San Francisco: HarperOne, 2006).

22   See Ben Witherington III, *Grace in Galatia: A Commentary on Paul's Letter to the Galatians* (Grand Rapids: Eerdmans, 1998).

CHAPTER 8

1   It is possible that *porneia* has its root meaning in Acts 15, which would mean it refers to temple prostitutes rather than to sexual dalliances with serving girls.

2   See David Instone-Brewer, *Divorce and Remarriage in the Bible: The Social and Literary Context* (Grand Rapids: Eerdmans, 2002).

3   See Ben Witherington III, *Women in the Earliest Churches* (Cambridge: Cambridge University Press, 1988).

4   A. J. Levine, "Anti-Judaism and the Gospel of Matthew," in *Anti-Judaism and the Gospels*, ed. William R. Farmer (Harrisburg, Penn.: Trinity International, 1999), 9–34, here 21.

5   See Mark A. Chancey, *The Myth of a Gentile Galilee: The Population of Galilee and New Testament Studies* (Cambridge: Cambridge University Press, 2002).

6   See the discussion in Witherington, *Matthew*, 1–34.

7   See Ben Witherington, "Matthew 5:32 and 19:9—Exception or Exceptional Situation?" *NTS* 31 (1985): 571–76.

8   J. A. Fitzmyer, "The Matthean Divorce Texts and Some New Palestinian Evidence," *TS* 37 (1976): 197–226.

9   A. Mahoney, "A New Look at the Divorce Clauses in Mt 5:32 and 19:9," *CBQ* 30 (1968): 33.

10 J. P. Arendzen, "Ante-Nicean Interpretations of the Sayings on Divorce," *JTS* 20 (1918–19): 230–41.

11 See my discussion of ancient vice lists in Witherington, *Grace in Galatia*, 403–6.

12 On this entire discussion, see the immediately preceding chapter, pp. 89–101, above.

CHAPTER 9

1   Krister Stendahl, *The Bible and the Role of Women* (Philadelphia: Fortress, 1966). This is a phrase I heard him use while taking Romans with him at Harvard Divinity School.

2   For a taste of the discussion, see Witherington, *Grace in Galatia*, 270–77.

3   On the former, see the fascinating article by W. A. Meeks, "The Image of the Androgyne: Some Uses of a Symbol in Earliest Christianity," *HR* 13 (1974): 165–208; and on the latter, Dennis R. MacDonald, *There Is No Male and Female: The Fate of a Dominical Saying in Paul and Gnosticism* (Philadelphia: Fortress, 1987).

4   On this subject, see Jouette M. Bassler, *Divine Impartiality: Paul and a Theological Axiom* (Missoula: Scholars Press, 1982).

5   James D. G. Dunn, *The Epistle to the Galatians* (Peabody, Mass.: Hendrickson, 1993), 207.

6   On this whole matter, see Ben Witherington III, *Troubled Waters: Rethinking the Theology of Baptism* (Waco, Tex.: Baylor University Press, 2007).

7   Richard N. Longenecker, *Galatians*, Word Biblical Commentary (Waco, Tex.: Thomas Nelson, 1990), 157.

8   See the detailed discussion in Witherington, "Rite and Rights for Women," *Women in the Ministry of Jesus*, 595–96, and the notes there.

9   See the detailed discussion in Witherington, *Conflict and Community in Corinth*.

10   See Ben Witherington III, *Friendship and Finances in Philippi: The Letter of Paul to the Philippians* (Harrisburg, Penn.: Trinity, 1994).

11   See Witherington, *Letters to Philemon, the Colossians, and the Ephesians.*

12   R. Loewe, *The Position of Women in Judaism* (London: SPCK, 1966), 52–53.

CHAPTER 10

1   For those wanting a fuller version of this essay, Robert Stewart and Broadman and Holman are producing a full-scale response volume to *Jesus Remembered* that will be forthcoming with a longer version of this chapter in it.

2   Dunn, *Christianity in the Making*, vol. 1, 6.

3   Dunn, *Christianity in the Making*, vol. 1, 119.

4   Dunn, *Christianity in the Making*, vol. 1, 121.

5   Dunn, *Christianity in the Making*, vol. 1, 126; emphasis in original.

6   Dunn, *Christianity in the Making*, vol. 1, 133.

7   Dunn, *Christianity in the Making*, vol. 1, 188.

8   Dunn, *Christianity in the Making*, vol. 1, 192.

9   Dunn, *Christianity in the Making*, vol. 1, 194–225.

10   See Dunn, *Christianity in the Making*, vol. 1, 198.

11   Dunn, *Christianity in the Making*, vol. 1, 200. He is quoting and following W. Kelber closely at this point.

12   On this point see pp. 132–35, below.

13   See C. F. Burney, *The Poetry of Our Lord* (Oxford: Clarendon, 1925).

14   Dunn, *Christianity in the Making*, vol. 1, 198–99 n. 138.

15   The most important of Bailey's works that is relied on is his *Poet and Peasant: A Literary-Cultural Approach to the Parables in Luke* (Grand Rapids: Eerdmans, 1976). It should be noted that this is in the main a study of Luke's parables. It is not a systematic comparison of what we find in the Gospels and what Bailey observed in the Middle East.

16   Dunn, *Christianity in the Making*, vol. 1, 209.

17   Dunn, *Christianity in the Making*, vol. 1, 209; emphasis added.

18   Dunn, *Christianity in the Making*, vol. 1, 210.

19   See Robert Tannehill, *The Narrative Unity of Luke–Acts: A Literary Interpretation: The Acts of the Apostles* (Minneapolis: Fortress, 1994). Somehow the influential work of Tannehill does not even make it into Dunn's large bibliography. We do find a passing reference to the first of Tannehill's two volumes (Dunn, *Christianity in the Making*, vol. 1, 94 n. 143), but Dunn does not seem to know his second volume and its significance.

20   See Ben Witherington III, ed., "Editing the Good News: Some Synoptic Lessons from the Study of Acts," in *History, Literature and Society in the Book of Acts* (Cambridge: Cambridge University Press, 1996), 324–47.

21   See Witherington, *Acts of the Apostles.*

22   Dunn, *Christianity in the Making*, vol. 1, 217.

23 See, for example, my discussion on repetition and amplification in *Letters and Homilies for Hellenized Christians*, vol. 1.

24 See Ben Witherington III, *The Gospel of Mark: A Socio-Rhetorical Commentary* (Grand Rapids: Eerdmans, 2001).

25 Dunn, *Christianity in the Making*, vol. 1, 223; see also 238.

26 Dunn, *Christianity in the Making*, vol. 1, 243.

27 See Dunn, *Christianity in the Making*, vol. 1, 244.

28 Dunn, *Christianity in the Making*, vol. 1, 249.

29 See S. Byrskog, *Story as History, History as Story* (Leiden: Brill, 2002), 33ff.

30 Byrskog, *Story as History*, 45.

31 Byrskog, *Story as History*, 109.

32 Byrskog, *Story as History*, 102–3.

33 Byrskog, *Story as History*, 105.

34 Byrskog, *Story as History*, 106.

35 Byrskog, *Story as History*, 167.

36 Byrskog, *Story as History*, 175.

37 Bauckham, *Jesus and the Eyewitnesses*, 5.

38 This is actually part of a memorable quote from Vincent Taylor, *The Formation of the Gospel Tradition* (London: Macmillan, 1953), 42.

39 Bauckham, *Jesus and the Eyewitnesses*, 8.

40 Bauckham, *Jesus and the Eyewitnesses*, 15–16.

41 Bauckham, *Jesus and the Eyewitnesses*, 19.

42 Bauckham, *Jesus and the Eyewitnesses*, 27.

43 Bauckham, *Jesus and the Eyewitnesses*, 28.

44 James Dunn, "On History, Memory and Eyewitnesses: In Response to Bengt Holmberg and Samuel Byrskog," *JSNT* 26 (2004): 463–84, here 483–84.

45 Bauckham, *Jesus and the Eyewitnesses*, 125.

46 Maurice Casey, *Aramaic Sources of Mark's Gospel* (Cambridge: Cambridge University Press, 2007).

47 Bauckham, *Jesus and the Eyewitnesses*, 211–12.

48 See the discussion in Witherington, *Gospel of Mark*, 9–36.

49 See at length Witherington, *What Have They Done with Jesus?*

CHAPTER 11

1 William Barclay, *The Making of the Bible* (London: SCM Press, 1961), 78.

2 Bruce M. Metzger, *The Canon of the New Testament: Its Origin, Development, and Significance* (Oxford: Oxford University Press, 1987), 286.

3 L. McDonald, *The Biblical Canon* (Peabody, Mass.: Hendrickson, 2007). This is now the third edition of this work and is considerably expanded over previous editions. See the review of David Chapman in the August 2007 online edition of the *Review Biblical Literature*.

4 See especially A. C. Sundberg, "Canon Muratori: A Fourth Century List," *HTR* 66 (1973): 1–41, where the first full form of the argument can be found,

and the more influential Geoffrey M. Hahneman, *The Muratorian Fragment and the Development of the Canon* (Oxford: Oxford University Press, 1992).

5   J. B. Lightfoot, *The Apostolic Fathers* (London: Hodder & Stoughton, 1890), now published by Digireads.com in 2007.

6   There is now a detailed, point-by-point refutation of most all of Hahneman's theories about the Muratorian Canon list by Joseph Verheyden, "The Canon Muratori: A Matter of Dispute," in *The Biblical Canons*, eds. J. M. Auwers and H. J. de Jonge (Leuven: Leuven University Press, 2003), 487–556.

7   See McDonald, *Biblical Canons*, 29, 291. See the quotation of Serapion's letter in Eusebius, *Hist. eccl.* 6.12.3-6, where he first allowed the Gospel of Peter to be read in worship, but when he discovered it was pseudonymous, he then reversed himself.

8   See McDonald, *Biblical Canons*, 243–304.

9   See the discussion in C. Kannengiesser, *Handbook of Patristic Exegesis: The Bible in Ancient Christianity* (Leiden: Brill Academic, 2006), 1395–1429.

10 Hahneman, 16–17.

11 See Gamble, *Books and Readers in the Early Church*.

12 Notice the nuanced conclusion of Bart Ehrman, *The Apostolic Fathers*, vol. 2 (Cambridge, Mass.: Loeb Classical Library, 2003), 169, who concludes it may be a document composed in several stages over the period between A.D. 110–40.

13 See the critique by E. Ferguson, "Review of G. M. Hahneman, *The Muratorian Fragment and the Development of the Canon*," *JTS* 44 (1993): 691–97.

14 The issue here is when Tatian's Diatesseron ceased to be seen in the East as a suitable substitute for individual or multiple apostolic gospels and was replaced by the Peshitta. This issue is still being debated, and the jury is out.

15 Verheyden, "The Canon Muratori," 556.

16 Harry Gamble, "Marcion and the 'Canon,'" in *The Cambridge History of Christianity: Origins to Constantine*, ed. M. M. Mitchell (Cambridge: Cambridge University Press, 2006), 195–213.

17 My thanks to Craig Evans for helping me nuance this argument properly. See his *Ancient Texts for New Testament Studies* (Peabody, Mass.: Hendrickson, 2005).

18 See G. W. Trompf, ed., *Cargo Cults and Millenarian Movements* (Berlin: Mouton De Gruyter, 1990), for the general tendencies.

19 McDonald, *Biblical Canon*, 165.

20 See Witherington, *Letters and Homilies for Jewish Christians*, for more on this text.

21 See above, pp. 16–17, on 1 Thess 2:13.

22 C. K. Barrett, "The First New Testament," *NovT* 3 (1996): 94–104, here 102–3. I have incorporated his note on Marcion into the text of the quote in a parenthesis.

23 See especially Bauckham, *Jesus and the Eyewitnesses*, on the Papias traditions.

24 For more on this theme, see Witherington, *Living Word of God*.

25 While I would not go as far as he does, I do think that David Trobisch is on the right track in suggesting that such apostles as Paul may well have themselves already reflected a sort of canon consciousness and so made collections of their writings for wider audiences than the originally intended one. See David Trobisch, *Paul's Letter Collection: Tracing the Origins* (Bolivar: Quiet Water Publications, 2001).

26 On this text, see Ben Witherington III, *Letters and Homilies for Gentile Christians,* vol. 2 (Downers Grove, Ill.: InterVarsity, forthcoming).

27 G. N. Stanton, "The Fourfold Gospel," *NTS* 43 (1997): 317–46; Martin Hengel, *The Four Gospels and the One Gospel of Jesus Christ* (Harrisburg, Penn.: Trinity, 2000). See also T. C. Skeat, "The Oldest Manuscript of the Four Gospels?" *NTS* 43 (1997): 1–34.

28 See Witherington, *What Have They Done with Jesus?*

29 See especially Bauckham, *Jesus and the Eyewitnesses.*

30 M. Mitchell, "Emergence of the Written Record," in her *Cambridge History of Christianity,* 178.

31 By apostolic, I mean those written by apostles or their co-workers. The author of 2 Peter seems to have had some contact with apostles and certainly draws on apostolic documents, such as Jude.

CHAPTER 11

1 Robert Frost, *Mountain Interval* (New York: Henry Holt, 1921), 9–10.

Scripture Index

Index of Subjects and Authors